AN AMERICAN
CATHOLIC
CATECHISM

A Crossroad Book
THE SEABURY PRESS • NEW YORK

The Seabury Press
815 Second Avenue
New York, N.Y. 10017

The material in this volume was originally published as "An American Catechism" in
Chicago Studies (vol. 12, no. 3, and vol. 13, no. 3).

Copyright © 1975 by The Seabury Press, Inc.
Designed by Carol Basen
Printed in the United States of America

Library of Congress Catalog Card Number: 75-7786
ISBN: 0-8164-1196-4
ISBN: 0-8164-2588-4 (pbk.)

Edited by George J. Dyer *with the cooperation of*

Gregory Baum; Eamon R. Carroll, O. Carm.;
Charles Curran; John F. Dedek; Avery Dulles, S.J.;
Joseph V. Farraher, S.J.; Bernard Haring, C.S.S.R.;
J. Bryan Hehir; Monika K. Hellwig; Richard P. McBrien;
Richard A. McCormick, S.J.; Charles R. Meyer;
Norbert Rigali, S.J.; Thomas F. Sullivan;
Cornelius Van Der Poel, C.S.Sp.; Jared Wicks, S.J.;
John H. Wright, S.J.

Contents

The editor wishes to express his deep appreciation to his associates on the staff of *Chicago Studies,* John F. Dedek, Associate Editor, and Marjorie M. Lukas, Executive Director.

Preface

Twenty years ago Karl Rahner told theologians that they were entering on an age "of the breaking up of things." Classical theological systems, categories, and vocabulary would not, he felt, be able to bear the weight that was being placed on them. Perhaps not even Rahner anticipated the extent to which his prophecy would be fulfilled. It has been four hundred years since Catholic theology experienced anything quite like these past two decades.

In retrospect we can see some of the dynamics that were operative in theology's changing world: the new centrality of the human person, the pluralism within the Catholic community, the flourishing ecumenical dialogue, the searching return to the biblical roots of the theological discplines. These new realities had a disconcerting impact along the whole range of theological thought; at least, Catholics felt disconcerted as they watched the disappearance of so many familiar landmarks. It is to these men and women that the authors have directed this small volume. None of them would say that the momentum of theological development is spent, but they do believe that it is possible to begin pulling things together again. The very shape of this volume is indicative of their hope. Each of them discusses one of the classical divisions of dogmatic and moral theology from the perspective of the seventies. While this "system" is not ideal, it does have the advantage of leading the reader down a familiar road to the present theological moment.

The authors have used a question and answer format in their articles, and for this reason we have presumed to call this volume a "catechism"; because it is addressed primarily to the Catholics of the United States, we called it *An American Catholic Catechism*. While it is in no sense an "official catechism," it does carry the professional authority of the individual authors. Their sincerest hope is that this volume will prove useful to the men and women of the Catholic community who feel, as they do, that it is time to pull things back together again.

George J. Dyer

PART ONE
The Belief of Catholics

Revelation

1. What is the meaning of "revelation"?

In common usage, even outside a religious context, the term "revelation" signifies some knowledge, awareness, or insight beyond that which a person can gain from his ordinary experience and his own unaided efforts. The term often connotes that the knowledge is received as a gift, that it comes in a sudden or unexpected manner, and that it is profoundly significant and capable of effecting a profound inner transformation of the recipient.

2. What is the meaning of "revelation" as a theological term?

In a religious or theological context "revelation" generally denotes the action by which God freely communicates to creatures a share in his own knowledge, including his intimate self-knowledge. The term frequently suggests a sudden or unexpected insight leading to a deep personal conversion on the part of the recipient.

3. What distinctions are necessary in order to avoid confusion in the use of the term "revelation"?

Two distinctions are of particular importance. First: revelation is said to be "immediate" in the case of those who originally receive the insights upon which a particular religion is based; "mediate" in the case of those to whom the insights are passed on. Second: revelation is said to be "public" when it is communicated to a prophet or apostle or other messenger to be communicated to the whole religious group; "private" when destined for the benefit of the original recipient or of a particular group within the community of faith.

4. Is "revelation" a key concept for Christianity?

Revelation is absolutely central, since the entire Christian life is built on the conviction that God has spoken to man and that the central teachings of Christianity rest upon public revelation given immediately to the prophets and apostles of biblical times.

5. Does God reveal himself in divine form?

No. It is impossible for man in this life to perceive the divinity in itself. God therefore reveals himself under the form of created signs or symbols that point to his presence and signify how he relates himself to his creation.

6. How did God communicate to man the revelation on which the Christian faith is based?

In the history of Israel, as interpreted by the prophets and writers of the Old Testament, God gave many signs of his love and care, and signified his intention to impart still greater blessings in the future. In the career of Jesus Christ, as interpreted by the apostles and writers of the New Testament, God completed the revelatory process begun in the Old Testament and gave the fullest and clearest sign of his saving purpose.

7. How is revelation related to the "word of God"?

The term "word of God" is one of the biblical terms that most nearly correspond to the modern concept of revelation. The "word of God," as understood by biblical authors, does not mean simply propositional statements but refers to the dynamic process whereby God freely expresses and communicates himself to man. Revelation according to the Bible comes not only through spoken and written words but also through dreams, visions, theophanies, and historical events.

8. What is meant by "salvation history"?

The term has various related meanings, but it usually signifies the story of God's saving action in history as interpreted by the prophets and apostles and as recorded in the Bible. In a wider sense, all the saving activity of God, even outside the biblical period, is part of salvation history.

9. How do the events of salvation history convey revelation?

The pattern of events in salvation history discloses the attributes and intentions of God who shapes that history. More specifically, these events manifest God as personal, free, loving, merciful, faithful, just, patient, and powerful. In showing forth these and other aspects

of God, salvation history exhibits man and the universe as objects
of God's powerful mercies and as destined by him for redemption
and glory. The exceptional events of salvation history, as narrated
in the Bible, bring to a focus the meaning of man and of the world,
and thus serve as interpretative keys to illuminate the riddles of
life.

10. What is the primary content of revelation?

The primary content of revelation is God himself insofar as he
makes himself present to man in a saving way. The events of salvation
history, as interpreted by the Bible and by the Church, pertain to
revelation insofar as they are means by which God effectively shows
forth his saving presence.

11. Where is God's revelation most fully given?

According to Christian faith the fullest disclosure of God is found
in the life, teaching, sufferings, death, and resurrection of Jesus Christ,
and in the sending of the Holy Spirit by the heavenly Father and by
the risen Christ.

12. In what sense is Jesus the fullness of revelation?

By sending his own Son to be our brother, companion, teacher,
example, and redeemer God shows forth his love and power in unsur-
passable measure. Besides revealing God, Jesus reveals us to ourselves, for in the light of his life we can best understand man as a being
who comes to himself by submitting totally and lovingly to God, even
when this submission requires suffering and death.

13. Did Jesus receive revelation?

Because Jesus was a man like others he needed revelation in order
to have a human knowledge of God. Inwardly enlightened by the
unique grace that was his, he learned of his Father's ways through the
Scriptures, through the persons he met, and through the events of his
earthly life, including his sufferings. After his resurrection, Jesus'
human consciousness was most brilliantly inundated by the divine
self-knowledge.

14. Is the sending of the Holy Spirit necessary for revelation?

Yes. To recognize the signs of God's presence in the world one must
be spiritually attuned to their meaning. The Holy Spirit, by his inner
presence in our minds and hearts, makes us perceptive to the evi-

dences of God in nature, in the events of history and in the persons with whom we come into contact. Thanks to the Spirit within us, we can discern that God personally communicates himself in love not only to others but also to ourselves.

15. What is the significance of Pentecost for Christian revelation?

The wonderful events of Pentecost, as described in the second chapter of Acts, signify the special outpouring of the Holy Spirit on the first Christians so that they would be equipped to believe and bear witness to the risen Christ. Thanks to the abiding presence of the Holy Spirit, these gifts of faith and witness are still imparted to individual believers, in varying measure, and to the Church as a whole.

16. Should the inner enlightenment of the Holy Spirit be called revelation?

The inner light of grace, bestowed by the Holy Spirit, enables us to experience the world in a new way, and to interpret the signs given to us. By itself alone, this inner enlightenment would not merit to be called "revelation," because it would not convey any determinate content. Revelation in the full sense implies both data gleaned from our contact with the world about us and a personal illumination that enables us to perceive in faith the divinely intended meaning of the data.

17. What is the meaning of "faith"?

In common usage, even outside a religious context, "faith" signifies conviction, commitment, and trust with regard to principles or realities that cannot be clearly seen or rigorously proved. Human life rests to a very great extent on faith, for in our everyday transactions and investigations we take many things for granted that we could not verify to a hardened skeptic. The religious believer holds by faith that the universe as a whole is ultimately controlled not by irrational or evil forces but by a beneficent personal power at work beyond and in all things. This beneficent power is called "God."

18. What is the meaning of "faith" in Christian theology?

"Faith" in theological usage means both a conviction that God has revealed himself and a confident commitment to that revelation as a path leading to salvation. More specifically, Christian faith means a firm conviction that the meaning of our life and our world is most fully disclosed in Jesus Christ. The fullness of faith includes personal commitment to the service of Christ and a trusting reliance upon him as Lord and Saviour.

19. Is faith reasonable?

Faith is reasonable provided one has found sufficient indications that God has in fact made a revelation. The reasonableness of faith does not require that each believer should be able to give a clear and distinct account of his reasons for believing. These reasons are often too personal to be put into words, but it is possible for a reflective believer, scrutinizing the grounds of his own convictions, to ascertain that they rest upon solid motives, excluding reasonable doubt.

20. Is faith certain?

The assent of faith has varying degrees of firmness, or certainty, depending on the strength of the signs that a particular believer has received and upon his own ability to interpret those signs. A spiritually perceptive person may at times achieve a very firm and unshakable confidence in what God has revealed. Without some measure of certainty one could not be said to have faith, for faith, as stated above, is a firm commitment. On the other hand human weakness often causes the believer to waver in his commitment, and even a committed believer may experience doubt as to whether a given statement is or is not guaranteed by divine revelation.

21. Is faith a risk?

Faith is not a risk in the sense of being a commitment to what is uncertain, for, as we have just explained, authentic faith rests upon signs sufficient to exclude reasonable doubt. On the other hand, faith is a full and free commitment to things that are not directly seen or compellingly demonstrated, and in that sense it may be called a risk or venture.

22. Is faith a gift?

Faith is a gift from God because, as we have seen, revelation is a gift. Both for the external signs of revelation and for the spiritual power of discernment, the believer depends on the free and loving self-communication of God. The act of faith, however, presupposes not only God's offer but also man's free acceptance. Nobody believes unless he wills to do so and actively uses his own powers.

23. Does faith affect one's attitude toward life?

Faith deeply affects the believer by delivering him from apathy, confusion, cynicism, and despair. It enables him to find meaning in life, to direct his energies toward that which he apprehends as supremely good, and to endure patiently the adversities that come his way, confident that God will be true to his promises in Christ.

24. Is faith necessary for salvation?

Nobody can receive the blessedness that comes from God's loving communication of himself unless he accepts revelation with the free response of faith. Without faith, therefore, man denies himself the happiness to be gained from sharing in God's own awareness, obscurely in this life and by vision in the life to come.

25. Does this mean that only Christians can be saved?

Christianity teaches that, although God reveals himself most fully in the incarnate life of Jesus Christ, God's saving will extends to all men, including those who through no fault of their own do not believe in Christ. If a person who is in a position to know the truth of revelation culpably fails to accept that revelation, he cuts himself off from the life of grace and from salvation. Those who believe, on the other hand, cannot complacently assume that they are securely on the way to salvation. They have a responsibility to live up to the truth to which they have committed themselves.

26. How can men be saved without believing in Christ?

In the New Testament Christ is described as "the light that enlightens every man who comes into the world" (Jn 1:9). This and other texts give us reason to suppose that in some way not fully apparent to us the light of the divine Word reaches all men, and that non-Christians, by being open to the light given to them, can have faith sufficient for eternal salvation. So too, Holy Scripture seems to indicate that the Spirit of Christ has been poured out, not on Christians alone, but on all men, enabling each individual to respond, if he so wills, to the light of Christ.

27. Does God give all men signs of his saving will?

He does. Even without the particular signs given in the history of Israel and in Christ, who fulfills that history, there are many signs that make it possible for men, enlightened by grace to achieve a lively faith.

For example, God's providence as known from the order of nature, from the experience of human love, and from events in the lives of individuals and nations may be sufficient grounds for a joyful acknowledgement of God's love for us and for a loving commitment to him in return.

28. Is there such a thing as "natural revelation"?
Revelation, as we are here using the term, is always something over and above what man can discover by his own unaided powers, and in that sense is "supernatural." But it may be called "natural" in the sense that it crowns and satisfies man's innate yearning for communion with the divine. The term "natural revelation" is sometimes used to signify a disclosure that God makes of himself through objects in nature, such as the sun, the stars, and the sea. To be truly revelation, this disclosure would have to be the result of the workings of grace upon the heart and mind of man.

29. Do the non-Christian religions contain and transmit revelation?
Religious men in various eras and countries, under the leading of divine grace, have achieved precious insights that are embodied in certain doctrines and practices. These grace-given insights, enshrined in the traditions of the various religions, may properly be called "revelation."

30. Do all the religions agree?
The various religions, insofar as they reflect the revealing presence and activity of God, are compatible with one another, for God does not contradict himself. A deep and sympathetic study of religions other than one's own often yields unsuspected spiritual treasures. To a great extent the faiths of different religious groups are mutually complementary and enriching. What is true and inspired in each of the religions comes in some way from God, and what is distorted in them is due to the failures of men. These distortions are responsible for certain disagreements.

31. Are all religions equally good?
No. Religions vary greatly in the depth and profundity of their insights and in their salvific power. In some religions the divinely revealed truth is heavily encrusted with error and corruption. Christians believe that God gives his fullest and deepest revelation in Jesus

Christ and that the Christian religion, though it has suffered from human deformations, remains accessible today. Therefore Christians, without denying the value and salvific power of other religions, claim a certain preeminence for the faith to which they adhere. This is not a matter for self-congratulation but a cause for humble thanksgiving, and it places upon Christians a special burden to understand their faith correctly and to bear witness to it in such a way that Christ may appear as universal Saviour.

32. How is revelation transmitted?

The founders and spokesmen of the religions, including Judaism and Christianity, have generally transmitted their privileged insights by instructing disciples in their doctrine and their way of life. In literate cultures this instruction is normally preserved, at least partly, in writings that are held in veneration by later generations in the same religious tradition. The characteristic doctrines and practices of a given religious family serve as channels by which its members enter into a revelatory communion with God structured in a way similar to that of the founder or founders.

33. Is human language capable of transmitting revelation?

God, as apprehended by faith, lies far beyond all that can be put into ordinary human concepts and words. The language of religious confessions, therefore, is to a great extent negative and figurative. It states what God is not, and suggests, rather than explicitly declares, something of what he must be. Religious communication occurs most effectively in situations of worship. Many of the Christian creeds were composed to be recited in a baptismal setting (and were later introduced into the Eucharist as well) so that the sense of the sacred would not be lacking. Unless his heart is disposed to worship, man will not achieve the sense of faith needed to interpret revelational language correctly.

34. Is the Bible revelation?

The Bible is a collection of books that express, in written form, the convictions of those who established the religion of Israel and that of the Christian Church. Insofar as the Judaeo-Christian religion is divinely revealed, the Bible may be said to contain or point to revelation. When read in a spirit of faith, the Bible effectively imparts a sense of God as he made himself known to the men of Israel and to the early

Christians. It does not, of course, answer all the religious questions of modern man, nor is it intended to do so.

35. Is the Bible inspired?

The Church, in its use of the Bible, has come to the conviction that God enlightened and directed those who composed and compiled the biblical books. This enlightenment and direction of the biblical writers is technically called "inspiration." Unlike revelation, inspiration does not involve an extraordinary communication of new insights. Inspiration is rather a special assistance given to a speaker or writer to express in a fitting manner the faith of the People of God at a given stage of salvation history. Although the gifts of revelation and inspiration are formally distinct, a given biblical author, such as Isaiah or Paul or John, may also have been a recipient of immediate revelation.

36. Is the Bible free from error?

In accepting the Bible as the basis of its own belief and teaching, the Church certifies that the Bible, taken as a whole, is a reliable witness to God's revelation as communicated to the Israelites and the early Church. The inspiration given to the sacred writers prevented them from falsifying what God had made known to his People by revelation. It did not, however, prevent the authors from sharing the common opinions of men of their day with regard to secular matters, not did it miraculously exclude all errors of a historical or scientific character. Even the religious teaching of the Bible shows a certain evolution over the centuries and thus individual passages, taken in isolation, are often inadequate and could be misleading. To take on its true value as revelation, each passage must be read in the context of the whole Bible as received by the Church.

37. Does the Old Testament retain its status as revelation for Christians?

The Old Testament is a record of God's self-disclosure to the Israelites before the coming of Christ. For many reasons this record remains important for Christians. Much of the Old Testament points forward to the New Testament as its fulfilment. Jesus and the apostolic Church, moreover, interpreted their existence and mission in terms of Old Testament categories, and hence their claims cannot be properly understood except against that background. In addition, the Old Testament contains many important insights that are simply accepted by

Christianity, without being repeated in the New Testament. On the other hand, certain ideas and practices that were appropriate for an earlier period are outdated since the coming of Christ. This is notably the case with regard to the ceremonial prescriptions of the Mosaic Law, which are not today considered binding on Christians.

38. Does the Bible contain the whole of Christian revelation?

The Bible is the most basic source available for reconstructing the developing faith of the Israelite community and that of the early Church. It bears witness to the fullness of revelation which, as we have seen, occurred in Jesus Christ. The Church's faith has no content that is not found, at least germinally, in the Bible. On the other hand, the Bible itself cannot be adequately understood except in the light of the ongoing experience of the Christian community. Some of its implications become clearer with the passage of time. Thus it would be a mistake to suppose that a believer of the twentieth century could gain a satisfactory understanding of Christian revelation by merely examining the text of the Bible.

39. What is the role of tradition in revelation?

By tradition is generally understood the continuous handing down of the faith of a community from generation to generation. The Church constantly meditates on the significance of Christ and understands the biblical message in new ways related to the situations that arise successively in history. Tradition, insofar as it reflects new insights into the meaning of revelation, adds something to the Bible. The Bible achieves its full value as revelation when mediated by tradition, which serves as a kind of environment or atmosphere in which the Bible is read. Tradition itself is known not so much by looking at it as an object as by subjectively dwelling in it through participation in the life of the believing community.

40. How is the Church related to revelation?

The Church, as the community of Christian believers, is the recipient of that revelation which God made of himself in Jesus Christ. Furthermore, the Church is the official herald of, and corporate witness to, that revelation. In every generation it has the task of proclaiming the Christian revelation, interpreting it, and rendering it credible by words and deeds.

41. Is the Church a reliable witness to revelation?

Christ has promised that the powers of death will never prevail against the Church (Mt. 16:18) and that he himself will remain with the successors of the apostles to the end of time (Mt. 28:20). Thanks to these promises it is certain that the Church will always remain in the truth of the gospel and will be able to distinguish sufficiently between truth and error so that the faithful will not be gravely misled in matters of vital importance to salvation.

42. What is the role of the official Church leadership with regard to revelation?

The official leadership, or the hierarchical magisterium (as it is sometimes called), has the task of overseeing the life and witness of the Church. It has a special responsibility for preventing the Christian revelation from being denatured or obscured. The magisterium exercises its doctrinal vigilance by scrutinizing the testimonies of Scripture and tradition, and by consulting the views of contemporary Christians, including specialists in theological questions.

43. Is the magisterium infallible?

The great majority of official doctrinal statements in the Church are subject to correction in the light of further evidence. But the universal magisterium (the college of bishops and the Pope as the leader and spokesman of that college) is assisted by the Holy Spirit so that in critical situations it will be able to say what is necessary to preserve the Church in the truth of Christian revelation. This assistance, guaranteed by Christ's promises in the New Testament, does not exempt the Church authorities from study, reflection, and consultation, but rather demands these measures. After sufficient study and reflection, the magisterium, by virtue of its infallible teaching power, may be able to commit the Church definitively.

44. Are infallible statements irreformable?

When the magisterium speaks infallibly its declarations have permanent validity. They are irreversible and in that sense "irreformable." But it is always possible and appropriate to plumb the truth of revelation more profoundly and to seek to express it more aptly in relation to the needs and possibilities of various times and situations. Thus the "irreformability" of the Church's dogmatic teaching does not prevent the further development of doctrine.

45. Are dogmas revealed truths?

Every dogma of the Church expresses an authentic aspect of the Christian revelation. The truth of revelation, however, consists not so much in the multiplicity of dogmas as in the indivisible mystery of God's saving self-communication to man that is touched upon from various angles in the different dogmas. The way in which revelation is parcelled out in dogmas depends on human thought-categories that are, to some extent, culturally and historically conditioned. The dogmatic formulas are not themselves revelation, but are human articulations of revelation. Revelation is assented to in and through dogmatic formulas, but also through many other intermediaries such as creeds, prayers, hymns, historical narratives, rituals, and other symbolic actions.

46. Did the history of revelation end with the apostles?

It is often said that the "deposit of faith," or the content of public revelation, was completed in the lifetime of the apostles. This statement conveys an important truth inasmuch as the apostles, enlightened by the Holy Spirit, were privileged to witness the career of Jesus Christ in whom God irrevocably and unsurpassably communicates himself. In the whole of future history God will speak no revelatory word that has not been in some sense already spoken in the personal gift of Christ, who is the divine Word incarnate. The Church does not teach new revelations, but it continues to proclaim the same revelation, the same gospel, that was divulged to the apostles through Jesus Christ.

47. Does revelation continue to occur in the Church?

Since the Ascension of Christ, God has not been silent; he continues to reveal himself to man, especially when the gospel is authentically proclaimed. The content of revelation today adds nothing essential to that which was proclaimed by the apostolic Church, but the revelation must be apprehended and transmitted in a manner that throws light on the deepest problems and anxieties of contemporary man. This requires not a mechanical repetition of what was said in past ages but a living and creative insight proportioned to the culture and situation of the day. In order that the gospel may be genuinely revelation for the men of every age, God grants the continued presence and assistance of the Holy Spirit.

48. Do individuals today receive revelation?

All believers receive sufficient light from the Holy Spirit to have a living faith. Through their own experience, interpreted by the light of grace, many are able to grasp more deeply the meaning of Christ for their personal lives and to help the Church discover and express the contemporary significance of what was originally revealed to the apostles.

49. Does revelation come through secular history?

As already explained, the history of Israel and of Jesus Christ, interpreted by the light of faith, was a medium by which the biblical revelation was first imparted. In principle there is no reason why the history of the Church and of the world, since biblical times, could not be interpreted in the light of faith so as to be a source of insight into God's designs and intentions. Such interpretations of history from the point of view of faith have occasionally been attempted, but have not won firm or universal assent in the Church. Thus secular history and Church history have not been revelatory to the Christian community to the same degree that biblical history is.

50. Will revelation be given in the life to come?

The saints in heaven receive revelation, no longer indirectly under the veils of faith, but directly through a face-to-face vision of God. At the end of history, the entire cosmos will be splendidly transformed, and will become radiant with the glory of God. Thus revelation will be given far more perfectly in heaven that it can ever be given on earth under the conditions of history as we know it.

Church

1. What is the Church?

The Church has been defined in various ways: as the Body of Christ, the People of God, the new Israel, the community of the elect, the sacrament of Christ, the congregation of saints wherein the gospel is rightly preached and the sacraments rightly celebrated, and so forth. Although the Second Vatican Council speaks constantly of the Church, nowhere does it offer a single, hard-and-fast definition which must be accepted by all Catholics without modification. In its deepest sense, of course, the Church is a mystery.

2. What does it mean to say that the Church is a "mystery"?

According to St. Augustine a mystery is a visible sign of some invisible grace. Pope Paul VI follows that Augustinian tradition when he defines the Church as "a reality imbued with the hidden presence of God." To affirm that the Church is a mystery is to confess that God is present to his creation in and through a particular group of people who believe in and celebrate the Lordship of Jesus.

3. In what sense is the Church a sacrament?

The word "sacrament" means sign. In its early theological usage (e.g., by St. Augustine), it referred not to the seven specific sacraments of the Church but to any outward expression of invisible grace. Thus, Christ himself is the fundamental sacrament. In his humanity, he is the great sign of God's invisible presence in history.

The Church, too, is a sacrament. It embodies Christ's presence for mankind. It is an outward, visible sign of God's grace in history. The Church's message is this: God has won the victory over sin and death in Christ; humanity is really possible!

Insofar as men and women can look to the community of the Church and see how the triumphant grace of Christ has transformed, and is transforming, people into selfless, compassionate, sensitive, free human beings, to that same extent can they have confidence in the outcome of human history. History will succeed because God is present to it. And mankind can see God's presence working in and through the Church. (See, for example, article 1 of the *Dogmatic Constitution on the Church:* "By her intimate relationship with Christ, the Church is a kind of sacrament or sign of intimate union with God, and of the unity of all mankind. She is also an instrument for the achievement of such union and unity.")

4. Why isn't the Church best described as the "Mystical Body of Christ"?

No single word or expression can capture the whole mystery of the Church. It is a mistake to build an entire concept of the Church on any one image, even if the image comes straight out of St. Paul, as "Body of Christ" does.

The strength of the Second Vatican Council's *Dogmatic Constitution on the Church* is its unwillingness to settle for any one term. It is true that "People of God" receives the dominant place in the council's teaching, but it is also true that "People of God" shares the theological stage with many other biblical images, such as temple, spouse, sheepfold, field, building, etc. (see n. 6–7).

A balanced theology of the Church will take each of these images into account and will not allow any one image to become so dominant that it suppresses the truth hidden in these other expressions.

5. Notwithstanding how difficult it may be to define the Church precisely, is there some definition that theologians today might agree upon?

The Church is the community of those who are called to acknowledge the Lordship of Jesus, who ratify that faith sacramentally, and who commit themselves thereby to membership and mission for the sake of the Kingdom of God in history.

The Church is, first of all, a community. It is people. It is not, in the first instance, an organization, or a means of salvation. It is not the hierarchy or the clergy. The Church is a community. (Note, for example, that the chapter on the People of God in the *Dogmatic Constitution on the Church* comes before, not after, the chapter on the hierarchy. This particular arrangement, however, was not achieved without a serious struggle at the council).

But the Church is not simply a community. It is not just people.

It is a special kind of community. It is a particular group of people who differ from other people in one important respect: Christians are those who affirm that the meaning and hope of human existence and of history itself reside in Jesus of Nazareth, whom God has raised up for our salvation.

6. Is it only this belief in the Lordship of Jesus which makes Christians different from everyone else?

This, and this alone, is what makes Christians different from the rest of mankind. Not that Christians are holier than other people. Not that Christians believe in God and give him due worship. Not that Christians believe in the brotherhood of man. Not that Christians believe in social justice and in the service of mankind. For these are things that Christians have in common with other religious and even nonreligious people.

What distinguishes the Christian from the non-Christian, and the Church from the rest of mankind, is the conviction and the faith that Jesus of Nazareth is the Lord, that he, and he alone, is the pattern and ground of all life. That what we call good and human, we call good and human because it participates in the reality of him. And what we call evil and inhuman, we call evil and inhuman because it recedes from, or rejects, the reality embodied in Jesus of Nazareth.

7. Why must we be so specific in our understanding of the Church? Could we not call all people of good will members of the Church? Doesn't the Church exist wherever the Spirit is?

No. These definitions tend to equate the Church with the Kingdom of God. It is to be hoped, of course, that the Church and the Kingdom of God overlap. We have a right to expect, that is, a fuller flowering of the gospel among those people who presume to preach it and to celebrate it publicly. The Church should be recognized as the initial budding forth of the Kingdom on earth (see the *Dogmatic Constitution on the Church,* n. 5). But the Church and the Kingdom are not one and the same reality. Where you have the Church, you don't necessarily have the Kingdom; and where you have the Kingdom, you don't necessarily have the Church either.

8. Our understanding of the Church thus far doesn't seem to make room for the special place of the Catholic Church within the Body of Christ. Do we no longer affirm that the Catholic Church alone is the one, true Church of Christ?

The expression "one, true Church of Christ" is misleading and it should be avoided. It implies that Catholics are the only real members of the Body of Christ.

There was some basis for this sort of reasoning even in contemporary papal documents, such as the two encyclical letters of Pope Pius XII, *Mystici Corporis* (1943) and *Humani Generis* (1950). In the latter document the Pope had written: ". . . the mystical Body of Christ and the Catholic Church in communion with Rome are one and the same thing. . . ." Therefore, it was not enough that non-Catholic Christians were baptized, or reverenced the Word of God in Sacred Scripture, or celebrated some of the sacraments. They lacked one thing that was presumably absolutely essential for membership in the Body of Christ; namely, communion with Rome. Thus, all non-Catholic Christians were related to the Church merely by desire *(in voto),* which means that if they actually knew the Roman Catholic Church to be the "one, true Church of Christ," they would spontaneously join it.

On first reading the eighth article of the Second Vatican Council's *Dogmatic Constitution on the Church,* it seems that the council is simply reaffirming the teaching of those earlier encyclicals. The text of the constitution reads: "This (one) Church (of Christ), constituted and organized in the world as a society, *subsists* in the Catholic Church" (italics mine).

As a matter of fact, however, the phrase "subsists in" was not in the original draft of the document. Rather it was selected as a more accurate and suitable replacement for the "is" that appeared in the first draft. The reason offered for this change was that *de facto* there do exist outside the visible boundaries of the Catholic Church genuine elements of sanctification (see, for example, the *Decree on Ecumenism,* n. 3). Vatican II was saying, therefore, that the means of Christian holiness are not confined to the Catholic Church, and that the Body of Christ is larger in scope and extent than the Catholic Church by itself.

One can conclude that the Body of Christ "subsists in" the Catholic Church, but one cannot say, without serious qualification, that the Body of Christ and the Catholic Church are simply "one and the same thing." Other Christians, who do not belong to the Catholic Church, share in the life of Christ's Body, even though the degree of such participation may differ from one Christian community to another, or from individual to individual.

9. What is apostolic succession?

Apostolic succession applies in the first instance to the whole Church. It means that every Christian has the responsibility to continue the work which the apostles themselves exercised by the will and commission of Jesus Christ.

The apostles, like Jesus, were to carry on his work of thanksgiving to the Father, of offering themselves and their communities as signs or sacraments of God's presence among men, and of using whatever resources they had for the sake of those in need.

This apostolic mission remains the mission of the People of God today (see chapter II of the *Constitution on the Church*) and what is said in this regard of the People of God applies equally to laity, religious, and clergy alike (n. 30), for indeed the lay apostolate is a participation in the saving mission of the Church itself and not merely a sharing in the ministry of the hierarchy (n. 33).

Apostolic succession also applies in a special way to the bishops of the Church who, by ordination, have a distinctive responsibility of guiding, assisting, and leading the rest of the People of God in the faithful exercise of their apostolic mission.

It is the Catholic conviction that the Church cannot remain faithful to the apostolic witness and mission without the assistance and direction of proper leadership. Overseers *(episcopoi)* have been given to the Christian community to help and inspire the Church to remain faithful to its apostolic foundation, to confess without equivocation the Lordship of Jesus, and to pursue without compromise his quest for the Kingdom of God.

It is always difficult for the Church to maintain a proper balance between the apostolic succession as it applies to the whole Church and the apostolic succession as it applies more narrowly to the college of bishops within the Church. The fidelity of the Church to the apostolic witness and mission must somehow grow out of the dialectical tension between these two realities. At times the strain of that tension seems disruptive of the Church's unity. But it is also the Catholic's conviction that the healing Spirit will preserve her life and insure her apostolic faithfulness.

10. What is the college of bishops and how is the Pope related to it?

Vatican II teaches that a fraternity of bishops exists within the Church, and that every bishop has power insofar as he is a member of this communion. The bishop is not, as some Catholics seem to think, merely the vicar or delegate of the Pope.

The college of bishops continues the college of the apostles, but one cannot argue that the two colleges are the same in every respect. However, the Council implies that just as the college of the apostles existed by the decree of the Lord, so does the college of bishops. In other words, we could not really conceive of the Church existing without some form of episcopal ministry.

True to its abiding concern to protect the primacy of the Pope, the council reminds us that this college of bishops exists only insofar as it takes in the Pope as its head. Without the Pope, there is no college. But this does not mean that the Pope is the sole principle of unity in the college. Unity is also insured by the presence of the Holy Spirit, fraternal love, common faith, and various other manifestations of communion. We know, for example, that the Church retains its unity even during the period between the death of one Pope and the election of another.

Furthermore, the college of bishops is the possessor of supreme and full authority over the whole Church (see the *Code of Canon Law*, c. 228, n. 1). This authority, although never independent of the Pope, is not bestowed upon the college by the Pope.

The Pope and the other bishops are members of the same college. There are not two centers of supreme and full authority, but only one, i.e., the college of bishops with the Pope at the center and head.

11. Is the acceptance of the papacy and the episcopacy so crucial that one who rejects them cannot be in the Body of Christ?

No. If that was true, only Roman Catholics would really be within the Body of Christ. But the Second Vatican Council in several places acknowledges the authentic ecclesial reality of other Christian communities. It refers to them, in fact, as "churches" (see, for example, the *Decree on Ecumenism*, n. 19), and it calls to mind certain matters of faith upon which there is a fundamental and essential agreement: Jesus is Lord; the Bible is the Word of God; Baptism incorporates one into the Body of Christ; the gospel of Jesus Christ is the norm of lives; and so forth (see the *Dogmatic Constitution on the Church*, n. 15).

The council does not teach, however, that all Christians whether Catholic or not, are incorporated into the Body of Christ to the same exact degree. According to the *Dogmatic Constitution on the Church* (n. 14), Catholics are "fully incorporated into the society of the Church." But it does not say Catholics "alone" are incorporated into the Church. It is not a matter of kind, but a matter of degree. This is a distinction which has important ecumenical implications, some of which are specified in the *Decree on Ecumenism.*

12. What is infallibility?

Literally, the word means "immunity from error." Every Catholic should know that infallibility was intended to mean only freedom from doctrinal error, not access to all truth, and that it could only be engaged under certain strict conditions: (1) the matter to be proposed must pertain directly to the gospel ("faith and morals"); (2) it is proposed for the belief of the whole Church; and, in the case of the Pope, (3) it is proposed *ex cathedra* (literally: "from the chair"), i.e., when the Pope is "acting in the office of shepherd and teacher of all Christians . . . by virtue of his supreme apostolic authority."

With regard to the Pope, the council suggested that his infallibility is the same infallibility "with which the divine Redeemer willed his Church to be endowed." It is the Church as a community which has been given the Spirit of truth and which cannot fundamentally err in its understanding of the heart of the gospel. The Pope is infallible only insofar as he enunciates and proclaims the infallible faith of the whole Church, Catholic and non-Catholic. He is not infallible unto himself, in complete independence from the Church.

13. Must Catholics accept all papal teaching as if it were infallible?

No. Only those teachings which fully and precisely fulfill the conditions enunciated by Vatican I can be regarded as infallible.

14. Are non-infallible teachings also non-authoritative?

No. If this were the case, Catholics would only have to take seriously infallible statements of the Church. And such statements are decidedly few in number. Indeed, since the proclamation of the dogma of papal infallibility at the First Vatican Council a hundred years ago, there has been only one exercise of this prerogative; namely, in the definition of the Blessed Mother's Assumption.

At their most authoritive level, the documents of Vatican II, for example, are in the category of "Catholic doctrine." They represent the teaching of the Church's magisterium in such wise that a Catholic must have good and solid reasons for disagreeing with such teachings. Much of the material in the documents of various ecumenical councils, as well as some material contained in papal encyclicals, falls into this category.

We should remember, however, that the attribution of the term "Catholic doctrine" to a particular teaching is itself a theological judgment, and, as such, the judgment is subject to later revision.

15. What is heresy?

The word "heresy" comes from a Greek word which means "to choose" or "to prefer." The heretic is one who chooses a particular aspect of Christian truth and takes it out of context, thereby exaggerating it and distorting its total meaning. In one sense, heresy is a matter of selective perception.

It is possible for a Catholic to fall into heresy (material, not formal) simply by repeating, *out of context,* some earlier doctrinal formulations of the Church.

Furthermore, if a Catholic today were to repeat the conciliar teaching that there are three persons in one God, and if he assumed that the early Church had the modern notion of person in mind (i.e., an autonomous subject endowed with its own proper consciousness, intellect, and will), that Catholic would be affirming tritheism: three Gods!

Orthodoxy, therefore, is not a matter of saying the right words, but of having the right understanding. Heresy, too, is not a matter of saying the wrong words, but of seeing only a part of the truth, out of context from the whole of Christian tradition.

16. Would a Catholic be justified in leaving the Church if he or she decided that he could work more effectively for the Kingdom of God outside the Church rather than inside?

If a Catholic, or any Christian for that matter, still believes in the Lordship of Jesus and in the mission of the community which confesses his name, then he is not free to work apart from the Church for the sake of the Kingdom. To believe in the Lordship of Jesus is to be implicated already in the community which keeps his memory alive.

When people raise this question of leaving the Church in order to do God's work more effectively, they are usually thinking of certain canonical and disciplinary aspects of the Church's life. "Leaving the Church" often means simply trying to function as a Christian without any further reference to, or regard for, the local chancery office or the local parish.

There are, of course, various levels of Christian missionary activity. There can be no precise uniformity. Pluralism and flexibility are

certainly compatible with the mission which Christ gave directly to
every member of the Church (*Constitution on the Church,* n. 33). But
for those who still believe in Jesus as Lord, leaving the Church as such
is not a real option. Instead, it may be a question of modifying one's
relationship with certain traditional ecclesiastical patterns of life and
work.

**17. We say that the Church exists for the sake of the coming of God's
Kingdom. We also insist that the Church has some obligation to the
world. What relationship exists among these three realities: the
Church, the Kingdom of God, and the world?**

They are not the same thing although it is always the hope of
Christians that all of these realities will converge at the end of time
(*Dogmatic Constitution on the Church,* n. 5, and *Pastoral Constitution
on the Church in the Modern World,* n. 39), i.e., that the world
(including the Church) might become the Kingdom of God.

The Church is that part of the world which alone confesses that
Jesus of Nazareth is the Lord and which, through preaching, worship,
example, and service to mankind, strives to make everyone and everything conform to the will of the Father and thereby enter into the
Kingdom of God.

The Church and the world are not the same thing, although they
overlap, because there are many people and institutions in the world
which do not acknowledge the Lordship of Jesus.

The Church and the Kingdom of God are not the same thing,
although we trust that they overlap, because there are many whom
God has that the Church does not have, and many whom the Church
has that God does not yet have (St. Augustine).

Finally, the Kingdom of God and the world are not the same thing,
although they may overlap, because much of the world is still under
the power of evil and refuses to submit itself to the sovereignty of God.

18. What is the mission of the Church?

The Church is that portion of mankind which is called to acknowledge the Lordship of Jesus and to fulfill the mission which Jesus
himself came to realize: the proclamation, signification, and facilita-
tion of God's Kingdom among men. The Church, like Jesus, exists to
announce the coming of the Kingdom, to be a sign of its presence in
history, and to usher in the Kingdom through its various good works.

19. Are we still bound to share our faith in Christ with those who do not yet believe in him?

Yes. There has been no theological or doctrinal development during the last several years which has eliminated "the missions" from the list of the Church's priorities.

If we believe in the Lordship of Jesus, i.e., that he is "the goal of human history, the focal point of the longings of history and of civilization, the center of the human race, the joy of every heart, and the answer to all its yearnings" (*Pastoral Constitution on the Church in the Modern World,* n. 45), then this is a perception which we are bound to share with others (*Constitution on the Church,* n. 17).

There may have been some Catholics in past years who tended to equate "the missions" of the Church with the very "mission" of the Church. This would be theologically inaccurate.

To the extent that we have broadened our understanding of the mission of the Church to include more than "the missions," there has been a change in our thinking about the missionary apostolate. However, such a change has not diminished the importance of preaching the gospel to those who do not yet believe in Christ. Rather, it has provided such activity with a wider theological foundation.

20. What part do the laity play in the mission of the Church?

Chapter II of the *Dogmatic Constitution on the Church* speaks of the Church as "People of God." Chapter IV of the document makes it clear that the council intended all members of the Church, including the laity, to be a part of this People of God. "Everything which has been said so far concerning the People of God applies equally to the laity, religious, and clergy" (n. 30). By baptism the laity are made one body with Christ and, in their own way, are made sharers in the priestly prophetic, and kingly functions of Christ (n. 31). By their very vocation, the document continues, they seek the Kingdom of God. And that quest, of course, is at the heart of the mission of the Church. Indeed, "the lay apostolate . . . is a participation in the saving mission of the Church itself. Through their baptism and confirmation, all are commissioned to that apostolate by the Lord Himself" (n. 33). There is no mention here that the laity shares in the mission of the Church only to the extent that the hierarchy allows. The mission comes from Christ through the sacraments, and not through the leadership personnel of the Church.

21. What was "Catholic Action"? Is it still a tenable notion today?

Catholic Action was defined as "the participation of the laity in the apostolate of the hierarchy of the Church" (see *Baltimore Catechism,* no. 3, and other similar sources). The assumption, clearly stated in many cases, was that the hierarchy alone was given the responsibility for the mission of the Church. The hierarchy, in turn, would decide whether or not to share that responsibility with the laity, and under what conditions.

It is difficult to reconcile that particular notion of the lay apostolate with the clear teaching of Vatican II given in the preceding answer.

22. How can the council's teaching on the lay apostolate be realized in practice?

Principally through the creation and effective operation of parish councils, diocesan pastoral councils, national pastoral councils, and through lay participation on various policy-making boards such as those supervising admissions to seminaries. Laity should also have some meaningful voice in the selection of their bishops and pastors, and in the ongoing evaluation of their pastoral performance.

23. How can the Church encourage the lay apostolate in this way and still preserve the distinctive authority of our bishops and pastors?

The distinctive leadership role of the bishop or pastor can be protected by the power of veto, but it seems that the council ought to be able to override such a veto by a reasonable majority, e.g., two-thirds or three-quarters. If such vetoes can never be overridden, under any circumstances, then we are right back where we started, with the bishop or pastor functioning, for all practical purposes, as a kind of absolute monarch.

It may appear that our primary concern today is to strip bishops and pastors of their power. On the contrary, our principal concern is to fulfill the theological and pastoral designs of the Second Vatican Council; namely, to incorporate the whole People of God into the decision-making process of Church life and mission, for which every member of the Church—laity, religious, and clergy alike—are responsible (*Dogmatic Constitution on the Church,* n. 30 and 33).

24. Do women have a special place in the Church? Could they be ordained, for example?

When the Second Vatican Council spoke on the question of women in society and in the Church, the council consistently argued on behalf of equality of rights for women and of a wider participation by women in the various fields of the Church's apostolate (see, for example, the *Decree on the Apostolate of the Laity,* n. 9, and the *Pastoral Constitution on the Church in the Modern World,* n. 9, 29, and 60).

Although the ordination of women raises some real problems for the Church, there is no overriding theological argument against the practice. Indeed, the reluctance of many churches to adopt this new practice springs from ecumenical rather than theological, biblical, or doctrinal reasons. These churches do not want to jeopardize the new spirit of fellowship which has emerged in recent years. Of course, as more and more churches accept the ordination of women, the less reason there will be for reluctance on ecumenical grounds.

25. What is the place of religious communities within the Church?

Those Christians who are convinced that they can best serve the Kingdom of God within a relatively stable, organized community should be allowed and encouraged to do so. Insofar as these communities promote the general work of the Church and the spiritual welfare of their members, they are an asset to the Church.

Ideally, religious communities do for the Church what the Church is supposed to do for the world, i.e., serve as a prophetic reminder of the gap that inevitably exists between rhetoric and reality, between the Kingdom-promised and the Kingdom-realized.

26. What is ecumenism?

Ecumenism is both a movement and a state of mind. As a movement it can be defined as the sum total of "those activities and enterprises which, according to various needs of the Church and opportune occasions, are started and organized for the fostering of unity among Christians" *(Decree on Ecumenism,* n. 4).

As a state of mind, ecumenism is an attitude of openness towards Christians of different traditions in order to learn from their distinctive experiences and example and in order to purify and deepen our own commitment to the gospel of Jesus Christ.

27. What are the goals of the ecumenical movement?

There are two very different approaches to the ecumenical movement. The first regards ecumenism as a new and more subtle means of bringing non-Catholics into the Catholic Church. Ecumenism, in the minds of these Catholics, is simply a matter of switching from vinegar to honey. But the ultimate goal is the same: the "return" of the Protestant to the Catholic Church.

A second approach to ecumenism rejects the notion of a "return" to Catholic unity and supports instead the idea of a "restoration" of Christian unity. The purpose of the ecumenical movement, in the second view, is to bring the various Christian churches together by encouraging mutual study and mutual respect, on the one hand, and collaboration in Christian mission, on the other (see, for example, the *Decree on Ecumenism,* n. 4 and 12).

It would appear that the Second Vatican Council favored the rhetoric of "restoration" rather than of "return" (n. 1). Without relinquishing its distinctively Catholic convictions, the council urges Catholics to "joyfully acknowledge and esteem the truly Christian endowments from our common heritage which are to be found among our separated brethren. . . . Nor should we forget that whatever is wrought by the grace of the Holy Spirit in the hearts of our separated brethren can contribute to our own edification" (n. 4).

The ecumenical movement requires a coming together, not toward one or another fixed expression of the Body of Christ but toward a common, living affirmation of the gospel of Jesus Christ. It is our prayer that as each community deepens its faithfulness to the one Lord of all mankind, the Spirit will restore to us that precious unity which, through the sin of all parties concerned, was lost so many years ago.

28. Are the Jews part of the Church?

No. Although the Church may potentially include all mankind, it can actually embrace only those who confess the Lordship of Jesus Christ, who can affirm with St. Paul that "no other foundation can any one lay than that which is laid, which is Jesus Christ" (1 Cor 3:11).

It is certainly true that Christians and non-Christians agree, or at least can agree, on many fundamental points. The principal point of convergence is in our common commitment to the coming of the Kingdom of God. Every person with religious faith affirms the presence of God and wishes to enable that divine presence to fill every portion of the world.

"Thy Kingdom come, thy will be done" is a prayer that can rise from the minds and hearts of every religious community, *(Constitu-*

tion on the Church, n. 15, and the *Declaration on the Relationship of the Church to Non-Christian Religions.)*

However, there is one area of religious conviction which must always distinguish the Christian from the non-Christian, simply because the Christian finds it meaningful and therefore credible, while the non-Christian finds it to be without adequate meaning and therefore without adequate force of truth. This area of conviction has to do with Jesus of Nazareth.

Whereas all religious people are committed to the realization of the will of God among men and to the worship of God, not everyone acknowledges that the will of God has been embodied definitively in Jesus of Nazareth or that the worship of God is, normatively, the worship Christ gives to his Father and which we share with Christ.

The ecumenical movement should certainly broaden our horizons to embrace the whole human community (indeed the word "ecumenical" refers to "the whole world"), moving us to seek new ways of cooperation with one another as we collaborate with God in the coming of his Kingdom. But the only way in which the non-Christian could be regarded in any sense as being a part of the Church would be by his confession of Jesus as Lord.

29. What is the proper relationship between the Church and the State?

The separation of Church and State can mean one of two things: (1) a constitutional separation whereby the independence of the Church is protected; or (2) a complete moral separation of social, economic, or political import.

A *constitutional* separation of Church and State means, on the one hand, that the State will do nothing to obstruct the work of the Church and, on the other hand, that the Church will neither seek nor accept any special privilege which might give it an unfair advantage over other comparable groups within the political society. These are really two sides of the same coin. If the Church accepts privileges from the State, it becomes indebted to the State and is proportionately less free. And vice-versa.

A total *moral* separation means that the Church will concern itself with religious matters only: worship, catechesis, preaching, doctrinal instruction, devotions, and so forth. How society is otherwise structured (e.g., system of taxation, housing, social services, labor-management relations, foreign policy, and so forth) is a matter of interest for the State alone.

Constitutional separation of Church and State has very much in its favor; complete moral separation has always been rejected by the Church, and most recently in the *Pastoral Constitution on the Church in the Modern World* (n. 43): "Nor, on the contrary, are they any less wide of the mark who think that religion consists in acts of worship alone and in the discharge of certain moral obligations, and who imagine they can plunge themselves into earthly affairs in such a way as to imply that they are altogether divorced from the religious life. This split between the faith which many profess and their daily lives deserves to be counted among the more serious errors of our age."

30. Does the Church have a future?

The Church will last as long as there are people who believe in the Lordship of Jesus Christ and who will thereby be moved to confess this faith openly and to celebrate it sacramentally. Whether the Church of the distant future will bear any major resemblance to the Church of the present day is, of course, an open question. But however it may change, it will always be the one community which accepts Jesus as Lord, which breaks bread in his name, and which is permanently committed to the coming of God's Kingdom among men.

God

1. What does the word "God" mean?

The meaning of the word "God," like the meaning of all other words, depends on its actual use, on what people intend to convey to one another when they use the sound or write the letters. From this point of view "God" has had and continues to have many different meanings. It may mean, for example, the supreme and ultimate principle of the being, unity, goodness, and intelligiblity of the world we encounter in experience, or, to put it more simply, the maker and lord of the universe. Or it may mean the object of actual worship, the thing or one to whom I unconditionally submit myself in adoration and praise.

However, such meanings of "God" constitute problems today, since some deny or at least question the suppositions implicit in these meanings: that the world is made rather than a purely chance and self-existent event; that anything or anyone deserves unconditional submission.

Still, an understandable meaning of the word "God," apart from whether this meaning is actually verified in anything or anyone, can be grounded in those universal human experiences which point beyond ourselves and the immediately given. Such experiences as questioning, wonder, spontaneous gratitude, a sense of the beautiful and the good, moral obligation (not mere taboos), and an awareness of the permanence of truth amid change, of the limitation of knowledge, of the relativity of space and time, of the irreducible difference between being and not-being, between affirming and denying—all these suggest (but do not necessarily establish or prove) an ultimate ground of value and reality we may call "God."

2. What then are some common misunderstandings of the word "God"?

(This question does not suppose that a certain understanding of

[31]

"God" has already been shown to correspond in fact to the divine reality, but that some ways of conceiving God are either inconsistent with the human experiences that point to an ultimate ground of value and reality, or else yield an understanding of God that makes it completely irrelevant whether we affirm or deny his reality.)

There are three common misunderstandings of the word "God." One removes him from all involvement with the world we know and live in. He is remote from us in every way, situated in the distant past or future and not at all in our present, residing in a "heaven" infinitely separated from our world, acting in ways that do not touch or influence our lives at any point. The classical form of this misunderstanding is "deism." The other misunderstandings tend to blur the distinction between God and the world. One of these conceives God as just another being, greater and more powerful, no doubt, but in the final analysis, just one more being among the many that exist. He is usually sought in those places where our knowledge fails, in the gaps where we can find no other explanation for a particular phenomenon. He is thus sometimes known as "the God of the gaps." Finally, God may be thought of as the sum of everything. The totality of all that is divine. There is no distinction between God and anything else except the distinction between whole and part. This, of course, is pantheism.

These three misunderstandings of "God" appear in many different forms, often subtly disguised. But still they either remove God from all contact with the world or else somehow confuse him with it.

3. How can we form any idea of God?

Ordinarily our ideas to some extent grasp and express the realities we know. But an idea of God can only point to him on the basis of something else we know and experience directly. For however close he may be to the world, he is distinct from it and his nature or reality differs from it radically. But since (as is shown elsewhere) the world exists through dependence on divine activity and through participation in the divine reality, the world provides a basis for forming some idea about God that directs our mind toward him without comprehending him or manifesting his own mysterious reality.

4. How then can we truly know God with certainty?"

Two things must be kept in mind when discussing the certainty we can have about God's existence and activity: 1) our knowledge of God is always much more the consequence of divine disclosure than of human effort and achievement, and 2) the ways of this disclosure are many and it is through their convergence rather than through any single one of them that our mind has certainty about God. Hence, we should continually inter-relate the various manifestations of God and not consider them in isolation from one another.

The many ways of divine disclosure can be grouped under four general headings, indicating the areas in which we may discover God's manifestation to us: 1) the world of nature; 2) individual experience; 3) inter-personal and community experience; 4) history. In each of these areas we may see that God is at work, and through his work, he is manifesting his presence to us.

5. Is certain knowledge of God a matter of reason or a matter of faith?

This question seems to separate what should merely be distinguished. On the one hand the human mind with the natural light of reason must be fundamentally capable of recognizing some divine manifestation with certainty, otherwise the mind is naturally closed to God and incapable of accepting any knowledge of God; somewhat as an eye must be able to see light if the use of a telescope is going to help it see better or farther. But on the other hand, the certain knowledge we actually have of God is never a matter of just reason or just faith, but always a matter of both reason and faith. For the knowledge of God always supposes a mind that is open to receive evidence of God; and faith is our willing openness to receive the disclosure of God's personal self-communication. Without this openness, reason itself would not as a matter of fact be prepared to acknowledge God as he is made known in his works.

6. How does God disclose himself in the world of nature?

In general, God manifests himself in the dependence and relativity of the world of nature, a dependence and relativity that are seen in such aspects of the world as change, limitation, multiplicity, unity, contingency, purposefulness, beauty, goodness, and intelligibility. The Five Ways of St. Thomas endeavor to explicitate the spontaneous movement of the mind from such aspects to God. It is not that the "proof" itself is the source of the mind's certainty about God's existence, but that the "proof" articulates and lays bare the prior spontaneous process by which the mind recognized the active presence of God in the dependence of the world.

Scripture touches on this matter in several places: Wis. 13: 1–9;

Acts 14: 15–17; 17:24–28; Rom. 1: 18–21. It is also implied in the psalms which speak of God revealing his glory in his works, e.g. 8, 19, 29, 65, 104.

7. How does God disclose himself in the personal experience of an individual?

This varies greatly from person to person, and depends also upon the perceptive awareness of each one. Some ways are the following. God is the horizon of abiding truth, the background against which all activity of judging truth or falsity takes place. He is the supreme value implicitly affirmed in every affirmation of self-transcending good. He is acknowledged as the source of one's life and being, which are experienced as continually being given. He is perceived as the ultimate reality sought in the questioning activity of the mind. He is the term of the experience of absolute dependence. The effective states of awe and joy, the sense of personal responsibility and unconditioned obligation, and the more intimate experiences of invitation, call, and challenge to grow manifest the presence of God. It must be remembered that all these personal experiences need to be considered as part of the converging evidence, and not self-sufficient "proofs" taken in isolation.

8. How does God disclose himself in the life of a community and in interpersonal relationships?

Here, too, there is much variety. Persons can discover in their relations with one another a dimension of unselfish concern that manifests the presence and activity of a power of love that transcends themselves and at the same time grounds the distinctive reality of their individual personalitites. The unity of a community is perceived as a gift, beyond the ability of the individual members to achieve, but graciously being communicated, healed, and preserved. The sense of purpose of the community, drawing the members into the future together, is perceived as a response to an ongoing, personal attraction arising from the ground of all possibility. The endless variety of human personalities responding to one another in freedom and unselfishness, discovering in one another unsuspected depth of vision and appreciation, manifests an enriching source of reality beyond these individuals themselves.

9. How does God disclose himself in history?

From the most extended perspective, we may see God as the goal, the good, whose attractive and unifying presence has stimulated and guided the whole evolutionary process from the first stirrings of life to the appearance of mind and the spread of the human race across the earth. As members of a particular people we can perceive in the decisive events of our past the protection and guidance of God who has brought us where we now are and continues to direct us into the future.

THE BIBLICAL AND CHRISTIAN UNDERSTANDING OF GOD

10. How does God reveal himself in the Old Testament?

The psalms, particularly those of praise and thanksgiving, show that God manifested himself to the Hebrews in all the ways mentioned above in question 4. The ancestors of the Hebrew people were polytheists, like all the peoples we know of in the Ancient Near East (see Jos. 24:2, 14). Through the self-manifestation of God they became, probably in stages, strict monotheists. In the earliest period, recalled in the sagas of the Patriarchs, there appear to be signs of a surviving polytheism, as when God manifested himself to Abraham as three visitors (Gen. 18:1–3). However, very early there appeared a practical monotheism, in which one alone was worshipped and acknowledged as God, though without any theoretical denial of the existence of other gods, worshipped perhaps by their neighbors. During this time God was considered a tribal or clan divinity, to whom they committed themselves and who watched over them. But soon they recognized that God's power to care for them meant that he was more than just a tribal god, and they gave him the title: Maker of Heaven and Earth (Gen. 14:19, 22) This realization of the creative power of God lies at the root of all subsequent development of Israel's understanding of God, both of his transcendence and his immanence. For as maker of all things, he is distinct and different from them; and this is his transcendence. But also, as maker of all things, he is intimately present to them, sustaining them by his power and guiding them by his wisdom; and this is his immanence. Thus, far from being opposed, divine transcendence and immanence are intimately related, the transcendent power of God being the root of his immanent presence in all things.

11. What does the Old Testament teach about the transcendence of God?

Referring often to the fact that God is creator of heaven and earth, the Old Testament teaches God's transcendence as his difference from all created things. He is unique, the One God, there is no other (Is. 45:18; Jer. 10:10–12). By his omnipotence he transcends creaturely weakness (Jer. 32:17; Ps. 135:5–7; Is. 55.) In his eternity he transcends the frail duration of creatures (Lam. 5:17–20; Is. 40:28; Ps. 90:1–4; 102: 25–27). In his immensity he transcends all limitation of place (1 Kg. 8:27; Jer. 23:23–24; Ps. 139:8–10). Through his Spirit he contains all things (Wis. 1:7), and by his Wisdom he orders all things (Wis. 8:1). He is beyond our ability to comprehend (Ps. 139:6; Job 42:3) or to praise sufficiently (Sir. 43:28).

12. What does the Old Testament teach about the immanence of God?

The whole narrative of the Old Testament recounts God's presence and activity in human history. Most significant are his election of the Hebrews as his own people (Gen. 12:1–3), the covenant he made with them (Ex. 19:5–6), the liberation from Egypt (Ex. 3:8) and the giving of the land of Canaan (Jos. 1:11), the establishment of the Davidic monarchy (2 Sam. 7:8–16), the sending of prophets (2 Kgs. 17:13), the captivity of the people in Babylon and their restoration (Is. 40:1–2), and the inspiration of sacred writings. God's choice and concern for Israel looked beyond them to the salvation of the whole world (Is. 2:2–4; 45:22; Jer. 16:19; Jonah; Ps. 116). God prepared them for a future, definitive saving act, by arousing and sustaining in them a messianic hope. This hope corresponded to an increasingly clearer word of promise: first to Abraham (Gen. 12:1–3), then to David (2 Sam. 7:7–17), with a prophecy of a new covenant (Jer. 31:31–34), and later a prediction concerning a mysterious Servant of Yahweh, whose suffering would remove sin (Is. 52:13–53:12), and finally the vision of a "Son of Man" who would inaugurate the universal Kingdom of God (Dan. 7:14).

13. What is the description of God that emerges from the Old Testament.

According to the Old Testament, the living and true God is the

Maker and Lord of Heaven and Earth, one, almighty, eternal, immense and unspeakably exalted, who for the salvation of all men chose a people as his own, and prepared them in many ways for the coming of a savior, the Messiah.

14. What is the central New Testament teaching about God?

In the New Testament, the word "God" (Gk. *ho theos*) normally designates the living and true God of the Old Testament (Jn. 8:54), the Father of Our Lord Jesus Christ (Heb. 1: 1–2), who sent his Son into the world (Gal. 4:4), worked in him and through him his prophetic and saving mission (Jn. 14:10), raised him from the dead (Eph. 1:20), glorified him, and conferred upon him the Holy Spirit to be given to all who believe (Acts 2:33; Jn. 7:39). It likewise teaches that God is also our Father (Mt. 6:9; Rom. 1:7), who has made us his sons and daughters in and through his Son Jesus Christ (Mt. 12:50; Eph. 1:5–6). This lays upon us the obligation to live as his children (Mt. 5:48), chiefly through forgiveness (Mt. 6:14–15), mercy (Lk. 6:36), and mutual love (1 Jn. 4:7); and it also inspires in us confidence and trust concerning everything that happens to us, even suffering and death (Mt. 6:25; 10:29–31). St. John sums up the whole Christian revelation of God in the expression: God is love (1 Jn. 4:7–21).

15. How does the New Testament teaching about God reflect Jesus' own human religious experience?

Jesus' own religious experience is expressed most essentially in the way he addressed God, calling him "Abba" (Mk. 14:36), a word that signifies not merely father, but a degree of intimate familiarity no one before him had ventured to presume. It is something like the English word "Daddy." He saw himself as entrusted by his Father with a prophetic and saving mission, and for this mission he knew himself endowed in a special way with the Holy Spirit (Lk. 3:22; 4:1, 14, 18; 10:21; Acts 10:38). His teaching proclaims the will of his Father (Mt. 7:21–27), and one who does the will of his Father is his brother, sister, and mother (Mt. 12:50).

16. How does the New Testament teaching about God reflect also the religious experience of the primitive Christian community?

The first generation of Christians experienced the power and the presence of God in the freedom, forgiveness, unity, peace, and charity that generally characterized their communities (Gal. 5; Eph. 4). They recognized here the gift of the Holy Spirit, given by the Risen Jesus to those who believed in him (Jn. 7:39; Acts 2:38), in fulfillment of the promise of the Father (Lk. 24:49; Acts 1:4). In this Spirit they acknowledged Jesus as Lord (1 Cor. 12:3) and called God by the same name Jesus had: "Abba! Father (Daddy)" (Gal. 4:6; Rom. 8:15). They recognized, too, that Jesus in sharing with them his Spirit, shared with them also his prophetic and saving mission (Jn. 20:21–23; Act. 1:8).

17. How did the Christian Church of the early centuries eventually formulate this teaching and its own continuing experience of God's presence?

The doctrine of the Holy Trinity is the formulation of the Christian experience of God. It was formulated gradually in reaction to forces within and without the Church. It maintained against the pagans that Christians are not atheists, since they worship Father, Son, and Holy Spirit as God. It maintained against patripassianists and monarchianists that Father, Son, and Holy Spirit are really distinct. It maintained against adoptionists and subordinationists that not only the Father, but also the Son and the Spirit are truly and fully divine. It maintained against the charge of tritheism that it acknowledges only one God. It maintained against Eunomius and his followers that God is an incomprehensible mystery.

The actual terminology developed slowly. It was finally agreed to say Father, Son, and Holy Spirit are distinct as *persons*, though it was recognized that *person* is a very inadequate term and could even be misleading, as if it meant that each of them had his own distinct intelligence and will. They are one however in the divine *nature*, in the godhead itself which belongs equally and totally to each.

18. What is meant by the distinction between the economic trinity and the immanent trinity?

The economic trinity means the three divine persons as they are communicated to us in the economy or plan of salvation: the Father sending the Son, the Father and the Son sending the Holy Spirit, and the Father coming to us with the Son and the Holy Spirit. The immanent trinity refers to the three divine persons within the divine nature itself. Some have suggested that the trinity is only economic, and that we can neither affirm nor deny an immanent trinity. The reasons advanced for this are that all distinction between the three is given within the plan of salvation, and that the inner mystery of God is quite beyond us. But the first reason is not entirely true (see, e.g. Jn. 17:5), and the second fails to note that if God truly communicates himself to us in the economic trinity, then God must be Trinity in himself.

19. But how can an immanent trinity be maintained without contradiction?

Unfortunately, for many it is the answer to this question rather than the communion we have with God, Father, Son, and Holy Spirit that has preoccupied their thinking about the trinity. Human reason reflecting upon the self-communication of God cannot know why the trinity is necessary or even possible for any positive reason. It can at the most show that it is not impossible, and then offer some suggestions to illustrate this non-impossibility. Briefly: all real distinction, whether in God or elsewhere, flows from relations of mutual opposition, relations which exclude one from being the other. Fatherhood and sonship are such relations. If then the divine persons are relations of mutual opposition with respect to one another, they are really distinct from one another. But if these relations are not so opposed to the single absolute reality of the divine nature, then while they are really distinct from one another as relations, they are really identified with the divine nature. There are three persons in one God. God is Father, Son and Holy Spirit. Each of them is the same God, though none of them is identified with any other. Such difficult and abstract reasoning is not calculated to nourish piety; but it is needed and useful to assure us that the mystery of God, as we experience and formulate it, is not an absurdity. The classical model for illustrating this kind of reasoning comes from St. Augustine and is developed by St. Thomas on the analogy of the human mind, where inner word proceeds from memory, and love proceeds from both. Here there are three: memory, word, and love, but only one mind. Ideally, too, each is equal to the others and is wholly present in them.

SPECIAL PROBLEMS: RELATIONS BETWEEN GOD AND THE WORLD

20. How is God active in the world?

It must be emphasized that God is not just another cause or agent alongside created causes and agents. God is not at work in the world the same way as creatures, only more powerfully and universally. God does not act in the world as a part of the world, but as the first beginning and last end and universal support of the whole world and the entire order of causes and effects within it. "For from him and through him and to him are all things" (Rom. 11:36). He is intimately and profoundly active in all things, as the ultimate interior source of their power and action, as the unifying center that draws them into the order of a single universe, as the ultimate good in whose goodness they share as they tend into the future, toward the realization of their native dynamisms. God does not interact with things as one cause among many; the whole multitude of causes in their many complex relationships with one another depend on the casual activity of God. He acts in the universal "within" of things, not outside them or between them. He both confers upon each thing the being and activity it possesses, and he subsumes that being and activity into the total order of the universe. It is because the activity of God is the universal presupposition of all activity that no experiment can be devised to test its presence in contrast to another situation in which it might be thought absent. In a word, God is transcendentally active in the world, not merely categorically, in some particular section or aspect of the world.

21. Is God in any way affected by the activity of his creatures?

God is not affected passively by his creatures in any way, i.e. their activity can neither add to nor diminish his supreme reality. But God does adjust or temper his activity to the conditions found in creatures, including the conditions that result from their activity. In choosing to make creatures, and especially in choosing to make free creatures, God chooses that his activity penetrates and influences the world according to the conditions of their activity and choice. Thus, although he is never passive with respect to the world but always totally active, his activity by choice is conditioned in its result by the activity of creatures.

As God truly loves mankind, he opens himself just as truly to joy and sorrow from those whom he loves. When they are willing to accept his goodness, they act according to his will, and hence please him and he rejoices over them. When they refuse to accept his goodness, they act against his will and block the communication of his goodness; thus they offend him and he sorrows over them. All these words, "love, please, offend, rejoice, sorrow"—point to the divine reality but do not adequately grasp or express it. They are more than mere metaphors, however, and signify however dimly the reality to be found in God.

22. But how can anything else be truly active if God is active in all things?

The activity of God does not compete with or suppress the activity of creatures, but precisely makes that activity possible. God does not merely share his goodness and reality with creatures, but he enables them to share with one another, and in the case of free creatures, to determine how this further sharing is to take place. Interior activity, that does not directly influence something else, as in seeing or thinking or willing, is not a sharing with another, but is an interior responsive act by which what has been received from another enters into the active possession of the creature, by a kind of interior communication.

23. Does God know all things?

God does know all things. It is his knowing things that makes them true. Here, too, of course, "know" points to rather than expresses the divine action. However, everything that is found in creatures derives from God according to his free determination to share; and as the total divine reality is wholly present to itself and is thus understood, so too this free determination is present and grasped as the source of the truth of things distinct from himself.

Some have thought that God does not know what is future to us, because as future it does not yet exist and is thus unknowable. However, Scripture and the constant teaching and belief of Christians hold that God does indeed know even what is future to us. The contrary opinion in a subtle way makes God part of the world, subjecting him to the creaturely conditions of time, making that future also to God which is future to us. But present, past, and future are temporal distinctions that are directly meaningful only to a mind in time knowing in the present. If God truly transcends the world, and if the world and its total order depends on God, then God knows whatever is in the world at any point of its temporal order. It is all "present" to him, not as though he and it were subject to some one identical temporal measurement, as when we say that something is present to us, but in the simple coincidence of the divine causal knowledge with all that proceeds from it, as when we say that action and effect are simultaneous.

24. If God knows the future, how is it that my free choices are not already predetermined?

God's knowing is causative as we said, and his causing is cognitive. He causes some things to act freely, that is, to act without being determined by him. Thus, as he causes according to the conditions that we freely place, so also he knows according to those conditions. He knows my future free acts according to the choices that I will actually freely make. His knowing does not determine what I am going to choose, but my future choosing determines the conditions according to which God's causative knowledge is active, since God has freely chosen to know and cause in this way.

25. How is evil (sin and suffering) present in the world if God is active there?

This question is probably the greatest challenge to belief in God. It has traditionally been answered in three affirmations: 1) evil is a privation of good, not something positive in itself; 2) sin arises from the abuse of created freedom, a freedom which God respects and does not suppress even when abused; 3) all suffering is traceable ultimately to sin, though not necessarily to the sin of the individual who suffers. It is this third point especially that has seemed weak to many, though clearly much suffering in the world would be relieved if men stopped sinning. Hence, another approach to this problem makes three other points: 1) some sin and suffering is statistically inevitable in this kind of universe which develops through an evolutionary process to become the arena for free human endeavor; 2) it is good, in spite of this evil, to have this kind of universe, where creatures through struggle and activity share profoundly the effective power of God; 3) God in many ways turns sin and suffering to good, especially by entering into the world through the redemptive incarnation of the Son. He takes upon himself the sin and suffering of the world, and from within transforms the human condition into one of hope, filled with the promise of eternal life.

26. How can prayer have any efficacy with God?

Prayer is effective not by persuading God to do something he is otherwise unwilling to do, but by manifesting in a new way our dependence on God. This dependence is the source of all the goodness that we have. A new manifestation intensifies and deepens the relationship, much as in the sacraments. Thus, if our prayer manifests real faith in God, it becomes the sign through which God works to bestow new benefits on us.

27. Does God have a plan for each one of us?

God does not determine ahead of time how our lives are actually going to be led in all their details. For this would both take away our freedom and make God the positive author of sin. But God does call each of us to eternal life; he renews this call and makes it possible for us to respond in every situation of our life short of final impenitence. Nothing happens to us that he does not turn to our good, if we are willing. This does not mean that everything that comes into our life comes directly from him. For much that touches us comes from the carelessness and sinfulness of others, which he does not will, and from chance occurrences of nature, which he does not directly intend, though he intends their possibility in general and knows eternally their realization in fact. Still, in all of this, he is present to benefit and protect us, especially in answer to our prayers.

28. How does "process thought" view God?

Much contemporary theology is being developed in terms of process. As applied to God this has various meanings, some acceptable and illuminating from a Christian point of view, others not really reconcilable with the biblical and Christian view of God. Thus process thought has made it clearer how we can affirm God's relationship to us, his involvement in our world, his responsiveness to our needs, the conditioning of his knowledge and activity by what we do. All of these are contained in the picture of God given us in sacred Scripture. But it is less easy to accept the idea that God himself is in process of development, that he is being fundamentally enriched by his contact with creation, that he is subject to time, etc. This seems to blur the distinction between God and the world and to oppose the teaching of Scripture.

29. What are some of the causes for the contemporary denial of God?

The problem of evil is still probably the greatest obstacle to accepting the reality of God (see question 25). But recent cultural advances have caused some to deny God, though usually they are rejecting a distortion of God and not the God revealed in the bible and authentic religious experience. Thus, modern science does not appeal to God for explanations of how the universe functions; here in fact it rejects the

"God of the gaps." Likewise, science often finds it impossible to suppose that any outside will is influencing what takes place in the world and history; usually, it is thinking of God as just another cause, operating in the same way as other causes, but more powerfully and universally.

Others have denied God, because religious persons have used the idea to legitimize their own selfish purposes. Religion, by merely preaching generosity to the rich and resignation to the poor, became an opiate of the masses, preventing them from achieving their true dignity.

Still others have denied God in the name of human liberty. If God is man's creator, gives him his nature and destiny, works in the world and in all human activity, it seems to them that belief in God has destroyed human freedom.

30. What positive service does atheism perform?

Atheism is a constant summons to purify our idea of God. We need to ask ourselves whether we wish to affirm precisely the understanding of God that the atheist is denying. If not, then we must clarify what we are affirming. If so, we must still try to appreciate his difficulty and to respond to it by a profounder faith and knowledge of God.

Creation and Fall

1. What has the Church said of the world's relation to God?

The ancient Christian creeds professed their belief in one God, the Father Almighty, who was the maker of heaven and earth, of all things visible and invisible. Later Councils of the Church repeated these statements but added that God freely created the world from nothing at the beginning of time. He did so in order to share his goodness, for his own glory and the sanctification of man. These statements are a summary of the doctrine of creation.

2. What is the origin of the term "creation"?

It comes from the Latin word *creare* which literally means "to beget." This in turn was an attempt to reproduce the biblical terms *bara* and *ktidzein*. The former was the word used in the Old Testament to describe God's uniquely sacred action upon Israel and upon the world. It appears in the first line of Genesis: "In the beginning God created (*bara*) the heavens and earth." The Greek Bible used the word *ktidzein,* which originally meant "to make habitable" or "to found" (a city), to express the same idea.

3. What is meant by the phrase "all thing visible and invisible"?

It expresses the belief that God is author not only of the perceptible world about us but of the angelic creation, both of which are part of God's single creative plan. There is nothing therefore apart from God that is not his creature.

4. What is meant by creation "from nothing"?

In a negative sense it means to produce something which in no way existed before. Positively, it means to produce the total reality of something.

5. Is this a valid definition of creation?

Yes, but it has its limitations. This theological definition developed during the Middle Ages and persisted until quite recent times. Medieval theologians concentrated their attention upon divine causality; and so, while they were well aware of God's activity in the on-going world, they focussed their speculations upon the world's origin. This type of causal speculation ran into difficulty with the rise of modern science. Science talks of causes as a type of perceptible interaction within a closed system. To interpret creation as a "cause" among other causes is to forget that it is a divine act quite outside human experience. To avoid this problem, theology retreated to a position where creation became further and further removed from the chain of natural causes and was restricted to the beginning of the world.

6. What effect did this have on the theology of creation?

The doctrine was in danger of being reduced to the divine initiative in launching the cosmos at some unthinkably remote and first moment of time with little relation to the on-going process of the world and man.

7. What important corrective has been made to this theology?

In 1973 the American bishops, recalling the work of contemporary biblical scholarship, said that creation is the beginning of the salvation accomplished by Christ and that God is present in history from start to finish.

8. What is the biblical basis of this corrective?

There was a clear link in the Hebrew mind between creation and the history of Israel's salvation. In fact it was only in reflecting on the latter that the Hebrews came to a realization of the former. Textually the two notions are clearly connected in the Priestly document which contains not only the first creation account (Gn. 1–2:4b) but also the story of the covenants (Noah, Abraham and Moses). In the second creation account the divine action is a prologue to God's saving work in Israel. Indeed Israel's salvation is promised in terms that recall creation: a new creation, a new triumph over the abyss and darkness, a new victory over chaos. Deutero-Isaiah, speaking to the disheartened Jews of the exile, reminded them that God, who shaped the world, shapes all history toward salvation.

9. Did this Judaic view of creation enter the New Testament?

The connection in the Jewish mind between salvation and creation helped prepare the Jews of the New Testament to see the link between Christ and creation. For Paul the redemption is a new creation with Christ the beginning and the goal. The author of the Apocalypse uses the imagery of Genesis to describe the plenitude of the divine work accomplished in Christ.

10. In the light of these considerations how may we view the doctrine of creation?

The doctrine expresses the unique divine action by which God is the author, ground and goal of the world and everything pertaining to it.

11. In what sense is God's creative action the "ground and goal" of all reality?

The enabling power of God is at the inmost core of all creaturely being and action without in any way detracting from the integrity of the creature. God's creative action empowers the world to bring itself about; at the same time he draws creation forward toward its fulfillment.

12. What is meant by "all reality"?

It means everything that exists, including man in his freedom. This is the positive meaning of the phrase "from nothing." Man and his world, therefore, move toward their consummation with their Creator who is both source and goal of their developing movement.

13. What is the "motive" for creation?

Creation is an act of generosity, the act of loving and giving. God created in order to share the goodness that was his with the world and with man. Man alone among earth's creatures, can accept this love and so bring about his own fulfillment—which is identical with the glory of God.

14. What is the role of Christ in creation?

As the Incarnate Word of God, he is the complete fulfillment of all that we mean by "man." And since the Word's enfleshment requires the world for his environment, God's creative will brought the entire world into being. Thus Jesus is not only the head of the human race but the summit of all creation. As such, he is the model and gracious source of man's "yes" to the loving creative act of God. For the

second Adam, unlike the first, was unequivocally focussed on the will
of his Father. "In him everything in heaven and on earth was created,
not only things visible but also the invisible order of thrones, sover-
eignties, authorities and powers." (Col. 1:15).

15. What is the pastoral relevance of the doctrine of creation?

This doctrine has had a profound effect on Western civilization.
With its insistence that both man and his world are good and that the
world is given to man's care, it set the stage for the appearance of the
scientific spirit and ultimately the technological revolution.

From the rise of capitalism to the recent past man's biblical dominion over the earth was seen as a charter to plunder the earth's
resources. We now see that "dominion" implies responsibility not
only for the future of mankind but for our evolving planet. This
responsibility would be entirely too heavy for mankind were we not
assured of God's continuing presence in the on-going work of creation.

In more personal terms the doctrine of creation is God's response
to man's anxiety. Each man is the author of his own autobiography,
but he is not alone. God's enabling and loving power undergirds man's
freedom and gives ultimate meaning to his life. It is the basis of
Christian hope.

THE CREATION OF MAN

16. What has the Church said about the origins of the human race?

The Councils of the Church have professed their belief that man,
a unity of flesh and spirit, owes his existence to the creative action of
God (IV Lateran and Vatican I). Moreover, man in the beginning was
specially favored by God but he sinned with universal consequences
for the members of the human race (Trent).

17. Why was the Church concerned about man's origins and his primal fault?

Fundamentally it was because she saw that both bore importantly
upon the redemptive work of Christ. Her reflection on Christ's salvific
work caused her to ask whether his forgiving grace is necessary for
every man in every age even before their freedom comes into play.

18. Has the Church committed herself to monogenism, i.e. to the existence of two individuals, Adam and Eve, who were the first parents of the race?

No, although the Church took a cautious stand for monogenism with the encyclical *Humani Generis* (1949). The reason for this position was that "it is not apparent how (polygenism) can be reconciled with the doctrine of original sin." In the quarter century since *Humani Generis* theologians have suggested various ways in which the two might be reconciled. At the present moment there is no necessary connection that can be seen between monogenism and the integrity of Catholic doctrine.

19. But have not the Councils spoken most solemnly of mankind's origin from the one man, Adam?

The Councils, Trent in particular, were addressing themselves directly to other questions. Trent was concerned with the problems of original justice and original sin. In their declarations they assumed that Adam was the father of the race. An assumption of this sort takes on the force of the definition itself only when there is a necessary connection between the two. In this case the assumption is not necessary to the integrity of the conciliar definitions on original justice and original sin.

20. Does not Genesis itself clearly speak of a single couple who were the protoparents of mankind?

The opening chapters of Genesis are concerned with the origins of mankind, *Adam* is not a proper name but a noun—man. The special creation of Eve was the author's way of showing that both sexes owed their origin equally to the special care of the Creator.

21. Does not St. Paul say clearly that sin and death entered the world through one man? (Rom. 5:12)

Yes, but two considerations are important to the understanding of this passage: Paul's purpose and his use of Genesis. Paul intended to show the universal extension of Christ's saving work; it extended to the entire race. To do so, he employed the Genesis text without giving it any meaning other than that intended by the author. And the author of Genesis was speaking of mankind's origin and the introduction of evil into the world through sin. Paul's purpose did not depend upon a literal interpretation of the creation account.

22. What is the Christian belief, therefore, about the origins of the human race?

Man, a unity of flesh and spirit, owes his presence on earth to the creative action of God. This creative action could well have found expression in an evolutionary process. Since the enabling power of God undergirds the world's movement there is no necessary conflict between the doctrine of creation and the theory of man's evolution.

23. Why does the Church speak of man as a unity of flesh and spirit?

This is a polemic statement directed against those who, like the gnostics or Albigenses, saw a dualism in man. In their view the material dimension of man was evil or the source of evil. The Church insisted in turn that man was one and good as he came from the hand of God.

ORIGINAL JUSTICE—ORIGINAL SIN

24. Why does the Church speak of the original justice and holiness of man?

The Church's teaching on original justice is a corollary of its belief in the redemptive work of Christ. As St. Paul describes it, Christ restored what Adam had lost. The clear implication of such a restoration is that mankind once had and somehow lost a gracious intimacy with God.

25. Does Genesis speak of man's justice and holiness?

It does not do so in a direct or extended way. The author is concerned with the origin of evil and he traces it to man and not to God who made all things good.

26. Does the New Testament speak of original justice?

An important theme of the New Testament is that through Christ man was restored to the image of his maker (Eph. 4:23; Rom. 5:10 ff.). The idea of restoration clearly implies that man once possessed and then lost what Christ gave back.

27. What is meant by original justice?

It means sanctifying grace as well as the gifts of integrity and immortality. The Councils did not define whether man was created in this condition or whether he was to dispose himself for it with God's assistance. In the latter case man faced a genuine invitation from God. Acceptance would have meant that man would have been transformed, deified, but without losing his human condition. He would not have known death as he now experiences it (immortality); nor would his commitment to good have been accompanied by the internal conflict that is a present part of the human condition (integrity).

28. What choice did man make?

Man rejected God's invitation to intimacy and union and so sinned gravely. Once this choice had been made, the possibilities open to mankind were closed; they could be re-opened only in Christ. Neither the explicit nature of this sin nor its time and circumstances were ever the object of a definition by the Church.

29. What were the consequences of this sin for the human race?

They are described by the phrase "original sin." By sinning Adam of Genesis affected for the worse not only himself but all mankind. The Council of Trent described this change as the loss of justice and holiness, the incurrence of divine wrath, the death of the soul as well as the body. The Council describes this condition as a true sin, present in all men and transmitted by propagation and not imitation.

Men imitate Adam's sin by their personal sin; but even prior to this they are affected by sin because they are human beings historically united in the human race. Because of Adam's sin human beings enter the world in special need of the grace of Christ. They are not capable of unswerving commitment to moral good without internal conflict (concupiscence) and they face the experience of death as we know it now (the loss of immortality).

30. Is original sin a personal sin?

It is in the sense that it personally affects each member of the race, not in the sense that it involves personal decision or choice.

31. Is this not unjust?

It would be unjust if God held men guilty of the sin of Adam. When we speak of the sin that affects mankind we are using the term in an analogous sense. Moreover, since God's self-communication in love is purely gratuitous, he could choose his own way of offering himself to mankind. He chose to make the gift dependent upon an initial choice at the beginning of the race and within the larger context of the redemptive work of Christ.

32. What biblical considerations prompted the Church's teaching on original sin?

The opening chapters of Genesis describe the entrance of evil into the history of man, but neither here nor elsewhere in the Old Testament is there clear evidence of the existence of original sin. The idea, though not the phrase, occurs in 1 Cor. 15:21; Eph. 2:3 but most forcefully in Rom. 5:12–19: sin and death have entered all men; in the transgression of one the rest died; through the disobedience of one the rest were constituted sinners.

33. How did this idea develop over the centuries?

The idea did not mature until the time of Augustine in the fourth century. In proclaiming original sin a dogma of the faith Augustine appealed both to Scripture and to the Church's practice of infant baptism. He felt that the essence of original sin was concupiscence. In the Middle Ages theologians sharpened their thinking about original justice, saying that it was basically sanctifying grace. They concluded that the essence of original sin was the lack of sanctifying grace —a fact for which Adam was responsible. Concupiscence was seen as the consequence of original sin, something remaining even after the sin had been removed. Trent defined the existence of original sin in every member of the race. According to this Council the sin consisted in the lack of that original justice and holiness that had graced the race. Essentially these remained the lines along with theology moved through the next four centuries. Recently theologians have begun to ask whether original sin could be better explained as the Sin of the World.

34. What is meant by the Sin of the World?

The phrase is a way of coming at the human solidarity in sin that is described by the Scriptures and the Councils of the Church. Man's whole history has been characterized by sinful action. The "Sin of the World," however, is not merely the sum total of individual sins, nor is it the guilt of one person passing to another. Rather it describes the fact that mankind is situated in an environment that is poisoned by sin. Situated in this way, man finds that his freedom is limited in its field of action, in the motives and insights presented to it. This situated liberty is the crucial factor in mankind's solidarity throughout its long history of sin. Being situated in a sinful environment, therefore, means the lack of the life of grace, death to the supernatural life, powerlessness. And this is the content of original sin as it has traditionally been described.

35. Are even infants affected by the Sin of the World?

Yes, because they cannot escape the environment in which their personalities will develop. They are pre-personally conditioned by the sinful situation into which they have been introduced through their conception.

36. Does this view of original sin conflict with Trent's statement that the sin is transmitted by propagation?

No. Propagation is the condition not the cause of original sin. Generation produces the man, but original sin is produced by the historical situation in which men are conceived. In this sense original sin is said to be transmitted by propagation.

37. Need the Sin of the World be traced to a single sinning parent of the race?

The critical factor in answering this question is the universality of original sin after the Fall. In one view the Fall should be seen as history, not as something that occurred in one well-determined sin. Sin gradually spread through the race until it became truly universal in the sin that was the rejection of Christ. Prior to this, sin had been a rejection of grace. From that moment on original sin became truly universal and baptism became universally necessary. In this explanation there would be no need for a single sinning couple who were men's first parents.

38. Is this an acceptable explanation of man's universal solidarity in sin?

It does not seem to do justice to the idea of mankind's universal solidarity in sin. The reason is that it diminishes the universal efficacy of Christ's redemptive role. It implies that not everyone in history has been in need of Christ's redeeming grace. For this reason it seems better to trace original sin to a primal fault which immediately affected the entire race.

39. Does a single primal fault demand a single sinning first couple, Adam and Eve?

No. Mankind could gradually have evolved to a point where it was capable of free choice. Here men stood on a new threshold, for God from the beginning had ordered creation so that it should produce not just a rational being but a man vivified by grace. This further step in man's development would be accomplished not through the evolutionary process but by man's acceptance of a divine invitation. The invitation was given to and the decision made by one man who acted for the race.

The biblical notion of the "corporate personality" in whom the community was incarnate helps us to see the possibility of an individual by whose action the situation of the collectivity before God was determined. If this were true of the Jewish patriarchs and kings, it would be all the more true of the first sinner.

40. What were the consequences of this first sin?

The evolutionary process did not stop but it took a new path. Had man accepted the divine offer, he would as a person have perfectly mastered his own nature, eliminated suffering, and passed ultimately to his definitive perfection without experiencing death as we know it. As things turned out, God's decision for man's divinization remained firm. But he would implement it in a different way. Each man would now be invited to share in the glory of Christ by sharing in the death of Christ. Man's destiny still remained within reach: the dominion of the person over nature, the triumph over suffering and death. But these will now be realized only in the eschatological order. As a result of the original opposition to God's plan, man comes into the world burdened by the spontaneity of a nature not totally mastered by the person (concupiscence) and faced by the prospect of suffering and death.

41. What then is original sin?

It is the state in which human beings are born precisely because they are members of the human race. As such, they are situated in a sinful history that affects their capacity to love God above all and to reach the form of existence for which they were destined. It is found in each man and can truly be called the death of the soul because it implies the lack of grace. The individual is not responsible for this state; yet because it is contrary to God's will, it is a sin, although in an analogous sense.

42. What pastoral relevance does this doctrine have?

It makes possible a realistic view of man in his world. He is essentially good as he comes from the hand of God. Nonetheless, he is situated in a history of sin. He may ratify this sinful history by personal choice or respond to the grace of Christ. Moreover, he must make his decision under concupiscence and in the face of death. Concupiscence and death are clear signs that the victory of grace is not yet complete. The eschatological character of this final victory rules out any possibility of man's achieving a world of perfect justice and love. He must strive for it; he cannot attain it in this world.

43. What has the Church said about the devil?

Three Councils recognized the existence of the devil—IV Lateran, Trent and Vatican I. Their intention was to assert that there is no absolute primal evil but only the evil due to the decision of free creatures. Nevertheless, their definitions imply the existence of personal, non-human beings. The devil is not mentioned in the early Creeds. The Fathers of the Church, however, were unanimous in their agreement that he existed. The New Testament is warranty for their conviction. Satan is mentioned in every book but two—the Second and Third Epistles of John.

44. What is the devil?

He is part of that spiritual creation of which we spoke earlier. And like all of creation he is subject to the sovereign will of God. Called to respond to God's invitation to union he rejected it. Prior to the free decision of men, therefore, the world already had an element of evil that was hostile to God.

45. What can be said of the present renewed interest in the devil?

As Richard Woods has said, "Overbelief in the power of Satan and the demons, or even accepting as Christian teaching the myths of the devil that sprang up over a thousand year period of Jewish-Christian speculation, is . . . a covert kind of devil worship, and from a psychological and spiritual point of view, more destructive than skepticism" (*Chicago Studies,* Spring, 1973).

The Church's teaching reminds man that he is not alone in this world. It also insists that all the world is subject to the Almighty Father, Maker of heaven and earth.

Grace

1. What is grace?

Grace is God's loving presence and man's transformation in it.

2. How is God present to man?

God is present in an ordinary way to the person who recognizes him in creation as the ground of all that exists. But through grace God becomes present to the human consciousness in a special way. Through faith he is perceived as Love itself offering to men a participation in his own life, an involvement with him in a relationship much more intimate than that between Creator and creature, one like men experience in their family life.

3. How does man know that God offers himself in this way?

Man knows through God's revelation of himself in Scripture. God is defined as Love.

4. What are the scriptural models of God's love for man?

In regard to the community of believers in God's word in the Old Testament, the model of love was that between husband and wife. The same model is used by St. Paul in the New Testament to express the love between Christ and his Church. More frequently, however, the New Testament employs the model of love between a father and his sons and daughters.

5. Is grace supernatural?

To the extent that the word "supernatural" means that man can in no way deserve or merit God's special love, in other words, that love must be absolutely freely bestowed, grace might be called supernatural. To the extent that man readily responds to this kind of love, thrives and flourishes on it and finds in it ultimate satisfaction and self-fulfillment, grace is rooted in and fully adapted to man's existential condition and hence ought not to be called supernatural.

[56]

6. How is man transformed by grace?

When man responds to God's offer of love by surrendering himself entirely to God in that love, he transcends his former sinful condition, receives an ability and incentive to grow further in that love, shares his life and freedom with God and becomes a fuller and more perfect image of the God-man, Jesus Christ.

7. Does grace rob man of his freedom?

All full commitments in love imply an initial surrender of personal and individual freedom to one's partner. But through love a new state of cooperative or shared freedom is attained. Through grace man comes to share in God's own freedom.

8. Does grace as a share in God's own freedom imply exemption from the law?

The graced person, as Scripture indicates, is free, like the Son of God himself, from the binding force of the law. He will most certainly, however, perform what the will of God demands, not because of the law, but because of his love of God.

9. Does the graced person remain a sinner?

The graced person cannot be regarded as guilty of serious sin, for it is impossible at one and the same time both to love God so completely and be turned away from him by sin. But the graced person remains liable to sin, and in this sense may be said to be both just and sinful.

10. Though still liable to sin, does the graced person receive an incentive to remain in and grow in love?

As one who loves, the graced person feels the need to fulfill the expectations of his beloved. So he is moved to avoid sin and develop more fully his love-relationship with God.

11. How does the graced person become in a fuller sense an image of Christ?

Christ is the paradigm of humanity. He is the perfect model of the kind of love that God expects from mankind. His being reveals the culmination of the divine-human act of love, for in him humanity and divinity are perfectly united. His human life reflects the fullest possible measure of divine love. The graced person in his own love of God and consequent participation in the divine life quite obviously becomes Christlike. The more he loves, the more closely he resembles the divine model of mankind.

12. Can grace produce some kind of identity with Christ?

Grace does not obliterate the unique and unrepeatable identity of either Christ or those who seek to follow him in loving God. But it does effect an analogical identity or identity of correspondence between Christ and his purely human brothers and sisters. This identity is more perceptible in the body of believers as a whole than in any individual member. Hence the Church as a whole is called the Mystical Body of Christ and perceives itself as primarily obliged to continue the salvational task of Christ in the world. But the individual Christian, too, especially through the sacraments of initiation, becomes "another Christ," and assumes some responsibility in promoting his cause in the world.

13. How do the sacraments of initiation proclaim the individual Christian's identity with Christ in grace?

In baptism water is understood to symbolize life and death. To be buried in water was, to the mind of the ancients, tantamount to dying. But they also saw water as the substance in which life initially began, and from which it continues to emerge. Through the symbolism of water the one who is baptized acts out the paschal mystery of Jesus, the mystery of his death and resurrection to a new life, the mystery which effected man's reconciliation with God alienated by sin. In so doing he proclaims his identity with Jesus. In confirmation the Christian is anointed with chrism, the Christ-oil. He literally becomes a Christ, a Messiah, an anointed one. So he proclaims his identity with Christ in the second great mystery of his life, the pentecostal mystery, the mystery that envelopes men in a closer, more loving union with God, the mystery that tends to set the world afire with divine love.

14. How does the Eucharist portray Christians' identity with Christ?

Man can die and rise only once; so baptism cannot be repeated. But faith in the risen life, the life of divine love, must be constantly nourished. The Eucharist in its symbolism is the sacrament of nourishment. In the Eucharist the bread and wine are symbols of the life of the people. Their human life is sustained by food and drink. When through the words of faith these are transformed into the body and blood of Christ, the people are shown in a very dramatic way who they really are: the body of the mystic Christ. Again when they introject the sacred species at communion time, they once more proclaim their identity with Christ.

15. Why is the Eucharist in a special way the source of grace in the lives of Christians?

The word "grace" (in Greek *charis*) means beauty. The graced person is beautiful in the eyes of God because he bears the image of Jesus. The word "eucharist" (in Greek *eucharistia*) implies reflection upon the graced condition of the believing community with consequent feelings of gratitude (in Latin, *gratia,* grace, thanks) to God. Thus in celebrating and rejoicing over its identity with Christ, the Christian community achieves in the very act a fuller identity with him.

16. If the image of Christ imparted by the sacraments is formally constituted by grace, that is, by a human response to God's loving presence in the sacramental rite, how can the sacraments be said to produce their effect automatically *(ex opere operato)?*

In the case of adults the sacraments do not produce their effect without proper dispositions on the part of the recipient. They are not magical rites which operate independently of the activity and cooperation of the recipient.

17. But if in the sacraments of baptism and penance, for instance, the disposition required on the part of the recipient is minimal: not charity, but attrition for sin, how can the recipient be said to reflect Christ in his love of God?

The recipient of any sacrament must want to receive it as it is received in the Church, that is, with all that the rite implies. Baptism and penance imply a total commitment to God in love: a fundamental option for God. So, as St. Thomas says, through the power of the sacrament, the recipient *"ex attrito fit contritus,"* that is, his minimal disposition, as he perceives it, is really converted into the more loving and Christlike one that the sacrament implies.

18. But how can baptized infants return God's love?

They can only when they are able. When an infant is baptized, the Christlike love of the Christian community is projected upon the child. Its sponsors promise that it shall be prepersonally conditioned (i.e. from the dawn of its personal consciousness) to know not sin, but the love of God. This guarantee removes the child from the influence of sin, and opens it to an experience of the power of divine love to the extent possible at this stage of its development.

19. To what purpose does grace effect in man an image of Christ?

The goal of the operation of God's grace in man is announced by St. Paul as *anakephalaiosis,* or the recapitulation of humanity in Christ, making Christ to be all in all. Christ the model, the head, together with others who bear his image represent the culmination of all creation. The process tending toward this goal is called Christo-genesis by Pierre Teilhard de Chardin. It is the infiltration and growth of God's Word in everything he has made. Thus in the final stage of creation God will be reflected in his image, in his Word, from without as well as from within the Godhead. And he will be revealed as Love unlimited.

20. What is merit?

Merit is that quality of a human act whereby it is deemed to be deserving of a reward.

21. Can the graced person merit if he has received love freely?

The graced person to the extent that he reflects Jesus merits a share in the reward of Jesus.

22. If grace is love and love is its own reward, how can the graced person be said to merit?

Basically love is a unifying force. It culminates in a union of the partners. Love can be called its own reward only insofar as the union it promotes is achieved. Affective love is only the first step to final union. It is only incipient union. Full union with God in accordance with each individual's capacity for love can be attained only in an eschatological situation when man can encounter God, as St. Paul says, face to face. Then and then only will love be its own reward.

23. What does the graced person through actions inspired by love merit for himself?

The graced person through actions inspired by love lays claim to ultimate union with God according to his capacity for love as well as an increase in his capacity to love. It seems equitable also that he be assured of a continuation of God's loving help.

24. Can the graced person merit anything for others?

Not strictly. But since he bears the image of Christ, a man for others, and has Christ's job to continue in the world, it seems equitable that God manifest his love for others through him.

25. What is holiness?

Holiness is completeness, soundness, healthiness of spirit.

26. Does grace make a person holy?

In transforming the human spirit and rendering it capable of participating in the divine, grace as God's love fulfills its most basic need and bestows upon it radical soundness and health.

27. Is anything besides grace necessary for salvation or the state of eschatological holiness?

Perseverance until death is necessary for salvation, that is, complete and total holiness according to one's needs and capacities.

28. What is final perseverance?

Final perseverance is death in grace. Though love tends to perpetuate itself, the human spirit remains liable to sin. Though grace bestows radical holiness or health, peripheral instability or ennui can lead one eventually to abandon God's love and pursue selfish goals. Perseverance implies God's special providence guarding the graced person from such a mishap until death. It is the greatest gift of God's love, but one which the graced person can easily obtain through prayer.

29. Are there two kinds of grace, actual and sanctifying?

There are not two kinds of divine love, but man's response to God's loving presence may be categorized as partial and complete.

30. What is meant by a complete response to God's offer of love?

When a person surrenders himself fully to God's love and tries to respond in kind to it, he is transformed and justified in the way described in questions 6–26.

31. What is meant by a partial response to God's offer of love?

It is possible when God offers his love, that a person will hold back and surrender only partially or tentatively to God. In this case he will not be fully transformed by that love. He may, however, come to believe in God, trust in him, regret his sins, etc. Thus divine love will work in him a more or less lasting, but only partial transformation, one, however, that always will point toward that full commitment which true love demands.

32. Can man accomplish any good without God's love?

The good that any man, be he atheist, agnostic, heretic or sinner, accomplishes will reflect at least the love of God that prompted him to create. But the good that merits ultimate union with God and a participation in his life can be achieved only through the influence of that special loving concern of God that is called grace.

33. Is it possible without grace to observe the law of God substantially, that is, without any consideration of the ultimate goal God has established for man?

Though a substantial observance of the law without grace would be possible in each and every human action, over a relatively long period of time man would fail without the support of God's love.

34. Does God deny his love to anyone?

In this life God offers his love to everyone, even sinners.

35. Is God's love owed to man?

Of its essence love must be freely bestowed and freely responded to. One has a right to demand justice, but never love.

36. Can a person dispose himself to receive God's love?

A person can remove what hinders the operation of God's love in his life, but without God's help he cannot positively dispose himself to love God. Scripture clearly indicates that God first loves man; man can only react to that love.

37. Does the priority of divine love take away man's freedom in responding?

No, man is free to resist God's offer of love.

38. If man can resist God, how does God retain mastery over the economy of salvation?

This is one of the most difficult problems in all of theology, and many theories have been elaborated to solve it. Briefly, it can be stated with St. Augustine that a human being does not resist an offer of love that is clearly and frequently made, but will freely surrender himself to love's delectation. Love is what human life is all about, and man freely devotes himself to it. God can retain mastery over the economy of salvation by manifesting his love to those whom he wills to save clearly, cogently and frequently.

39. Does God, then, will to condemn certain persons?

Not initially, before any consideration of their demerits. As Scripture indicates, God first wills to save all men. So he manifests his love to all in a way that would be sufficient to elicit a positive response. But because love is free, he may love some more than others, and even before any consideration of their merits, manifest his love to them in such wise as to assure their free response. Others he may permit to resist his offer of love, though it is in itself sufficient to move them. If they persevere in their rejection of him, God has no alternative but to condemn them.

40. Is it necessary to believe that some persons are condemned?

Though the Church demands belief in the salvation of certain persons, it has never demanded belief in the condemnation of anyone. It is quite possible that all men will be saved, though there is no revelational guarantee of this. There is only God's initial statement of his willingness to save all men, for which he sent his beloved Son. If one holds to the proposition that all men are actually saved, it is certain that he may not live out his own life on that presumption. The threat of punishment in Scripture is very real, and every man in his own case must take it into account; even if he believes that all other men will be saved, he must acknowledge the genuine possibility that he could be the only reprobate.

41. What does predestination mean?

Predestination is an act of God by which he determines to save those whom he wishes, even before any consideration of their merits. Predestination implies that God's love is prior to men's; that his love is perfectly free, and that consequently he may love some persons more than others; that he may therefore assure their salvation by clearly and lavishly manifesting his love to them and so bring them into final union with him.

42. Is it possible for man to become aware of God's loving presence?

Adults must become aware of God's loving presence in order to respond to the divine offer of love.

43. How does one become aware of God's loving presence?

A person becomes aware of God's loving presence at least in his own response to it: in his belief and trust in God; in his commitment of himself in love to God; in his strivings to please God by always trying to do what is right.

44. Is it possible for man to experience the presence of God in other ways than this minimal one?

Many people experience the presence of God in other more significant, yet still ordinary ways; some have an unusual or peak experience of the presence of God in their lives.

45. What are some of the occasions when an ordinary but more significant experience of God's loving presence is likely to be enjoyed?

Some occasions on which a person is apt to have a fuller experience of God's presence are these: 1. a particularly moving liturgical or ritual celebration; 2. an effective involvement in prayer; 3. in receiving strength and help in difficult or trying circumstances of life, particularly when one has incurred some deep loss; 4. in perceiving a basic meaningfulness to one's life; 5. in being aware of one's ability to love another person who really is unworthy of one's love; 6. in recognizing one's ability to place oneself in the position of another person before judging or reacting to him, as Christ placed himself in our position.

46. What is a peak experience?

A peak experience is a singular and unusual one that is likely to be remembered always and has a profound influence on subsequent behavior. St. Paul had such an experience when he was unhorsed by an apparition of Jesus on the road to Damascus.

47. What makes peak experiences so different?

They often combine opposite reactions: at one and the same time a person feels small and weak, and yet great and powerful. The subject-object dichotomy is broken down or lessened: one feels himself as a part of what seems to be taking place outside of him. They are usually thematized around ultimate issues: life or death; self or non-self; meaningfulness or meaninglessness. They seem just to happen; one does not cause them.

48. What are some of the characteristics of peak religious experiences?

They are: 1. numinous, or other-worldly; 2. nebulous, or unclear, concealing as much or more than they reveal; 3. symbolic, containing elements which are related to religious themes; 4. ecstatic, filling the subject with joy and rapture; 5. liminal, featuring elements so great as not to be able to be fully focussed in consciousness; 6. ineffable, or incapable of being fully communicated or explained to others.

49. How is God apprehended in a peak experience?

Normally God is thought of in terms of analogy (e.g. Father, like a human father, only more admirable), or in terms of a negation of the imperfection of creatures (in-finite, not limited like all created good things). But the apprehension of God in a peak experience is pre-conceptual. God's presence is not thought of or understood, but felt. It may be so powerfully felt that one never doubts at all that one's experience was of God. Or, it may be less directly felt, but the circumstances of the peak experience support the conclusion that it clearly was God-given, and since that is so, God must have been present in it.

50. What lasting effects does an experience of God produce in a person?

1. A deeper faith; 2. greater respect for and confidence in oneself, as Abraham manifested when he dared to bargain with God over Sodom; 3. a truer appreciation of one's position *vis-à-vis* God: humility; 4. more energetic love of one's neighbor; 5. a basic joy and contentment not disturbed by peripheral problems or the disbelief of others in the experience; 6. a desire for recurrence of the experience without being "hooked" on the extraordinary in one's spiritual life.

Christology

1. What is the core of the Christian faith?

At the center of Christian faith stands the conviction that Jesus of Nazareth, the first century Jew whom we call the Christ, makes the decisive difference in the future that is possible for each human person and for mankind.

2. Why do we call Jesus of Nazareth Christ?

Ever since the Apostles' experience of the Resurrection, the followers of Jesus have given him the Jewish title, Messiah, in its Greek form, Christ. Messiah was a rather vague and ambiguous title when the Apostles took it over. It meant one anointed and specially chosen by God to bring the fulfillment of God's promises to his people. In Christian usage the title came to mean the unique savior of all mankind throughout history.

3. What are the more important beliefs of Christians concerning Jesus Christ?

Christians believe that Jesus, who was executed by Roman crucifixion, was raised from the dead on the third day by God the Father who made him Christ and Lord (Acts 2:36); that the Christ originates from the Spirit and the Virgin (infancy narratives and Creeds); that having suffered total rejection, humiliation and pain, Jesus is exalted to be the judge of all men and all history with God the Father and will one day be manifest to the world as such; that he is present in history to and through his church by sacrament, word and Spirit; that he who is human, exactly as we are, is at the same time of the very being of God, divine, Son of the Father, Word by which God expressed himself in history, the shining in the world of the light that is God (Niceno-Constantinopolitan Creed); that in him the world and all men are redeemed from sin and despair.

4. What is the origin of the doctrine of the Resurrection?

Resurrection was taught in Judaism even before the time of Jesus. Both Jesus and Paul declared themselves in agreement with the Pharisees and in opposition to the Sadducees over the question of resurrection. The Jews did not teach the immortality of the soul but they were convinced that if a man is faithful to God and lives in quest of the Reign of God on earth, God can not be less faithful, and when his Reign is established will, so to speak, awaken from the sleep of death all those who because of their fidelity ought to participate in the rejoicing.

5. How is the Jewish teaching relevant to the Resurrection of Jesus?

The Apostles, in trying to explain in words their unique and inexpressible experience, used the language of the existing Jewish teaching. In doing so they were making a claim that the Reign of God had come in and through Jesus because of his death by crucifixion. The scandal to Jewish listeners was not the claim that someone had risen from the dead, but the claim that the Risen one was Jesus the crucified, whose claim had been judged inauthentic by the official Jewish leadership.

6. How does Christian tradition explain the Resurrection of Jesus?

From apostolic times onwards people have asked some questions about the Resurrection of Jesus and the resurrection of all the faithful which could not be answered. The Apostles did not speak of the Resurrection of Jesus as merely the resuscitation of a corpse to continue the same life as before. They spoke and wrote of a transformed life and a transfigured presence that eluded all attempts to explain. To them that transfigured presence meant a total and radical change in their capacity for perception and response, a passage from despair to unshakeable hope. It meant the presence of Jesus to them (and to those who throughout history would believe in Jesus as the Christ) in a new way that could never be destroyed by force. It also meant the total vindication of Jesus, his life, his teachings and claims, and his works, as well as the breaking into present history of the Reign of God.

7. What is the official Catholic teaching on the Resurrection of Jesus?

The Catholic Church teaches that the Resurrection of Jesus is central to Christian faith; that Jesus rose to a transformed life to die no more, by his own power as Son of God; and that his Resurrection is the pledge that we too shall rise.

8. What is the origin of the doctrine of a virgin birth by the power of the Spirit?

The recital of the virgin birth is given in the infancy narratives (introductory chapters) of the gospels of Matthew and Luke. Those narratives parallel in various ways a series of stories about miraculous, promised births in the Hebrew Scriptures. In each case the point of the recital is to emphasize the power and mercy of God intervening in the history of his people to accomplish what appeared impossible.

9. Is the virgin birth an important point in Christian doctrine?

The early churches thought this doctrine central enough to incorporate it in the creeds of both East and West.

10. What relevance has this doctrine to salvation?

It would seem to be closely related to the scandal concerning the messianic claim made for Jesus. The early Christians had to answer the objection that Jesus could not possibly be the Christ (Messiah) because it belonged to the very definition of the term, Messiah, that such a one must be acknowledged or authenticated ("fathered") by Israel. The religious leaders of Israel had rejected the claim. Jesus had been disowned by them and executed by the Romans without effecting the profound change that would bring the Reign of God. By what right could the newly assembled Church claim to bring forth Messiah to the world? Jesus certainly looked like a bastard claimant to messiahship. The only answer to this could be that the "fatherhood" of Israel was not needed because the Christ was authenticated (fathered) by God himself. Mary (and the Church) virginally brought forth the Christ to the world by the power of the Holy Spirit.

11. What is the origin of the doctrine of the Ascension?

The Acts of the Apostles relate that the followers of Jesus, having enjoyed the extraordinary experience of an especially intimate presence of the Risen Christ for forty days, underwent a dramatic experience of separation. This is told in spatial terms but obviously means much more.

12. What is the meaning of the doctrine of the Ascension?

There appears to be a two-fold meaning. On the one hand, it is a clear statement that the responsibility for making the Reign of God a publicly manifest reality in all the affairs of men now lies with the followers of Jesus who are to be his body (his presence) in the world, living in the power of the Holy Spirit which is the Spirit of Jesus. On the other hand, the doctrine of the Ascension is a statement about Jesus Christ, "raised to the right hand of the Father" as judge of all mankind and of all history, one who is to "come again in judgment."

13. What is the doctrine of the Second Coming?

Though we commonly refer to the Second Coming, the "Final Coming" would more accurately express the sense of the early Christian expectation that has become standard Christian teaching. The early Christians referred to the *Parousia,* a presence of Jesus Christ that was not yet realized and must finally come about to fulfill the promises. Concerning the manner of this presence Scripture and tradition tell us nothing except in most general terms that it means the completion and fulfillment of all history and all human striving.

14. What is the meaning of the Parousia for Christian life in history?

The doctrine of the Parousia puts the whole Christian message in the perspective of hope. It implies that not all the events significant for salvation have yet happened. It asserts that Jesus Christ is relevant not only to each individual but to the public affairs of men today and tomorrow. This doctrine asserts that political, economic and social structures and decisions are to be judged by the values discerned in the light of Christ (cf. Eph. and Col.)

15. How is Christ present in history?

Christ is present in history not only as an inspirational memory, legendary hero, a dream. He is personally and concretely present by sacrament, word and Spirit. When the followers of Jesus gather in the Eucharist to make the redemptive moment of his death present by their present participation in it, and allow their lives to be assimilated to the mystery of that death, they become the body (or presence) of the Risen Christ to one another and to the world. When the gospel is preached, mediated and assimilated so that it becomes effective, Jesus himself is present by the power of his work. Moreover, through his death Jesus breathed his Spirit into his followers that they might not only imitate what he had done and execute what he had told them to do, but that they might extend into history the spontaneity and creativity of his own response to the divine call and the human situation.

16. How does Jesus Christ differ from other religious leaders and founders?

Christian teaching makes a set of claims for Jesus Christ which are not made for any other figure in history. It claims that Jesus alone is the key by which the meaning of human life can be understood; that he is the only source and channel of salvation for all men; that he alone is the mediator between God and man because he and he alone is by nature of the same being and reality as the one transcendent God.

17. What does Christian doctrine say about the uniqueness of Jesus as man?

The Christian teaching about Jesus as man is that he was throughout his life so unequivocally focussed on the Father who beckoned him that he is accurately described as sinless; that his death, therefore, is in no way due to sinfulness in him but is the outcome of, and an answer to the sin of others; that he so totally realized in his person all that man is called to be in response to God, that he is the cornerstone of God's creation and the anticipation of the complete development of all mankind; that in his own person he made the breakthrough by which the power of evil in the world is broken and redemption becomes possible once and for all for all mankind because of Jesus.

18. What is contained in Christian tradition concerning the character and personality of Jesus?

The Christian tradition and the scriptures of the New Testament have passed on a very stylized picture of Jesus. We have no data on his character, temperament or personality.

19. Was Jesus really human?

The orthodox Christian teaching has always insisted not only that Jesus is an historical personage (for which there is ample substantiation) but also that he truly thought, felt, enjoyed, suffered, worried and made painfully difficult decisions. Moreover, the Christian teaching is that he learned by experience as every human person does, though he is generally credited with further knowledge pertaining to his mission, that is described as gift-knowledge rather than acquired knowledge.

20. Did Jesus really die?

From time to time the thesis has been put forward that Jesus did not really die on the cross but just seemed to die. This has been suggested by those who wanted to deny the humanity of Jesus and who suggested there had been a substitution of another person to die in his stead, or that there had been a kind of visual trick. The thesis has also been advanced by those who want to undermine the foundations of Christian faith by showing that the Resurrection of Jesus is a hoax. The Christian answer to this is that the Resurrection is a matter of faith but that the death of Jesus is an ordinary factual datum checked and attested by the competent civil authorities of the time.

21. Given the claim of sinlessness and the claim of divinity, is Jesus in any true sense a model to be imitated by other men?

Christian tradition has presented Christianity as a matter of the following or imitation of Christ. One of the early titles given to Jesus is that of the Second (or last) Adam. Because *Adama* means not one individual man *(ish)* but man in the sense of mankind, the title Second Adam implies a new model for what mankind can be. It suggests that men can find a new corporate unity in Jesus. It does not suggest that any individual can be exactly like Jesus, but rather that Jesus extends the power (grace) to grow to be like him and to be one in him to mankind. It implies that he is uniquely capable of integrating mankind and reshaping human affairs so that individual men and mankind can fulfill their vocation.

22. Is the divinity of Jesus defined doctrine?

The divinity of Jesus is defined and reconfirmed in the most solemn tones by a series of early ecumenical councils of the Church. It must, therefore be considered as a central doctrine in the tradition of the Christian churches.

23. What is the origin of the divinity claims for Jesus?

The New Testament makes many statements about Jesus and gives him some titles, such as *kyrios,* Lord, which imply divinity but do not give clear definitions of what is meant. The gospels show Jesus addressing God the Father on very intimate terms not usual among Jews of his time. They also portray him in various ways as claiming equality with God, claiming to judge all men and all history, and making reference to a personal pre-existence. This represents the post-Resurrection testimony of the first generation of Christians. We have no resources to go back in time beyond the post-Resurrection testimony of the Apostles, and demonstrate that the divinity claim was made by Jesus before his death.

24. Are there parallels in Jewish history for the divinity claim?

No. It is unthinkable within the Jewish frame of reference to claim divinity or equality with the one transcendent God for any human being. Jewish tradition will not even claim sinlessness for any human being and is at pains to show that the greatest heroes of the tradition, such as Moses, were sinful men able to do what they did only because of the liberating power of God's Spirit taking hold of them. Christian teaching from earliest times has emphasized that the Spirit of God by which Jesus did wonderful works was not in any way alien to him but strictly his own.

25. Is it possible to specify more precisely what Christians mean by calling Jesus divine?

With the divinity claim we are unescapably in the realm of a mystery of faith or revealed truth. That means we are dealing with a conviction that is not the outcome of discursive reasoning but of an experience that defies reduction to strictly appropriate concepts. There can be no explanation of a mystery of faith that "decodes" the poetic or analogous language and presents the content of the mystery in "literal terms." In those matters which Christian tradition has called revealed truths, we are dealing with a type of gift-knowledge (not actively acquired knowledge) which is at the outer limit of what human language can express. At this boundary language only works by hints, analogies and paradoxes.

26. If the divinity claim for Jesus, so central to the Christian message, can not be precisely defined, how is it to be explained in order to carry meaning for Christians?

In the history of the Church, the divinity claim has been explained for the most part in three ways: by elaboration of further poetic images; by paradox; and by very specific negations.

27. What are the traditional poetic explanations that may help Christian believers to understand what is meant by the divinity claim?

Traditional poetic explanations include the following: Jesus is the Son of God by nature not adoption; he "came down from heaven" and was made man; Jesus is the Word of God spoken in eternity as well as in history; Jesus is the full self-expression of the transcendent God through which all things came into being; Jesus is the thought of God expressing his self-knowledge and, therefore, is the design or pattern of all creation; Jesus is the light or radiance of God, related to the Father as the shining is to its source, the light.

28. What are the practical implications of these images?

The most important implication of the poetic images in which Christian tradition explains the divinity of Jesus is this: to learn what God is like, what God's promise is to us and what God's call and exigence are on our own lives, we should contemplate and meditate the person, teaching, life and death of Jesus. This is where a true understanding of God will emerge because no man has seen God but it is Jesus the Son who reveals the true features of the Father. To see the Son is to see the Father. God is love but we only find out what that means by an experience of the love that Jesus is, showing that God loves first, that divine love is anticipatory, creative, healing, making possible the impossible and making a gift of the power to respond.

29. How is the divinity of Jesus explained by paradox in Christian tradition?

Paradoxical assertions include the following. Jesus is of the same being (substance, reality) as God and yet of the same being (substance, reality) as ourselves. Son of God though he was, he learned the discernment of the will of the Father through what he suffered (hostility, rejection, etc.). Being by nature equal to God he did not disdain to take the form of a servant and humble himself even to a death by criminal execution. Of Jesus we can rightly make some assertions that are true only of God, yet we also properly make statements true only of man. He is one with the Father, co-eternal with the Father, yet he is not the Father but proceeds from him. He is co-equal with the Father, yet in some sense the Father is greater than he. There is one God, yet the Son and the Spirit are distinct "persons" within the one Godhead.

30. How do these paradoxes affect Christian life practically.

These paradoxes serve first and foremost as a warning not to deal with the mystery of faith as though it were a philosophical thesis or a conclusion from empirical science. They safeguard the divinity claim without pretending to comprehend or intellectually master it. They insist that we can trust God's self-revelation in Christ though we can not properly explain it. They also insist that God has truly intervened in human history not alongside man's work and the freedom of man, but precisely as the extraordinary enabling power within the freedom of man, liberating man to achieve with human work what goes beyond his powers. This is very important for the practice of Christian life in the world, because it gives the model for the relation of man to God in terms of man's freedom in and responsibility for human history.

31. What specific negations contribute to our present understanding of the divinity of Jesus?

The important negations made officially by the Church after much struggle and reflection include the following. The union of God and man in Jesus is not an "accidental" or transitory or merely functional one but "substantial," that is, a union in the very being that Jesus is, a personal union, a union in his person. Further, the human will and human mind of Jesus are not to be seen as simply assimilated or absorbed into divine initiative but are exercised in their greatest fulness and freedom. Nor is the humanity of Jesus to be thought of as simply appearance or illusion. Jesus is not to be identified with God the Father, nor with the Spirit, but is to be thought of as the Word incarnate.

32. What is to be learned from these negations?

These negations are important because Christian teaching, while emphasizing the uniqueness of Jesus and of the union of God and man in Jesus, also makes Jesus paradigmatic for the relation of God and man. On the one hand, these statements are concerned with rejecting any idea of a "deus ex machina," a cosmic furniture mover, achieving with the ease of magic what would take great human effort and sacrifice, eliminating the need for arduous effort and creative initiatives and leaving man only passive roles of grateful acceptance, ritual participation and mechanical execution of a fully fashioned plan. On the other hand, the process of negation has also been concerned to assert that God has indeed intervened in history, so that the power by which we are called to act is much greater than our own resources, and the reconstruction of mankind and the world that we are summoned to undertake is also far beyond what we see as possible by our own resources.

33. Why did Jesus die by criminal execution?

Jesus was executed by the occupation forces of the colonial power because in his person, life and preaching he was seen as a threat to the social order sanctioned by the Roman colonizers. It was a political execution. A contributory reason for the execution was that the official religious leadership did not endorse him or stand by him and bargain for him with the Romans because his stand was too radical for them and threatened the compromises they had worked out within the status quo. Christian teaching, however, has focussed not on the reasons for which Jesus was killed but on the reason for which he himself chose to go up to Jerusalem and accept death by execution.

34. What does Christian tradition say about the death of Jesus?

Christian tradition maintains that Jesus died in his prime by criminal execution not because he was trapped by circumstances and had this fate forced upon him, but because he freely accepted it as the "will of the Father." The Christian teaching is that Jesus went to his death in "obedience to the Father" and out of love for mankind which could be redeemed by this death.

35. Why do Christians see the death of Jesus as redemptive?

Christians claim that the death of Jesus is redemptive not directly because of the suffering involved, but because they see it as the ultimate possible act of creative love. Within the world whose structures and values are badly distorted by sin, Jesus accepted his death in full freedom, discerning in it the most creative response of love that could be made to the panic-stricken resistance that polarized against his person and his message.

36. Is it not abhorrent that the crucifixion of Jesus be seen as the command or will of the Father?

Christian teaching certainly does not intend that the transcendent God we worship is vindictive (as men are when they are personally insecure), exacting a proportionate amount of suffering for the sum total of the sins committed in history. Nor does it intend that God, whom the Bible introduces as just, merciful, compassionate, an inexhaustibly faithful lover, simply wills the suffering of the innocent.

37. In what sense, then, is the crucifixion seen as the will of the Father?

The Christian teaching is that God wills the personal fulfillment of all men, that he takes the part of the poor and the oppressed and wills the liberation of mankind from the network of sin that destroys men by oppression, fear, hatred, distrust, greed. Therefore it is properly described as the will of the Father that Jesus should confront and radically challenge the network of sin in human society even though this polarized all the forces of sin against him to destroy him.

38. What are the practical implications of this for Christian living?

The nuances of the Christian explanation of the will of the Father and the obedience of Jesus with regard to the passion and death are central to an understanding of the commitment made by Christians. If suffering as such were willed by God and were redemptive, Christians would not need to be concerned with the oppressed and poor of the world except to exhort them to suffer patiently. Nor would the Christian be concerned with the structures of oppression in the world. If, on the other hand, God wills the fullest liberation (redemption) of men from all that oppresses them and hinders personal fulfillment, then the Christian task is to enter into the stance of Jesus by challenging the structures of sin and oppression and by championing the poor and the oppressed and all who suffer without counting the personal cost or risk.

39. What is meant by saying that it is not suffering but love that is redemptive?

Christian teaching does not condemn pleasure and enjoyment and does not propose that deprivation, pain and oppression are "better for man" than their opposites. It condemns hatred, greed, the exclusion of other persons and the exclusion of God from one's life and values. The opposite of hatred, greed and the exclusion of others is love, that is, caring, providing, giving life and hope and support and accommodating oneself to make room for others. The life and message of Jesus is seen by Christian tradition as being essentially a revelation and breakthrough of such love within a context of rejection, and the death of Jesus is seen as the carrying of that creative, healing love "to the end" by consummation.

40. Why do we have less explicit, defined Church teaching on how Jesus redeems than on who Jesus is?

The scarcity of defined teaching on the Redemption is probably due to the dynamic and practical character of this mystery of faith. It does not yield much understanding to rational or scholarly inquiry. Nor can its teaching and preaching easily be cast into a permanent, unchangeable formula. The mystery of redemption is understood in the praxis of the following of Jesus, and the explanations to be taught and preached must be forged ever anew out of that praxis.

Mariology

1. What is Mariology?

Mariology is the study of the Blessed Virgin Mary in relation to Christian teachings. Catholic teaching on Mary's place in doctrine and devotion was set forth at length in the Second Vatican Council's dogmatic constitution on the Church, *Lumen gentium,* November 21, 1964, where the eighth and final chapter is, "The Blessed Virgin Mary, Mother of God, in the Mystery of Christ and the Church." (A good commentary by Donal Flanagan is in Kevin McNamara, ed., *Vatican II: Constitution on the Church,* Franciscan Herald Press, Chicago, 1968.)

2. Why do Catholics call Mary the "Mother of God?"

The ecumenical Council of Ephesus, 431 A.D., proclaimed as legitimate the title "Mother of God," which had already been used for more than a century in some parts of the Church. The Council's purpose was Christological: to teach solemnly that Jesus, Mary's Son, is the Son of God made man. "Mother of God" enshrines this doctrine.

3. Why do some Christians not care for the title "Mother of God"?

Although this phrase has been common since the fifth century, especially in the liturgies of East and West, some find "Mother of God" not only post-biblical but liable to misinterpretation as if a divine claim were being made for Mary herself.

4. How can one show the special place "Mother of God" (the Greek *theotokos*) holds in liturgical prayer?

The eucharistic prayers recall our communion with Mary "virgin Mother of God." In the calendar, since 1970, January 1 has been called "solemnity of Mary, Mother of God"; the traditional entrance prayer to the Father speaks of "Jesus Christ, your Son, the source of life, whom you gave us through the virgin mother Mary."

[78]

5. What is the gospel sense of Mary's blessedness?

"Blessed" is the biblical word most characteristic of the Mother of Jesus, who appears always as "hearing God's word and doing it"; her life was a "pilgrimage of faith," in the Council's phrase *(Church,* n. 58: *Church* is the abbreviation for the dogmatic constitution on the Church, *Lumen gentium).* In the first human words addressed to Mary, Elizabeth salutes her as blessed in the fruit of her womb and blessed in her faith.

6. What is the bond between Abraham's faith and Mary's faith?

Abraham, "our father in faith" (eucharistic prayer no. 1), journeyed to an unknown land to find God, and in his old age was told Sara would bear him a son, in whose descendants all nations would be blessed. He was prepared to sacrifice this child, Isaac, still counting on God, "for whom nothing is impossible," to realize the great promise embodied in the boy. Greater things were promised to Mary and more was asked of her: she would be virgin mother of the Messiah, Emmanuel. Gabriel assured her as God had assured Abraham: "nothing is impossible with God" (Lk. 1:37). Isaac was spared, but Mary "lovingly consented to the immolation of this Victim which she herself had brought forth" (*Church,* n. 58).

7. What did the Council mean by describing Mary as the "exalted daughter of Zion" and as outstanding "among the poor and humble of the Lord" (Church, n. 55)?

Recent biblical studies have shown what the liturgy has long celebrated: the dependence of the New Testament on the Old in the references to the Mother of Christ. St. Luke's nativity chapters apply to Mary words and themes first used of her people many centuries before, as in Zephaniah prophesying messianic joy to the "daughter of Zion," that is, the people of God (Zeph. 3:14–7). Mary is the great example of the lowly ones (*anawim*) who were looking for the consolation of Israel; God "has looked upon his servant in her lowliness" (Lk. 1:48). (See Lucien Deiss, C.S.Sp., *Daughter of Sion,* Liturgical Press, Collegeville, Minn., 1972, and A. Gelin, S.S., *The Poor of Yahweh,* Liturgical Press, Collegeville, Minn. 1967, also paperback, with preface by Barnabas M. Ahern, C.P.)

8. What is the meaning of "the virgin birth"?

"Virgin birth" is the common term for the virginal conception of Jesus as related by St. Matthew and St. Luke and consistently and constantly repeated by the Church in its ordinary teaching. The biblical evidence is not conclusive (silence of the other New Testament writers; the intricate nature of the nativity chapters with difficulty of separating "fact" from "literary form"); and the main purpose of the phrase, "born of the Virgin Mary," in its early occurrences was to call attention to the true humanity of Jesus. Yet even very early writers (Ignatius, Justin, Irenaeus) repeat the biblical claim he had no human father, seeing therein a miraculous sign of God's redemptive intervention. In its ordinary teaching the Church continues to affirm the virginal conception of Jesus.

9. Is there not another view of the "virgin birth" found among Catholic theologians today?

The *New Catechism,* better known as the Dutch Catechism, first published 1966, gives meanings for the "virgin birth" without answering the question: did Jesus have a human father? Some Catholic theologians have suggested (e.g. P. Schoonenberg) there is a doubt as to whether or not a literal virginal conception must be regarded as a binding part of the Church's teaching. The Supplement to the Dutch Catechism, added at the insistence of the Holy See, defends the virginal conception. A deeper understanding of Christ himself, and also of our Lady's role in his human origins, can be hoped for from the present discussions. (See the careful study by Raymond E. Brown, S.S., *The Virginal Conception and Bodily Ressurection of Jesus,* Paulist Press, New York, 1973, also Joseph Ratzinger, *Introduction to Christianity,* Herder and Herder, New York, 1970, chapter, "Conceived by the Holy Ghost, born of the Virgin Mary.")

10. Who were "the brothers of the Lord"?

Since the 4th century the Mother of Jesus has been regarded as remaining a virgin life-long, having no other children, never using her marriage rights, exclusively dedicated along with her husband Joseph to the will of God manifested in Christ. This life-long or "perpetual" virginity is an early instance of a growth in understanding, beyond the biblical evidence. "Brothers of the Lord" can equally well be cousins according to gospel word usage.

11. Why is Mary regarded as "the new Eve"?

After the New Testament, the oldest Christian description of Mary is as "new Eve"—"who put her absolute trust not in the ancient serpent but in God's messenger" (*Church,* n. 63). "What the virgin Eve bound through her unbelief, Mary loosened by her faith" (St. Irenaeus, died ab. 201, as quoted in *Church,* n. 56). By St. Jerome's day (d. 420), it was axiomatic to say: "death through Eve, life through Mary." The comparison of Mary to the first Eve is by contrast, and whereas the first Eve was wife of Adam, Mary, the second Eve, is mother of Christ the new Adam. Other women in biblical history play "new Eve" roles also, and indeed all women are called "to contribute to life, just as a woman had contributed to death" (n. 56).

12. What does the "Immaculate Conception" of Mary mean?

That Mary was "immaculately conceived" means that by his grace God kept her free from original sin ("immaculate") at the very beginning of her existence as a human person in her mother's womb (her passive "conception"). This was in anticipation of the merits of Christ, the one Redeemer of all mankind, and was a "preservative redemption" in contrast to the liberation from original sin accomplished for others by baptism. In 1854 Pope Pius IX "defined" the Immaculate Conception, declaring this aspect of Mary's holiness to be a doctrine revealed by God.

13. What bearing on the Church's self-understanding has Mary's "Immaculate Conception"?

Mary was kept free from original sin that she might give herself wholeheartedly to her Son's person and work, in total service to the redemptive mystery (*Church,* n. 56). Mary's "privileges" put her at the service of her Son's kingdom, even as Christ's love for his bride, the Church, enables the Church to enter into the sufferings and death of her Lord for the sake of his brethren. The Church contemplates Mary's "hidden holiness" (*Church,* n. 64), "admires in her the most excellent fruit of the redemption; discovering through this faultless model what the Church herself desires and aspires to be (*Liturgy* Constitution, n. 103). "She was the first beginning of your Church; its very pattern as the Bride of Christ, perfect in its beauty" (Preface for December 8).

14. What transition has taken place from a "privilege-centered" view of the Immaculate Conception to the view regarding Mary Immaculate as the perfect model of the Church?

A dogmatic definition is not the last word in the Church's understanding even of the doctrine thus proclaimed. Under the Holy

Spirit's guidance, in answer to new needs of changing times, the Church finds further meanings in old truths. We now see in the Immaculate Conception, defined as dogma by Pius IX in 1854, a great sign of Christ's love for his Church, with the warning that the gift of grace is also an invitation to become "mother of sorrows" even as for the 1870 definition of papal infallibility the Church has learned that the Pope is always also "crucified Peter" in his service of the servants of God.

15. What is the dogma of the Assumption?

The Assumption is the doctrine that the "Immaculate Mother of God, the ever-virgin Mary, was at the end of her days on earth, taken up, body and soul to heavenly glory" (wording of the definition, November 1, 1950). The choice of words is deliberate: "body and soul" are our customary way of referring to the total person; "taken up" is biblical language for the transfer to "heavenly glory," where the Risen Christ reigns at the Father's right hand. Nothing is said of how our Lady ended her days on earth. According to the more commonly held view, one may suppose she died, even as her Son had done, but the defined truth leaves that question unanswered. What does matter is that the corruption of death visited upon mankind at the expulsion from Eden no longer holds. Thanks to the power of her Son's Resurrection, Mary, the perfect Christian, has been freed from all forms of corruption, including the last enemy, death. As representative of the Church, Mary stands for the Church and for each member of it.

16. What is the ecclesial meaning of the Assumption?

In the 1950's Louis Bouyer coined this phrase for the Assumption: "Eschatological Ikon of the Church." The Council's words are similar: "sign of sure hope and solace for the pilgrim people of God" (n. 68). Mary "exalted by the Lord as Queen of all, in order that she might be the more thoroughly conformed to her Son, the Lord of lords (cf. Apoc. 19:16), and the conqueror of sin and death," (Church, n. 59) is herself "daughter and member of the Church." She is a living pledge to the rest of the Church of the Bridegroom's promise. In Mary the Church is already one with Christ, himself the "first-fruits from the dead." She is the earnest of the union with the Risen Christ. The Assumption of Mary is the response of the Church-bride to the invitation of Christ the bridegroom, reminder to the entire Church of the consummation still to be achieved in full. "Today the Virgin Mother of God was taken up into heaven to be the beginning and the pattern of the Church in its perfection" (Preface for August 15th).

17. What is meant by calling Mary model or type of the Church?

The likeness between Mary and the Church is based on the unity of God's loving dealings with them both: what the Father of mercies did for the Virgin Mary, preparing her for the motherhood of Emmanuel from the beginning of her life, joining her to Jesus' redemptive work, bringing her to final reunion with the victorious Christ is not only the sign but also the first and most perfect achievement of his saving plan for the entire Church. Mary is the "spotless image of the Church" (*Liturgy,* n. 103).

18. Is it a new idea that Mary is model of the Church?

The Mary-Church analogy reaches back to New Testament times; the Gospel "blessed Mary" already stands for all who hear God's word and keep it. Early Christian writers saw Mary, the Virgin Mother, as model to the Church, called to virginal fidelity to Christ and to be the mother of all his brethren in water and the word by the power of the Spirit. The order, "word, faith, maternity," is verified in both Mary and the Church. "That which God intends for his Church he manifests clearly in the perfect image of the Virgin Mother" (from E. Schillebeeckx, O.P., *Mary, Mother of the Redemption,* Sheed and Ward, New York, 1965).

19. What value has Mary's example for modern women in their strivings for freedom and dignity?

At the Annunciation, the Father asked for Mary's free consent before the overshadowing of the Holy Spirit brought about the Incarnation of the Son: "The Virgin Mary received the word of God *into her heart* and her body at the angel's announcement and brought forth Life to the world" (*Church,* n. 53). Mary was perfected as person, by her free choice in faith, even before she became the Mother of the Savior. Mary achieved her destiny by freely cooperating with God's love, reacting responsibly to the demands of God and neighbor on her during all her pilgrimage of faith.

20. Is there biblical evidence for devotion to Mary?

The Gospel description of the Mother of Jesus shows the special respect of the earliest Christians. She is the "blessed" one, *par excellence,* especially in St. Luke. In St. John's account of the wedding feast of Cana, the Mother of Jesus shows faith in her Son even before the "first of his signs," by which he revealed his glory and "his disciples believed in him" (Jn. 2:11). The veneration in which the early Church held Mary is shown by her representative role throughout her life. In the Nativity chapters she is the "daughter of Zion," model of the Lord's "poor and lowly," blessed in her faith, as Elizabeth proclaimed. In the public life Mary is the "woman" of Cana and Calvary, and the other references to her provide Jesus the occasion to speak of true blessedness as rooted in faith, in the incidents of the enthusiastic woman (Lk. 11:27–28) and the true kinsmen (Lk. 8:19; Mt. 12: 46; Mk. 3:31).

21. How do Catholics understand the "communion of saints," and where does Mary fit here?

In Catholic understanding, the "communion of saints" is a fellowship in Christ found not only between believers on earth but also between earthly pilgrims and those who have "fallen asleep in the Lord." Hence the Church prays for the dead, and honors in a special way the saints, above all the Mother of Jesus, always mentioned first in the prayer of remembrances at the Eucharist. "In the earthly liturgy, by way of foretaste, we share in that heavenly liturgy . . . celebrated in the holy city . . . toward which we journey as pilgrims and in which Christ is sitting at the right hand of God . . . venerating the memory of the saints, we hope for some part and fellowship with them" (*Liturgy,* n. 8). Mary occupies a special place in the Church's consciousness of the communion of saints, for she is the image and first flowering of the Church as it is to be perfected in the world to come" (*Church,* n. 68).

22. What is meant by the intercession of Mary, the Mother of Jesus?

Though a traditional term, the word "intercession" is easily misunderstood. We have direct access to Christ the one Mediator who "lives forever to make intercession for those who approach God through him" (Heb. 7:25). Hence the "intercession" of our Lady and the other saints is totally dependent on the supreme and all-sufficient intercession of the Risen Christ. It means the Blessed Virgin, who gave herself entirely to God's will on earth, remains "inseparably joined to her Son's saving work" (*Liturgy,* n. 103). By her prayers and presence with her Risen Son, she is solicitous still that all men be united with Christ. "By her maternal charity, Mary cares for the brethren of her Son who still journey on earth surrounded by dangers and difficulties, until they are led to their happy fatherland" (*Church,* n. 62).

23. What is meant by the title "mediatrix" as applied to Mary?

The Council used "mediatrix" one time only (*Church,* n. 62), explaining carefully that Mary's mediatorial activity draws its power entirely from the unique mediatorship of Christ (1 Tm. 2:5–6) and fosters the immediate union of the faithful with Christ. The Council's concern was both ecumenical and pastoral: ecumenical, in that words like mediatrix, dispensatrix and co-redemptrix strike Protestants as damaging to the centrality of Christ the Savior; pastoral, in reminding Catholics that Mary is completely dependent on Christ, her will one with his. It would be a travesty of Christianity to regard Mary as somehow in charge of mercy as against the justice of Christ the Judge.

24. Can it be said, then, that the term "mediatrix" has fallen into official disfavor?

Mediatrix had become a common word in Catholic thought and devotion, especially since the 1920's, and there were some on the eve of the Second Vatican Council who thought it might even be dogmatically defined. This did not seem opportune to the Council, sensitive to the wider Christian world and to possible pastoral misunderstanding. In the Church's outlook, Mary is regarded still as truly mediatrix, but the Council favored simpler language, e.g., "inseparably joined to her Son's saving work" (*Liturgy,* n. 103). Mary is joined to the total redemptive work of Christ, both his earthly life and suffering and his present exaltation. Another good example is from the decree on the priesthood: "Led by the Holy Spirit, she devoted herself entirely to the mystery of man's redemption" (n. 18).

25. In what sense is Mary called our Mother?

Consenting in faith Mary became Mother of Jesus by the power of the Holy Spirit. Equally by faith she is the blessed one who hears the word of God and does it, thereby bringing Christ to others. "Maternity" means transmission of life, and our Lady gave Life to the world. Christ came to form for himself the body which is his Church. "God sent forth his Son born of a woman . . . that we might receive our status as adopted sons" (Gal. 4:4–5). Mary's spiritual motherhood began in her consent in faith at the Annunciation; this continued to

Calvary, and will last until the body of Christ is complete in "the eternal fulfilment of all the elect" (*Church,* n. 62).

26. What is the meaning of the title, "Mother of the Church," proclaimed by Pope Paul VI, November 21, 1964?

In the Holy Father's intention and explanation, "Mother of the Church" states in a single phrase Mary's spiritual motherhood towards the members of the Church, the "mystical body" of which Christ is the Head. "Church" comprises both pastors and people.

27. What significance have such events as the appearances of Mary at Guadalupe (1531), Lourdes (1858) and Fatima (1917)?

Even where the Church has given its approval to devotions, prayers and penitential practices associated with pilgrimages to such shrines, the initial events remain matters of free choice for Catholics. This is true even of so well-researched a case as Lourdes, where there is no doubt of the holiness of the visionary, St. Bernadette. Such private revelations are, all the same, valuable reminders to believers of the special place of the Mother of God in the saving economy, and of the basic Christian values of prayer, penance and the sacraments, especially the Eucharist.

28. What is the place of our Lady in the liturgy?

"In celebrating the annual cycle of Christ's mysteries, holy Church honors with special love Blessed Mary, Mother of God" (*Liturgy,* n. 103), for "Mary was involved in the mysteries of Christ" (*Church,* n. 66). The Church's liturgies, in all their rich variety of place and time, both past and present, are proposed as the standard of devotion to Mary.

29. What does our current liturgy offer with respect of the Blessed Virgin?

In spite of the fall-off of popular devotions, the reformed liturgy has even more than before included praise of our Lady, always in clear dependence on Christ and in relation to the entire Church. The Lectionary has many readings from Old Testament and New for our Lady's days. Pope Paul's Roman Missal (1970) provides prefaces for the Immaculate Conception and the Assumption as well as two common prefaces. Many Marian feasts have new prayers, biblical, conciliar and ecclesial in their outlook. The simplified calendar leaves open more choices than before for commemorations of our Lady, Saturdays and other days also.

30. How can the liturgy lead Catholics to renewed devotion to the Virgin Mary?

Since "true devotion consists not in superficial sentiment or empty credulity . . . but proceeds from true faith" (*Church,* n. 67), the liturgy, which is centered on Christ and ever conscious of the whole community of the Church, provides the norms for all other cult of Mary. Marian piety can take many legitimate forms, displaying veneration, love, invocation and imitation (*Church,* n. 66). Tested devotional forms from the past, especially the Rosary, long beloved of individuals and of families, are still valuable and well reflect the liturgy. Good devotions to Mary will always "cause her Son to be rightly known, loved and glorified, and all his commands observed" (n. 66).

31. Is it possible to describe in single phrases the shift in emphasis about our Lady, both doctrinally and devotionally, that has taken place in the Church in recent years?

The conciliar teaching and the clarifications of the Pope and bishops since the Council show clearly there has been no denigration of Mary's true place in Catholic life. What has occurred is a significant shift from a "privilege-oriented" Marian piety to a "sharing-concept." She is "Mother of the Church" indeed, but at the same time Mary is seen much more now as also "daughter and member of the Church," showing forth in her life and vocation the Church's, and every Christian's, call to faithful service and to glorious union with Christ.

32. Is the Virgin Mary still a sign of division to Christians in the West?

It is unfortunately true that bitter polemic has often swirled round the figure of Mary during the centuries of Reformation and Counterreformation, and Christians are still divided in their understanding of her proper place and fitting reverence for her. Yet, in the new postconciliar Catholic climate and also on the part of many other Christian churches and groups there is a willingness to study her true role openly, charitably, especially on a common biblical basis. Mary as model of faith, humility and obedience is a unitive factor, even if we are still divided about the "growth in understanding" of revelation illustrated by such doctrines as her Immaculate Conception and Assumption, and about Mary as the type of man responding to God's grace and thereby taking an active meritorious part in his own salvation. What the Church has said about the effects of redemption in Mary, it has affirmed in other ways and at other times of us all. Still ahead lie the fulfilment both of the Savior's prayer, "that all may be one," and the prophecy of his mother, "all ages to come shall call me blessed."

Eschatology

1. What is the central biblical notion by which Christ announced man's glorious destiny?

The kingdom of God. The first recorded words of Christ were: "The time has come. The kingdom of God is at hand. Repent, and believe in the gospel" (Mark 1:15). The kingdom of God remained the principal content of Christ's preaching. In our day, Christians again try to express in terms of this kingdom the faith of the Church in regard to man's future.

2. What is the kingdom of God?

The kingdom of God, promised to Israel and proclaimed by Jesus Christ, is God's ultimate victory over all the enemies of human life —over sin, evil, injustice, oppression, suffering and death. The kingdom is the rule of God's Word in the history of men. The kingdom is men's entry into a new heaven and a new earth.

3. What is the relation of Jesus to the kingdom?

Jesus preached the coming of the kingdom. He was, moreover, God's instrument in inaugurating it in history. In his own life, Jesus anticipated the kingdom: In him God was victorious, even over the power of death. Christ's resurrection reveals men's glorious destiny. At the end of time Jesus shall return to establish the kingdom in glory. Then God shall be all in all.

4. What is the meaning of Christ's message that "The kingdom of God is at hand"?

Jesus preached that God's victory over evil was upon the people and about to usher in a new age. The early Christians held that the total delivery from evil would come soon and abruptly. Later, Christians had to learn that history would go on. Yet God's kingdom continues to press upon people, freeing them from sin and injustices

[89]

and enabling them to become a reconciled humanity. When we pray, "Thy kingdom come, thy will be done on earth as it is in heaven," we ask God to invade with his power our sinful and unjust world to recreate our common humanity. Christians retain a great sense of urgency in regard to the kingdom.

5. Can the promised kingdom be equated with heaven?

No. Jesus proclaimed the coming kingdom in terms that transcended the split between heaven and earth. Heaven and earth are spatial terms. Jesus preferred to announce the promised future in temporal terms: he spoke of the new age. The scriptures speak of the new heaven and the new earth (*cf.* 2Pt. 3:13; Apoc. 2:1). God's coming victory over evil will take place within history and yet transcend history. By reducing the kingdom of God to heaven, Christians tended to forget that the earth and its history are the place where God encounters men and recreates their personal and social life. This led to a certain spiritualization of God's promises made to men.

6. Can the promised kingdom be equated with personal salvation?

No. Jesus proclaimed the coming kingdom in terms that transcended the split between person and society. The salvation promised for the future embraces persons and the social and political structures to which they belong. God shall usher in a new age. The whole fabric of human life shall be recreated. By reducing the message of the kingdom to personal salvation Christians neglected the social dimension of divine grace and often forgot that the divine promises included the transformation of society. For Jesus, salvation was not private: It was public and social. Equating the kingdom with personal salvation has led to a privatization of God's promises.

7. Can the kingdom of God be equated with the immortality of the soul?

No. Jesus proclaimed the kingdom in terms that transcended the split between body and soul. The salvation promised for the future and pressing upon the present situation, affects the whole of man, his mind, his body, his social existence and his earthly abode. God shall be victorious in man's flesh. By equating the coming kingdom with the immortality of the soul, Christians tended to forget that the new age Christ has promised and inaugurated transforms man's historical existence. This trend has led to a certain spiritualization and privatization of God's promises.

8. How are we to understand the Church's teaching on heaven, personal salvation and the immortality of the soul?

These teachings must be related to the wiser and more inclusive message of the kingdom. This relation to the kingdom enables us to overcome an interpretation of the divine promises that makes them exclusively spiritual and private. The kingdom of God consists in God's victory over evil in all its forms and phases. These promises include man's glorious future after death: but this future will take place in a context, as yet unknown and unimaginable, of the world's new creation. We believe that God will always create life out of death, but what this life will be like we have no way of knowing.

9. Why do Christians so often think of eternal life first of all in terms of personal immortality?

The early Christians understood the divine promises for a glorious future as the salvation of mankind and the recreation of the cosmos. They were less preoccupied than we are with the question of their private future. However, throughout the centuries the individualism of western culture has made Christians concentrate on the topic of their personal future. What will happen to me after I die? This became a question of over-riding importance. Today we have become critical of the individualism we inherited. We think that the question of personal salvation isolated from the full extent of Christ's promises makes the gospel too private and too spiritual. Today we again prefer the original Christian perspective that saw the divine promises as referring to the new heaven and the new earth. We do not like to make belief in personal survival after death something that weakens our yearning for God's coming into human history to deliver all people from the power of evil. We want to long for eternal life as God's approaching kingdom, pressing upon us now, to save us from the enemies of life. The message of life eternal is, therefore, significant for man's present existence. "This is eternal life: To know thee who are truly God, and Jesus Christ whom thou has sent" (Jn. 17:3). The message of God's coming kingdom profoundly modifies the earthly life of men.

10. Can eternal life, according to its full meaning, be equated with God's kingdom?

Yes. God's gracious and victorious coming, which is with us now and yet is still future, is called kingdom in the first three gospels (Matthew, Mark and Luke) and life eternal in the fourth gospel

(John). The image of of kingdom suggests that God's victory is pressing upon us from the future, while the image of eternal life suggests that already now we are alive by a vitality that transcends us, that moves us ahead toward fulfillment over many obstacles, and that will never permit us to die.

11. How is man's personal life affected by the message of eternal life?

The Christian believes that God's victorious grace is operative in his life. He trusts that he has a special destiny. God has promised him a glorious future. He believes that the conditions of life, however trying and hostile they may be, do not lock him into an iron cage where his life is an endless repetition of trivialities and pains: he expects the new to take place in his life. He hopes for repeated breakthroughs of divine grace; he anticipates never-ending and yet unexpected openness. He regards his own personal history as the locus of God's victorious coming, even if the world should break down around him and even as his body is being destroyed, he clings to the message of the kingdom and trusts that through these trials he will become more truly human, more truly conformed to Jesus Christ.

12. What are the social and political implications of the message of eternal life?

The Christian believes that God's victorious grace is operative in history. He trusts that his people, his society, his culture have a special destiny. Jesus has revealed that the kingdom of God is at hand. Hence history is not an iron cage in which societies are locked into patterns of endless repetitions. The new takes place. The kingdom's call to repentence reveals the inner contradictions in the institutions sinful men have created and the lasting alienation these institutions inflict on human life. The coming kingdom empowers people to recognize their plight, to acquire new vision, to act in unison and to transform their societal life. God's victorious grace operates in the human heart: it is also operative in the social order. The message of eternal life, therefore, makes the Christian critical in regard to present institutions, ready for social change that makes these institutions more human, and eager to engage himself in the transformation of society.

13. Why have we been so little conscious of the socio-political consequences of the message of the kingdom?

A certain privatization and spiritualization of Christ's message, mentioned above, made us forget that the gospel was addressed to individuals as well as societies and that it intended to mediate personal transformation as well as a new age of society reconstructed. One reason for this privatization was the wish of society, religious and secular, to escape criticism. For by confining sin to personal transgressions and by limiting the message of the kingdom to individual persons, the ecclesiastical and the secular institutions were able to pretend that they were not under God's judgment and not destined to be radically transformed. By privatizing the gospel, the institutions were able to set themselves up as sacred and beyond criticism.

14. What is the meaning of the final resurrection?

The Christian doctrine of the resurrection of the body is the central affirmation that prevents the message of the kingdom from being understood in an exclusively spiritual and private manner. For God's victory, we are told, is not confined to the soul nor limited to individuals; what is affected is the whole of humanity. The redemption that is promised us includes the earthly and communal aspects of human life. The resurrection of Jesus anticipates the new age, to which all men are destined. In him is anticipated the final end of history. Christians affirm the final resurrection to express their unwavering hope that God's grace has power over the cosmos and the course of history.

15. What is the final judgment?

The kingdom of God is accompanied by God's judgment on sin and evil. The kingdom evokes repentence. The kingdom reveals to men the extent of their malice and the powers of destruction operative in their midst. When Christians looked upon the kingdom as God's imminent victory putting a stop to history, they expected God's final judgment to be pronounced at the end. But as the kingdom came to be understood as future and present, and as pressing upon us now, God's judgment was also seen as being upon us now, bringing to light human sin, personal and social. This judgment of God reveals to us our brokenness, our involvement in sin and destruction, and hence makes us conscious of the ever-present need of redemption. The doctrine of the final judgment, which is future as well as present, reminds us of the unfinished character of the world and the conditional validity of human institutions. Life on earth remains provisional. History remains under God's judgment. The Church, too, situated in history remains under the divine judgment. Only as the kingdom of God is established in glory and every tear is wiped away, will God's judgment on earth be complete. This completion, we are told, will be the time of Christ's return.

16. What is the meaning of the judgment for society?

It places every aspect of man's institutional life, including the Church, under an ongoing divine critique.

17. What is the meaning of God's judgment for the individual?

A certain privatization and spiritualization of the gospel has made us look upon God's judgment as the judgment to be pronounced on a person after he dies. Yet we have seen that God's judgment, implicit in his approaching kingdom, is operative in personal and social life even now. God's judgment is upon individual persons and their society. The Christian believer recognizes the divine summons present in his life, accusing him of sin, revealing the hidden destruction in which he is involved, convicting him of false consciousness and initiating him into successive conversions of mind and heart. According to biblical teaching, God's grace is judgment before it is new life. God leads us to the recognition of our illness before he applies the remedy and heals us. God's judgment is operative in our personal history as a gracious, life-bringing reality. We can make ourselves deaf to God's voice; we can refuse to hear; but when we do, we exclude ourselves from the source of life and are in danger of death from which there is no awakening. God's judgment on people is a judgment unto life, but they may choose it to be judgment unto death.

18. Did Jesus Christ give us information about the world to come?

Divine revelation is not information about another world, but an initiation into new awareness and new life. Christ's message of the kingdom, as we have seen, does not separate present history from the total fulfillment of God's promises at the end. God's kingdom is in the future and is already with us. The promises regarding God's victory have to do with the present age as well as with the age to come. The message of the kingdom, therefore, creates the faith in God's active and powerful presence in our lives, as judgment and new life, leading us on towards his ultimate victory over all the enemies of life. We want to understand the Christian teaching regarding the end, therefore, not as information about another world but as a message about the-present-as-well-as-the-future and hence as mediating a new perspective on human history.

19. What is the meaning of heaven, hell and purgatory?

These teachings, according to the preceding reply, are not information about a future world but a message about the present-as-well-as-the-future. They initiate us into a new consciousness. They mediate divine salvation. Heaven, then stands for God's victory over sin and evil, operative in our midst at this time but achieving its completion only at the end. The doctrine of hell reminds us of the chaos from which God's grace saves us. It makes us aware of the possibility of total loss, of making ourselves so completely deaf to the divine Word that we shall no longer be able to hear God's voice when he addresses us in mercy. The doctrine of heaven and hell reveals to us the seriousness which lies in moral decisions. Heaven and hell indicate the dimensions of man's possibilities. Finally purgatory must also be understood as a message about the present-as-well-as-the-future. The doctrine reveals to us that man becomes holy through many transformations, some very painful, which God graciously operates in him. The way to God passes through many conversions at various levels of personal depth. Only if we consistently understand the Church's teaching about the future as having to do with the-present-as-well-as-the-future are we able to regain a faithful understanding of the coming kingdom announced by Christ, which is already here and yet is still approaching.

20. Why have many ardent faithful Christians today ceased to believe in eternal life?

Many Christians have ceased to believe in the Church's teaching about the future because they regard it as information about another world. They have not been taught to understand this teaching as shedding light on the present and the future simultaneously. They hold that the preoccupation with another world supposedly recommended by ecclesiastical teaching, distracts from the importance of earthly life, trivializes man's historical existence, and creates the illusion of escape from his grave responsibilities. At the same time, some of the Christians who reject the ecclesiastical teaching on eternal life retain great faith in history as the locus of God's victory, they remain open to the new, they refuse to regard any phase of man's history as definitive and complete, and they look forward to man's ongoing transformation by divine grace. In other words, they continue to believe in the coming kingdom of God. While they reject the terminology, they continue to believe in life eternal.

21. Is the fear of death a universal cause of anguish?

In our culture the fear of death seems to be widely spread and a cause of much anguish. Some of the great philosophers have regarded the dread before the ineluctable reality of personal death a central dimension of human existence. There is good evidence, however, that the acute fear of death which many people experience today is related to the extreme individualism characteristic of western culture. The attitude towards our own death is inevitably connected with the imagination that accompanies our reflection on the future. If in my imagination of the future, my own personal life is central—and this is the stance of modern individualism—then the thought of death will cause me great anguish. But if a person's imagination about the future is dominated by his family, his children and his children's children, or if he dreams of the great things that will happen to his people or of the great achievements to be accomplished by the movement to which he belongs, or if—as a Christian—his imagination of the future is tied to God's kingdom coming upon people and delivering them from misery, then his own personal fate will not be central in his awareness and he is not likely to be anguished about his inevitable death. A wise atheist once said, it is easy to die if what one loves is protected. If my principal love is myself, then the thought of death greatly frightens me. But if I love something that is not threatened or endangered by my death, then I can relax. The Christian who yearns for the coming kingdom that will deliver people for happiness, can die easily; for what he loves is protected. God's victory has been assured him in Christ. From this it follows that if Christian teaching on the last things concentrates on what happens after the individual dies, it does not deliver people from fear. But if Christian teaching concentrates on God's kingdom and refuses to separate the promises made to an individual from the promises made to all men, then it actually purifies the imagination and removes the fear of the future. For God's victory is assured.

22. How do we know whether we believe in eternal life?

To believe in eternal life cannot be equated with acknowledging the doctrine about the world to come. For it is possible not to affirm belief in the world to come, and yet be carried by a confident faith that whatever we are, whatever the crisis we have to face, whatever destruction threatens us, God's victorous grace will accompany us and will forever create new life out of our shattered ruins. It is this hope —which ever remains a free and unsolicited gift—that is the sign of personal faith in the kingdom that is to come.

PART TWO
The Christian Sacraments

Sacraments in General

Note. This presentation of the ecclesial sacraments gives extensive reviews of the historical background both of the word "sacrament" and of the Christian understanding of sacramental events. The seven ecclesial sacraments do not exist in a timeless realm of fixed natures, but are immersed in an ebb and flow of development through the centuries of the church. In Question 7 we begin a review of five perspectives from which sacraments can be profitably understood today. The fifth perspective, developed in Question 11, provides the framework of understanding operative both in our definition of a sacrament (Question 12) and in the subsequent treatment of the individual sacraments.

1. Where did the word "sacrament" originate?

In the ancient world, the Latin word *sacramentum* was the term for the oath of allegiance by which a soldier pledged his services upon induction into a legion of the Roman Empire. With this in mind, the Christian writer Tertullian called Christian baptism a "sacrament" in the early third century.

In introducing this usage, Tertullian was underscoring the importance of the renunciation of Satan and the commitment to Christian discipleship made by a person receiving baptism. The ancient term *sacramentum* is a constant reminder of the new lifestyle and allegiance to which we dedicate ourselves in receiving the sacraments—a point St. Paul developed at length in treating baptism (Rom 6:3–11) and the Eucharist (1 Cor 10:14–21; 11:17–34).

2. Does the word "sacrament" occur in the Bible?

In the Latin Bible *sacramentum* translates the Greek word *mysterion* (mystery), the term which St. Paul used in referring to the hidden plan according to which God in his eternal good-pleasure intended to save, renew, and unite all things in Christ (Eph 1:9; 3:3,9). Thus, God's great "sacrament" is now revealed in the Gospel which proclaims the outpouring of his blessings as we are called to freedom from self-seeking and death. Climactically, this "sacrament" leads to our

[101]

incorporation into God's Son now risen and glorified. The old divisions that scar our humanity are overcome and a new life and spirit is offered us (Eph 2). This is the unfolding of God's plan or "sacrament" of salvation.

3. How were the sacraments understood in the ancient church?

The early teachers who wrote in Greek spoke often of the Christian "mysteries" as they referred to many of the prayers, rites, and practices that were growing up in the church. A privileged place among these Christian mysteries was held by the complex series of acts making up one's initiation into Christianity: Lenten instructions, exorcisms, anointing, profession of faith, and the solemn rite of baptism which led to one's first full sharing in the Eucharist on Easter Sunday.

In the Latin world, Tertullian expressed the awareness that a spiritual effect is linked in the sacraments to a bodily action. "Indeed, the flesh is the hinge of salvation . . . The flesh is washed, so that the soul may be made clean. The flesh is anointed, so that the soul may be dedicated to holiness . . . The flesh is shaded by the imposition of hands, so that the soul may be illuminated by the Spirit. The flesh feeds on the body and blood of Christ, so that the soul too may fatten on God."

The most influential early Christian teacher was St. Augustine, the bishop of Hippo in North Africa (died 430 A.D.). Augustine formulated four important principles that have entered into Christian consciousness as fundamental to understanding the sacraments. (1) A sacrament is a holy sign (image, symbol, expression) through which we both perceive and receive an invisible grace. (2) In its rite, the sacrament or sign is made up of two essential parts, a material component or element and a spoken word of consecration and conferral. "The word is joined to the element and the result is a sacrament, which becomes in a sense a visible word." (3) Some sacraments, including baptism and ordination, are never repeated. Their lifelong effect is like the military brand, or "character," by which a soldier was marked for life as a member of a Roman legion. These sacraments are therefore once-for-all enlistments for service amid God's people. (4) Because it is Christ who ultimately confers a sacrament, the gift of grace and holiness is not prevented or impeded by the possible moral failings of the priest administering the sacrament.

In spite of these initial precisions, writers and teachers continued long after Augustine to speak of a considerable number of rites as

Christian sacraments, including the sign of the cross, the conferral of
ashes on Ash Wednesday, and Christian burial. About 1150, St. Bernard of Clairvaux even used the word in the more ancient sense as he
reverently referred to the mysterious oneness of the three divine persons as "a great sacrament to be worshipped rather than investi-
gated."

4. How were the sacraments understood in the medieval church?

Between 1100 and 1300 the sacraments were vigorously discussed
in the schools and universities of Western Europe. Church teaching
on the sacraments soon came to be marked by the orderliness and
careful precision of academic theology.

There was early agreement that "sacrament" should be used in the
strict sense only for those seven rites instituted by Christ in which
God is offering us grace and life *through the rite itself,* whereas other
prayers and actions are principally occasions for our personal devotion and prayer for God's grace. Thus, there are seven ecclesial sacraments, but many other "sacramentals."

One of the chief contributions of St. Thomas Aquinas (died 1274)
was the explanation that the indelible sacramental "character" given
in the unrepeatable sacraments is in fact a spiritual reality on the order
of a commission or appointment. Persons baptized, confirmed, or
ordained are singled out to share in the priestly calling of Christ and
thenceforth to live lives of worship and service in the likeness of
Christ.

Aquinas dared to use the ideas of the ancient Greek philosopher
Aristotle in building his theology. Thus Aquinas spoke of the sacraments as the *instruments* God uses in causing in us or communicating
to us the graces of salvation. To show the overall harmony of God's
plan, Aquinas compared the sacraments to the human nature of Jesus
Christ, for in being assumed into union with the Eternal Word, this
human nature was God's primary instrument in working out his plan
of reconciliation and salvation.

**5. How were the sacraments understood in the era of the Reforma-
tion?**

The Protestant Reformers were greatly concerned to simplify the
sacramental rites so as to give the people a deep personal experience
of God's forgiving grace as they received the sacraments. Martin
Luther (died 1546) and John Calvin (died 1564) argued that according

to the strict word of Scripture only two sacraments, baptism and the Lord's Supper, were instituted and ordained by Christ as trustworthy signs and means of grace.

Early in the Reformation, Ulrich Zwingli (died 1532) and others began teaching that the sacraments were to be seen as expressions of *our* remembrance of Christ and of *our* devotion stirred by the Holy Spirit. Luther responded sharply that the sacraments are "the bridge, the path, the way, the ladder . . . by which the Spirit might come to you." Thus, for the main Reformers, the preached word and the bibical sacraments are the divinely instituted "means of grace."

John Calvin urged people to understand baptism and the Lord's Supper by way of analogy with the seal stamped or embossed on a charter or document to give it official standing. Calvin taught that sacraments are the actions that confirm and corroborate the word of the Gospel in which God promises us forgiveness of sins. Therefore, one received the sacraments by trustfully casting oneself upon God's word as the only basis of assurance and not by seeking to influence God by offering him good works to gain his mercy.

In responding to the Reformers, the Council of Trent (1545–62), impressed on Catholic consciousness the conviction that there are in fact seven sacraments in the Christian dispensation, even though Scripture's witness to each of these is not of the same clarity. The Council also reaffirmed that sacraments are not simply stimulants to our weak faith, but are the means or instruments by which God confers upon the devout recipient his gift of grace and new life.

Trent also formulated a number of answers to particular questions about the sacraments raised by the Reformers, for instance, the real presence of the body and blood of Christ in the Eucharist, the effectiveness of baptism in really removing original sin, and the necessity of telling all serious sins in receiving the sacrament of penance. But most of all, the Catholic response to the Reformation was a strong affirmation of the importance of the sacraments over against the eventual Protestant tendency to greatly subordinate them to the preached sermon.

6. How are the sacraments being understood in the church today?

The word "sacrament" is again being applied more widely than to just the seven principal rites of sanctification and worship in the church.

Christ himself, both as the Incarnate Word of God and as the man so totally "for others" that he gave his life, is seen as the *primordial sacrament* of our encounter with God. In Christ, God's loving kindness becomes visible in a great sign and God's saving mercy becomes effective in the world of men and women needing salvation.

Also, the church, as the community of believers in Christ, is grasped as the *fundamental sacrament* by which God both reveals in sign and effects in action the unity of all mankind. The people of God show forth already that ultimate unity of mankind toward which all of God's works are tending. In her mission of witness and service, the church is actively engaged in promoting this reconciliation that anticipates the final kingdom. Thus the church is both sign and cause (as instrument) of what is to be God's ultimate gift to mankind.

This wider use of the term "sacrament" is but one indication of a many-sided movement of *integration* by which the ecclesial sacraments are being understood less as detached events of grace between God and man and more as meaningful moments within God's universal dispensation of salvation. Because Scripture reveals this dispensation as a many-splendored reality, we must look at it from a series of different viewpoints or perspectives. The following five questions will indicate the place of the sacraments within five different perspectives or frameworks of understanding which emerge from Scripture and the tradition of Christian teaching.

7. What is the role of the sacraments in the renewal of creation?

Scripture affirms that the ultimate intent of God's saving work is the creation of "new heavens and a new earth in which righteousness dwells" (2 Pt 3:13). The end of our world will signal the beginning of a new *world,* and not simply an ethereal dwelling-place of ghostly spirits. It is in this vein that our creed confesses, "We look for the resurrection of the dead."

But this new creation is not simply way off in a distant future. The risen Christ is "the beginning, the first-born from the dead, that in everything he might be preeminent" (Col 1:18). And through his Spirit, Christ, the first-born, is now preparing mankind to pass into the coming new creation. His primary work is of course the conversion of men and women, as he renews human hearts and effects reconciliation. But the earth is to be renewed as well. "Creation itself will be set free from its bondage to decay and obtain the glorious liberty of the children of God" (Rom 8:21).

Therefore, by Christ's use of water, oil, bread, and wine in his present work of sanctification and renewal, the sacraments introduce a profound truth into our religious lives. Already, Christ incorporates the *things* of this world into his encounters with human persons, and this expresses that his pre-eminence extends through the whole of creation. As a teacher of the kingdom, Jesus referred to sowing seed, finding pearls, and catching fish to make his point. Today, we meet him, not by escaping from the earth, but through acts of dialogue and exchange that include earthly elements expressing his saving work and bringing it to bear on our lives.

The sacraments are thus expressive of Christ's lordship over creation; they point to the day on which all things are to be subject to the Son (1 Cor 15:27f). His is not the domination of abject elements by one with power, but a sovereignty that confers righteousness, holiness, and new being. Our earth too is to share in this renewal.

8. What is the role of the sacraments in the course of personal living?

Each of the seven sacraments responds to a deep personal need we have of God's redemptive presence at the *critical moments* in our individual life-histories. In the sacraments, God works to place our major life-decisions in a meaningful context of graced service of him and of others. God recalls us from rootless wandering and the morass of isolated choices in the face of life's central problems. We need not seek in darkness for the meaning of life, growth, guilt, illness, sex, vocation, death, and relating to other people.

Baptism envelops the beginning of life in God's loving kindness and stamps it with the irrevocable concern of Christ and his assembled people. As a person approaches maturity, confirmation renews the gift of God's Spirit as the source of strength and support in a life of discipleship and service. In ecclesial penance, we can deal with the cancer of sin and the wounds of guilt and infidelity by approaching the Lord, "a God merciful and gracious, slow to anger, . . . forgiving iniquity and transgression and sin" (Ex 34:6f). When serious illness threatens to engulf us in self-concern, sacramental anointing brings God's presence and assimilates us to Christ who suffered on behalf of many. Ordination and marriage are sacramental dedications of mature Christians to the life-long vocations of loving service to which God calls them.

Our basic problem, however, the one that accompanies us for a lifetime, is the way we relate to other people. Can we overcome the stifling effect of self-seeking so as to live in peace with others? Can we grow in prompt readiness to help and serve the Christ who calls to us through people in need? Thus, God would have us return constantly to the eucharistic meal where we and those near to us are made one body in Christ and where we are inserted into Christ's selfless giving of himself on behalf of every human person.

Through the sacraments, therefore, the course of our personal lives is repeatedly punctuated by God's loving presence at just the moments of our greatest need of him.

9. How do sacraments serve as signs of the single mystery of God's saving love?

When we speak of the single mystery of God's saving love, we mean to express the deep Catholic conviction that in truth "God our Savior . . . desires all men to be saved and to come to the knowledge of the truth" (1 Tim 2:3f). In this view, God does in fact make a genuine approach to every human person to offer each one the gift of transforming intimacy with himself through grace.

Thus, the life of every man is in fact enveloped by God's Spirit, whose incognitos are more varied than we can imagine. The Spirit's intent and purpose is solely to open hearts and transform them in loving submission to the Father. Consequently we do not see the church or even the whole of Christianity as the exclusive area in which God's love unfolds itself in human lives. Christians are not those selected out of humanity to live in communion with God. Christians, rather, make up the elect people who give witness to God's one mystery of love and who by their service seek to facilitate the universal reconciling work of God's Spirit.

Therefore, the life of God's people is shaped by those expressions or articulations of the one mystery that repeatedly raise it to a heightened level of memory and consciousness, that engage a person in receptive response to God's love, and that unfold the implications of this mystery for the lives of individuals and communities.

In the community of God's people, the sacraments explicitate and celebrate the many facets of the loving kindness with which God already embraces the life of every human person. This one mystery of love aims at our birth into new life (baptism). This love is strengthening and supportive (confirmation), cleansing and forgiving (penance), healing and faithful unto death (anointing). God's love conforms us to Christ's selfless service of others (orders and marriage), and it repeatedly breaks the barriers of selfishness that divide and alienate us from one another (Eucharist).

In the sacraments we celebrate the many-splendored mystery of

God's saving love as it works continually in the lives of all men and women.

10. What is the role of the sacraments in the saving history of God's covenant people?

It is a truism that God does not deal with us as isolated individuals independently of our families, our work-situation, and our community of faith and worship. But there is another kind of context for our moments of conversion, growth, and worship of God. Scripture inserts the lives of both individuals and communities into the vast panorama of "the history of salvation."

In very ancient times, God spoke and worked in manners that repeatedly promised a new and fuller presence of his love. The old covenant with Israel became pregnant with hope and expectation of a new, more intimate convenant (Jer 31:31–34). In the death and exaltation of Christ, this promise reached a fulfilment in which we now share, "because God's love has been poured into our hearts through the Holy Spirit given us" (Rom 5:5). But the ultimate stage, the consummation, has not yet come. We still look forward to that fullness of time when all things will be united in Christ (Eph 1:10) and creation will no longer groan in futility (Rom 8:21f).

The Christian sacraments are the events in which the climactic moments of this salvation history are brought to bear on our lives. The phases of God's plan become contemporaneous with moments in the lives of individuals and communities. The liturgy of baptism, in the Easter vigil celebration, involves each of us in God's creation of the world, his liberation of Noah's family from the flood, and the passage of God's people out of Egypt to a land of promise. Our baptism is our insertion into the death and rising of Christ (Rom 6:3–11), a fact made vividly clear when the sacrament is given by completely immersing the person in water and then bringing him out in the likeness of a resurrection.

In the Eucharist, Christ is present in a living memorial of his death on our behalf and we are called to dedicate ourselves to the Father with him in a sacrifice of praise. In the eucharistic meal, we anticipate the final union God intends to grant, a communion of intimate nearness which Scripture often presents as a banquet. Confirmation, ordination, and marriage celebrate anew the sending of God's Spirit to consecrate his people in their individual vocations.

Thus, as we share in the sacraments we come to be inserted more fully into the history of salvation. Our memories are stamped more deeply with God's purpose; we are conformed to the central event of Christ's obedient death on behalf of men; and we are emboldened by hope as our future is bathed in the light of the coming triumph of God's peace over our hostilities and hardness of heart.

11. What is the role of the sacraments in the life of God's priestly people?

The sacraments are key events both for expressing and for further developing the self-understanding of the people God has gathered and made a priestly body. This people does indeed acknowledge the presence of God's Spirit touching the life of every man and woman. God's saving work, under whatever guise, is coterminous with the complete span of human existence. Still, we who are in the church sense that God has chosen and marked us out for a special role.

We are not the sole recipients of his grace, but are rather a people called to a special service within the unfolding of God's saving work. In the image of Christ, the church is anointed for messianic and priestly service in the midst of the world. As a priestly people, the members of the church are called to witness to the world about what God is accomplishing, to become a focal point of unity in the service of human reconciliation, and to approach God in prayerful worship in place of and on behalf of all men.

In the sacraments, therefore, this priestly people strives to become more and more possessed by the self-understanding of Jesus as he lived and died on behalf of the many and for the benefit of all. Baptism incorporates new members into the priestly community. Penance reconciles repentant sinners to the community of worship. Anointing heals the inner wounds which prevent illness from becoming an act of witness and redemptive suffering. Marriage and ordination dedicate couples and individuals to their special roles of service in building up the priestly people. In the Eucharist Christ gathers his people about himself, incorporates them as his body and leads their worshipful approach to the Father.

Thus, in the sacraments, God's people is fitted to pursue its role and vocation to be a priestly and messianic people. Ever aware of its unworthiness, the church seeks to deepen its sense of being called out to extend into our world the mission of Christ, the Lord's Servant and High Priest.

12. What, then, is a sacrament?

The definition of a sacrament will differ according to the specific perspective one adopts. Using as a framework the life of God's priestly people, as developed in the preceding response, we can both insert the sacraments into the larger dispensation of the Spirit in the world beyond the church and also highlight the communal dimensions of Christ's sacramental work of forming and preparing his priestly people.

Accordingly, the sacraments are *rites of incorporation* in which Christ is drawing men and women more fully under the influence of his redeeming grace and his saving mission. Sacraments are *events of grace,* in which the Spirit of God is imparted by the Lord who is ever sending his Spirit into the world. In the sacraments, incorporation and grace are extended through *symbolic* or *ritual acts* of human communication and human worship in the church, such as initiation, reconciliation, a festive meal, or a marriage commitment.

In receiving a sacrament, a person is both *receptive* of God's loving nearness and *responsive in worship.* Receptivity to grace, or "faith," is basic to a life near to God. In sacraments both the community and individuals give expression to their faith and under the influence of the Holy Spirit develop and deepen this fundamental receptivity to God's presence and influence. In sacramental events, we are not, however, exclusively passive or receptive. Sacraments entail worship and in every sacrament we respond to God in acts such as confession and thanksgiving, sorrow for sin and dedication to a new life, heartfelt petition, self-forgetting praise, and yearning for ultimate union and intimacy with God. Of such strands is woven the worship of God's priestly people.

Sacraments are not performed to benefit an individual or the Church. As in the Gospel, so in the life of his people now, Christ *gathers* his followers so that he might *send them out* as heralds of God's loving design for the world. God has deemed it right to use our services in his approach to men, and in the sacraments he is gathering, forming, strengthening, and commissioning his people for their mission in the world on which he sheds his lovingkindness.

Thus, sacraments are the symbolic or ritual acts of incorporation into the sphere of Christ's grace and mission; in sacraments we demonstrate our receptivity to the Spirit and responsive readiness to worship and serve the Lord, who is both gathering and sending his priestly people into the world.

Sacraments of Initiation

BAPTISM

1. What does the Bible teach concerning baptism?

Israelite religious practice included various washings or ablutions, principally to make a person fit to take part in acts of worship. But more important for the Christian understanding of baptism was the role of water in the great events of early salvation history. At the beginning God subdued the waters of chaos by his Spirit (Gn 1:2). At the time of the flood, Noah and a small representative group were brought together by God and saved as the floodwaters began to engulf them (Gn 6–9). Israel's liberation from Egyptian bondage came by a passage through water (Ex 14), and after the years of wandering the tribes entered the land of promise by another passage, this time through the River Jordan (Josh 4). Thus, water was closely associated with the origins of Israel's covenanted relation with the Lord God.

When Ezekiel gave voice to Israel's hope of a new covenant, he mentioned cleansing with water in his description of the newly gathered people who were to receive a new heart and a new spirit (Ez 36:25). When John the Baptist came forth as a herald of imminent judgment, baptism was the sign and gesture by which men expressed conversion from sin and readiness for the "mightier one" who was coming (Mt 3).

At Jesus' baptism, the Holy Spirit descended and the Father solemnly designated Jesus for his messianic work (Mt 3:16f). Later, Jesus hinted at a significance in baptism far deeper than that of cleansing or washing. Referring to his approaching death, Jesus declared, "I have a baptism to be baptized with; and how I am constrained until it is accomplished" (Lk 12:50). With these words Jesus planted a seed that flowered in St. Paul's teaching that Christian baptism is an act assimilating us to Jesus' death and resurrection.

In the documents of the apostolic church we see an incredibly rich unfolding of the significance of the baptismal act with which the convert began his new life in the Christian faith. The earliest practice of the church was probably to baptize converts "in the name of Jesus" (Acts 10:48; 19:5) since in baptism it was his Lordship they confessed and into his body they were incorporated. In an early letter, St. Paul explained succinctly this incorporation in terms of passing from the tutelage of the law to authentic sonship. "For as many of you as were baptized into Christ have put on Christ." This means that the divisions set up by our old categories are torn down, "for you are all one in Christ Jesus" (Gal. 3:23–28).

Another important baptismal passage is Romans 6:3–11, where Paul states that baptism is an act conformed to the central mystery of salvation, the death, burial, and resurrection of Christ. As Christ now lives "to God," the baptized are to walk in newness of life. They have passed through a fundamental change and are now beyond the dominion of sin. In a later epistle (Col 2:8–3:17), the theme of baptismal dying and rising leads to a sketch of authentic Christian morality. One raised by God in Christ must not be enslaved to the ritual prescriptions, but should live a life of compassion and gratitude, spreading love and peace. "If then you have been raised with Christ, seek the things and that are above, where Christ is, . . . for you have died and your life is hid with Christ in God" (Col 3:1f).

The First Epistle of Peter begins with an eloquent passage on the significance of Christian baptism (1:3–2:9). The writer addresses those who have been born anew by the living and imperishable seed that is God's word (1:23f). This new birth transforms one's vision of the future, since it is a birth to living hope, "and to an inheritance which is imperishable, undefiled, and unfading, kept in heaven for you" (1:4). But this new life and hope is not simply a matter of individual consolation, for the baptized are now aggregated to God's new people, "to be a holy priesthood, to offer spiritual sacrifices acceptable to God through Jesus Christ" (2:5). Through baptism God's mercy is manifest (1:3; 2:10) and Christ's redemption is effective (1:18f). The effect of baptism is the gathering and building up of a people bearing priestly and prophetic responsibilities. "You are a chosen race, a royal priesthood, a holy nation, God's own people, that you may declare the wonderful deeds of him who called you out of darkness into his marvellous light" (2:9).

Scripture, therefore, yields a many-sided witness to Christian baptism. From the beginning, there was complete certainty that Jesus had mandated this manner of entry into the community of his discples. The developing understanding of a new life lived to the Father and in the power of the Holy Spirit led naturally to the trinitarian formula of baptism (Mt 28:19). Probably the New Testament church administered baptism solely to adult converts. Baptism was thus the climactic moment of their conversion and renewal of heart as they began a life stamped by their confession of Jesus as Lord and Savior. The New Testament passages reviewed here remain the finest articulations of the meaning of adult conversion and the new life of Christian freedom and responsibility issuing from baptism.

2. What do we learn from the present liturgy of baptism?

The new liturgy of infant baptism (from 1969), places considerable stress on the commitment of the parents to foster in their child the life of faith. Immediately before the water is poured over the child, the parents state their own rejection of sin and make profession of their faith in Father, Son, and Holy Spirit. Their child is then baptized "in the faith of the Church," which they have professed. Baptizing an infant is thus a pledge made on the part of the parents and the ecclesial community that this child's life will be enveloped in God's loving concern. Christian conviction and ideals are to form the context and atmosphere in which the child will be growing up.

Immediately after baptism, the new Christian is addressed, "God the Father of our Lord Jesus Christ has freed you from sin, given you new birth of water and the Holy Spirit, and welcomed you into his holy people." Baptism is, therefore, at once an act of liberation, rebirth, and incorporation. This is given striking expression in the three concluding actions: anointing with the oil of priestly and royal dignity, clothing with a white robe symbolizing the new creation in Christ, and conferral of a candle lighted from the Easter candle to encourage the newly baptized to live in the light of faith.

3. What then is the fundamental meaning of baptism?

Baptism is before all else the action by which Christ associates with himself the individual members of the people through whom he continues to worship the Father and shed his love on the world. In baptism, Christ gathers to himself disciples who are to share his destiny and mission.

Hence the water of baptism is first the place of a spiritual death, burial, and rising in conformity to Christ. Baptism is an act of passing through to a new existence under the influence of the risen Christ, who became a "life-giving spirit" (1 Cor 15:45). This new existence in Christ entails above all a personal intimacy with God who has revealed himself as Father, Son, and Holy Spirit. Risen with Christ, the baptized have access to the Father and can address him familiarly as the Spirit suggests and makes possible.

Because Christianity rests above all on the entry of God's Son into our race, baptism has a rich human context. It is an act of insertion or incorporation into a people. In baptism, the community of the people of God receives a new member and confers a share in its priestly dignity and responsibility. The baptized person begins to be initiated into the vision of faith and the set of values by which this people lives. Above all, a baptized person is oriented to taking part in the mission Christ has conferred on his people in extension of his own priestly and prophetic service of mankind.

4. But, still, why baptize small infants who can neither grasp this meaning nor accept this responsibility?

We cannot claim that small infants were baptized from the very earliest Christian times, even though the New Testament does relate that whole "households" were baptized (Acts 16:15; 1 Cor 1:16). Only by the year 250 A.D. is it clear that in different places Christians were, without any sense of a problem, bringing their new-born infants for baptism.

Infant baptism became very significant in the fifth century as churchmen developed arguments against Pelagius, who downplayed the role of God's grace as the absolutely necessary means of overcoming sin. Infant baptism was for many an incontrovertible argument that everyone is born in bondage to sin and from the start stands in dire need of God's grace, which is given as a pure unmerited gift. Further, the word of Christ began to be cited in his connection, "Unless one is born of water and the Spirit, he cannot enter the kingdom of God" (Jn 3:5). The baptism of small infants thus came to be both highly appropriate and urgently necessary.

Infant baptism came under fire when the adherents of the radical Reformation in the sixteenth century, the radicals, or Anabaptists, demanded that the church disestablish itself and become a consciously committed band of adult Christians living up to the full requirements of the Gospel. Consequently, Christians of the Baptist and Mennonite traditions do not baptize their infant children.

More recently, other objections have been raised against the practice of infant baptism in areas of Europe where vast numbers of Catholic Christians have only a nominal relation to the church. Would it not be better to allow the name of Christian to quietly die out where the realities of living faith, active worship, and transcendent hope have already dried up?

5. What meaning is to be ascribed to infant baptism?

A traditional defense of baptizing infant children has been based on fear that they would be lost if they died as young children. However, this argument frequently treats our original sinfulness as basically the same kind of sin of which responsible adults can be guilty and by which they alienate themselves from God. God does will to save an infant child from sin, but we must believe that his ways of doing this cannot be limited simply to Christian baptism.

Others have argued that infant baptism is a most dramatic and needed expression of aspects of God's love that we all too easily forget. They point out that in saving us God's Spirit takes the initiative in an act of sheer graciousness. The beginning of God's saving work in the human heart is not dependent on some precondition of our making. Baptism is God's deed, not something of our creation, and administering it to infants posits a drastic reminder that God's grace is not his response to our efforts.

A still more adequate line of thought looks especially to the influence of the personal environment on a person's development. All of us born into the human race are inserted into a web of human relations now twisted and scarred by self-seeking, exploitation, and hatred. The world of mankind is not what God intended it to be, and even an infant can be injured or poisoned by this environment. Sinfulness has a snowballing effect and if unchecked it will inevitably overrun the young adult and sweep him along in willing agreement.

However, through the work of Christ this sinful process has been reversed and in Christ's church men and women are creating a counter movement in which God's grace and concern find expression in human care and loving, not the least in the love of parents for their growing children. From this viewpoint the baptism of an infant is a solemn pledge made by the parents and by the ecclesial community to do their best in the rearing of this child to reverse the seemingly inevitable processes of sin. For the child this is an act of liberation as he is drawn into a community of faith and love. His life has a new horizon, that of the vision of faith as articulated by the Christian confession. By baptismal incorporation, God's love for the infant becomes concretized in the concern of his parents to free him from the inherited human destiny of sin and estrangement from God.

Thus, if the parents are dedicated to bring up their children in a personal environment of faith and loving concern, the baptism of these children as infants is a most significant sacramental expression of the beginning of life in Christ.

CONFIRMATION

6. What does the Bible teach concerning confimation?

For apostolic times there is no clear evidence that a special separate rite was regularly performed to impart the Holy Spirit to baptized believers. However, two passages in the Acts of the Apostles tell of the apostles giving the Holy Spirit by laying hands on persons already baptized (Acts 8:14–17; 19:5–6). These two incidents appear to have been the result of special circumstances in the earliest Christian mission, but they did lead to the eventual inclusion of such a rite in the baptismal liturgy of the early church and later to the development of a separate rite of conferral of the Holy Spirit by the bishop after baptism by an ordinary priest.

What Scripture does make clear, however, is that by Christ's promise the Spirit of God was poured out abundantly on the band of early believers to give them courage and eloquence in witnessing to the world about Christ. This work of the Holy Spirit had been amply foreshadowed in ancient Israel, where early leaders like Samson and Gideon, then kings like David and Solomon, and finally prophets like Elijah, Amos, and Ezekiel were all made capable of extraordinary deeds by the Spirit of God which raised them up and strengthened them.

The Spirit descended upon Jesus as he began his public preaching (Lk 3:22), and he came to declare, "The Spirit of the Lord is upon me, because he has anointed me to preach good news to the poor" (Lk 4:18). After his resurrection, Jesus assured two of his disciples, "I send the promise of my Father upon you; but stay in the city until you are clothed with power from on high" (Lk 24:49).

After the great outpouring of the Spirit on Pentecost, the earliest expansion of Christianity was illumined, inspired, and emboldened by the Holy Spirit (e.g., Acts 4:8,31, 8:29; 9:17; 10:42; 13:2,4,52). In writing to Corinth, Paul gave his famous listing of the manifold gifts found in the church, concluding, "All these are inspired by one and the same Spirit, who apportions to each one individually as he wills" (1 Cor 12:11).

In the Gospel of John, we find the Spirit viewed from another perspective. He is that "other Paraclete" (the Advocate or Counsellor) who after Jesus' departure will give the disciples a full disclosure of Jesus' teaching (Jn 14:25f; 16:13f).

This manifold witness to the Holy Spirit indicates there is more to the work of the Spirit than the renewal and rebirth given in baptism. Those granted new existence at the beginning of their Christian life receive the further promise and reality of guidance, inspiration, and fresh courage in serving the advance of the Gospel message. It was only a matter of time before the church's liturgy made a place for conferral of this gift, first by the imposition of hands and then by the anointing with oil.

7. What do we learn from the present liturgy of confirmation?

Ordinarily confirmation is conferred within Mass, so as to clearly demonstrate its role as a further stage, beyond baptism, in the single process of incorporating, or initiating, a new member into the full life and worship of God's people.

The material element in the rite of the sacrament is a special oil, called chrism, consecrated by the bishop on Holy Thursday. The significance of anointing with chrism is that of strengthening one's Christian life for arduous service of the Gospel.

After Scripture readings and a homily on the manifold works of the Spirit, those to be confirmed renew their baptismal rejection of Satan and adhesion to the faith of the Church. As a preparatory rite, the ministers place their hands on all those to be confirmed. Imposing hands is found all through the Bible as a gesture of blessing. This is articulated in the Bishop's prayer: "All powerful God, Father of our Lord Jesus Christ, by water and the Holy Spirit you freed these candidates from sin. Send your Holy Spirit upon them to be their helper and guide. Give them the spirit of wisdom and understanding, the spirit of right judgment and courage, the spirit of knowledge and love, the spirit of reverence in your service."

The sacrament is then conferred by anointing the forehead with chrism in the form of a cross and saying the words, "Receive the seal of the Holy Spirit, the Gift of the Father." The reference to the seal echoes Paul's expression of God's strengthening work: "It is God who establishes us with you in Christ, and has commissioned us. He has put his seal upon us and given us his Spirit in our hearts as a guarantee" (2 Cor 1:21f). The sacrament, thus, expresses God's further dominion over persons chosen to serve him in his priestly people. God's seal is impressed upon them, and his claim strengthened, by a further gift of his creative Spirit.

8. What then is the fundamental meaning of confirmation?

Confirmation stands in the process of initiation into the life of the priestly people of God. It is the point at which God confers a gift of his Holy Spirit to turn the Christian outward to face the world to which the church is sent with its saving mission. Confirmation is a sacramental perfecting or strengthening of the new life begun in baptism. The maturing of this life entails quite naturally a new degree of responsibility for sharing in the mission of witness and service which God has given to his elect people.

The role of the bishop in consecrating the chrism and as the "original" (although not exclusive) minister of the sacrament makes explicit the close link of this gift of the Spirit with the mission of proclamation and service which Christ gave to his church in solemn mandate through the apostles.

It is to be noted that the themes of personal maturity and adult commitment to Christian living are not in the forefront of this understanding of confirmation. These are questions of education, adjustment within the family, and increasingly meaningful participation in the Eucharist. Confirmation should not be "used" in an attempt to meet these problems.

Although national episcopal conferences have been urged to make adaptations regarding the proper age and appropriate preparation for receiving confirmation, such adaptations are clearly to respect the nature of the sacrament as a stage within the process of Christian initiation.

9. What is the pentecostal or charismatic "baptism in the Holy Spirit"?

"Baptism in the Holy Spirit" is a religious experience granted to Christians who are pursuing a spirituality focused on the manifold works and gifts of the Holy Spirit. In this experience, one becomes aware in a decisively new way of the presence of God in one's life. The occasion for such an experience is usually intense intercession for the person by a community prayer oriented to the Holy Spirit.

The gift given in this "baptism" is not the beginning of the Holy Spirit's activity in one's life, but rather a release or further development in the realm of experience of the gifts given originally through the sacraments of baptism and confirmation. The Spirit comes to a new visibility, bringing a deeper sense of the presence of the Risen Christ, a fresh vigor in prayer, and greater zeal to witness to God's work in the church and in the world.

Consequently, in the term "baptism in the Holy Spirit," the word "baptism" does not refer to a sacramental rite with water, but to an experience of immersion in, or innundation by, the Spirit's presence. This meaning is, in fact, very close to the root-meaning of the word which has come to be used for the first rite of Christian initiation.

Sacraments of Forgiveness and Healing

PENANCE

1. What does the Bible teach about sacramental penance?

Over the centuries, this sacrament of forgiveness and reconciliation has been understood as originating on the evening of the first Easter. St. John records that the risen Jesus appeared in the midst of his fearful disciples and after a greeting of peace issued this emphatic commission: "As the Father has sent me, so I send you." Then he breathed upon them and said, "Receive the Holy Spirit. If you forgive the sins of any, they are forgiven; if you retain the sins of any, they are retained" (Jn 20:21–23).

In this saying of Jesus, the disciples' forgiving or retaining are said to be effective (". . . they *are* forgiven . . . *are* retained"). In all probability these second clauses are phrased passively in accord with the Hebraic way of attributing something to God without mentioning the divine name. The appointment to the work of forgiving or retaining sins is given considerable solemnity by the parallel Jesus drew between his own mission from the Father and the mission he imparted to his disciples.

A fuller understanding of the origins of ecclesial penance can be gained by reviewing, first, Jesus' own ministry to sinners, then, his conferral of power to "bind and loose" upon his disciples, and, finally, the way the earliest communities dealt with the reality of sin as it cropped up in the lives of its members.

One of the most startling aspects of Jesus' ministry was that he, the herald of God's new reign, so frequently sat at table with sinners and tax collectors. When challenged by Jewish officials, he gave this succinct description of his mission: "Those who are well have no need of a physician, but those who are sick; I have come not to call the righteous, but sinners" (Mk 2:17). When he encountered the receptivity of faith, he spoke at times the consoling words. "Your sins are forgiven" (Mk 2:5; Lk 7:48). Jesus offered a moving account of God's readiness to forgive in the story of the son who sinned against his father but upon repentance was not only forgiven but was led into a joyous feast (Lk 15). And at his last meal with his followers, Jesus indicated that he was going to death for the benefit of sinners: "This is my blood . . . which is poured out for many for the forgiveness of sins" (Mt 26:28). Thus, the Easter commission recorded by John confers on the apostles the power and responsibility to continue a central part of Jesus's own work and to communicate to sinful men the benefits unleashed on the world by his death for others.

2. What does the New Testament say of forgiveness after baptism?

Baptism is, of course, the primary way the power of sin is overcome in the life of the believer. But the New Testament also contains varied evidence of a disciplined but ultimately saving response by the church to the sin its members commit after their baptismal incorporation into Christ. This latter response to sin, like the commission to forgive or retain, is also marked by an alternative, that is, between "binding" and "loosing."

The Gospel of Matthew records that Jesus assured Peter and the larger group of disciples that whatever they bound on earth would be bound in heaven and whatever they loosed on earth would be loosed in heaven (Mt 16:19; 18:18). In these words Jesus spoke in the idiom of the rabbinic tradition and thereby passed on to his church a capability for dealing with sin in the lives of its members. The power to bind and loose was held by synagogue authorities in Jesus' day. By this power they exercised over sinful members a discipline of exclusion from (binding) and restoration to the synagogue community (loosing). Jesus took over this practice for his new community, the church, and promised that both the exclusion imposed and the restoration granted would have significance and validity before God.

Other texts of the New Testament afford us glimpses of a practice of this kind at work in the life of the earliest Christians. St. Paul wrote in a very early letter that the community was to "note" members not living up to the apostolic norms, and in more flagrant cases they were to keep away from such a person (2 Thes 3:14.6). However, this is a loving discipline looking to renewed conversion: "have nothing to do with him, that he may be ashamed. Do not look on him as an enemy, but warn him as a brother" (3:14f). A later letter echoes the rules laid down in the gospel: "As for a man who is factious, after admonishing him once or twice, have nothing more to do with him" (Ti 3:10; see Mt 18:15–18).

These directives reached their climax in Paul's reaction to the report of a case of flagrant immorality that occurred among the Corinthian Christians (1 Cor 5:1–5). This should sadden the community and lead to the guilty man's exclusion. Paul's directive took the form of a judgment pronounced on the man in the name of the Lord Jesus. And so the community is to deliver the man over to the realm outside the church where Satan reigns, in the hope that he might in the end be saved when Christ comes in judgment. Paul evidently felt that his apostolic authority included the power of "binding" in the name of the Lord those who fell into serious sin after they had entered the Church through baptism.

The severity of this primitive church discipline should, however, be seen in the light of the concerned words in which Paul later directed the Corinthians to manifest the love of Christ for sinners (2 Cor 2:5–11). They should turn to a person once punished to forgive and comfort him. In this loving forgiveness Paul concurs: "Anyone whom you forgive, I also forgive. What I have forgiven . . . has been for your sake in the presence of Christ" (2:10). Here is the ultimate result of the church's binding a person with the punishment of exclusion: the body of believers lovingly reaccepts the person and thus extends the gentle loosing that imparts Christ's forgiveness.

Thus, the New Testament does not simply witness to a great outpouring of forgiving and renewing grace upon those called to faith and baptism. There are also glimpses of a way of forgiveness for the baptized who fall into sin, a way involving both their relation to their fellow believers and the pronouncement of punishment and release by apostolic authority. Built on this foundation, the practice of ecclesial penance has, however been carried out in a notable variety of forms in the history of the church.

3. What forms did sacramental penance take in the early church?

Churchmen of the second century had occasion to urge a further conversion or change of heart upon their people. They made some brief references to "confessing" sins, but we find no clear account of the liturgical forms this took or of the role of pastors and priests in this confession. The third century saw the rise of rigoristic movements which called in question the church's power to extend penance to those guilty of capital sins like murder, adultery, and apostasy. The great majority of leading bishops responded that there was no reason to limit the kinds of persons who could be reconciled after completing an assigned penance. Still, the spirit of rigor was abroad and ecclesial penance was quite arduous, lengthy, and limited to but one reception in a person's lifetime.

The central conceptions of early Christian penance were these: partial excommunication from the body of the faithful because of one's sin; the assignment of a specific penitential lifestyle by the bishop; the support of penitents by the church's prayer of intercession; and eventual restoration to full communion by episcopal imposition of hands.

Early Christians were convinced that serious sins committed after baptism could *not* be forgiven in an act of sheer grace or amnesty. The malady was deepseated, and conversion must include a laborious experience over a period of time. Purification was sought through fasting, wearing coarse garments, humble begging for help, and sexual abstinence. This arduous purification was, however, neither self-imposed nor carried out in proud isolation. The penance was assigned by the church and accordingly had a quasi-sacramental value. One's fellow Christians were deeply concerned for the penitent. Their support created a web of solidarity as one advanced toward reincorporation into the eucharistic community. Pastors led their people in prayer for penitents. Gifted Christians were there to counsel penitents and pray with them. As St. Jerome said, the bishop readmits a sinner to the altar only after all the members of the church have wept together with him.

But since this process of purification, conversion, and reconciliation was strictly limited to once in a person's lifetime, great numbers of persons put off penance until late in life. This increased both the number of persons excluded from the eucharist and the number of death-bed confessions with immediate reconciliation. Gradually, the ancient form of penitential reconciliation became a pastoral liability.

A creative breakthrough occurred in Irish and Anglo-Saxon monasteries in about the 6th century. Monks had long valued visits to "spiritual physicians," that is, to perceptive fellow monks for healing advice and prayer. Expanding from this practice, abbots began granting repeated penance and reconciliation to their monks and to the people of their district. Reconciliation still followed the performance

of penance, but the increasing use of the procedure gave rise to ordered schedules of the length and kind of penances appropriate to
various sins. Soon handbooks for confessors were drawn up and these
spread over Europe during the missionary campaigns of the monks in
the seventh and eighth centuries. This penitential discipline played no
small role in the creation of a Christian civilization amid the savage
peoples who had entered Europe with the decline of the Roman
Empire.

4. What form did sacramental penance take in the medieval church?

A development of great significance occurred about 1000 A.D. when
circumstances brought on the gradual introduction of reconciliation
immediately upon confession of sins. Suddenly, attention became
focused on the penitent's act of confession and the priest's act of
absolution. Previously, these had been steps in the process, but steps
greatly subordinated to the penance performed with the support of the
church. Now the specific sacramental act was seen to be the absolution spoken by the priest.

The recital of one's sins to the confessor soon took on a penitential
character because of the shame and humiliation associated with it.
Laying open one's guilt was taken as a significant sign of conversion
and renewed good will toward God. Reflection soon concentrated on
the relation between the priest's absolution and this change of heart
signalized by confession. If conversion had already occurred, why was
confession and absolution still required? If one was only partly converted from sin, say, more in fear of punishment than in love for God,
was this sufficient for receiving absolution?

The theologians of the twelfth and thirteenth centuries labored over
a satisfactory account of sacramental penance. Confession was
becoming more frequent in the church and in 1215 the Fourth Lateran Council made an annual confession obligatory on any Christian
guilty of serious sin. By the mid-thirteenth century, especially in the
work of St. Thomas Aquinas, most of the main questions about the
sacrament of repeated individual forgiveness were answered.

The penitent's part was to dispose himself by a repentant sorrow
already under the influence of the power of the keys. The sacramental
act is completed by the interaction of repentant confession, with
readiness to do penance, and the absolution of the priest. Absolution
confers the grace of interior loving sorrow which brings to completion
the penitent's preparation. Absolution, therefore, does affect the sin-

ner's guilt, but not in such a way that forgiveness is a declaration received passively. The penitent must open himself to full conversion under the grace of the sacrament and be responsive to this grace which may only prove effective some time after confession, for example, while one is doing the assigned penance or at the time of next receiving Holy Communion.

This, then, was the sacrament which the Protestant reformers attacked for imposing the impossible, and unbiblical, obligation of detailed confession upon the faithful. Also, the reformers saw in the satisfactory penance after absolution an audacious attempt by sinful man to appease God and merit a reduction of punishment which God gives in pure grace to believers.

In the Reformation era, the Council of Trent reaffirmed the sacramental nature of ecclesial penance and underscored the obligation to make an explicit confession of the serious sins one was aware of after a normal examination of conscience. Confession is one moment in the movement of a believer from alienation from God back into the sphere of his love and friendship.

5. What changes have affected sacramental penance in the recent past?

The most striking fact concerning sacramental penance is the dramatic decline in the practice of confession by Catholics. Many causes have converged in bringing this about: a declining sense of personal guilt; the impersonal, threadbare rite of confession; the ineptitude of many confessors in articulating personal concern and help for ordinary people; the realization that the great ills of our time are so deeply inscribed in institutional structures that personal sin pales into insignificance; etc. However, we must also point to significant efforts made toward renewing the meaning of this sacrament.

First, there were many efforts toward developing unofficial liturgies of penance that place sacramental forgiveness in a setting of communal prayer and worship. Clearly this is a crying need of believers who are becoming deeply aware of their corporate identity as God's priestly people. The church has the serious obligation to show itself forth in the world as a community that expresses God's mercy in its own life.

However, the movement toward effective communal celebration of penance was bedevilled by questions about the obligation to confess sins in a specific way (Can this be done later? Is it absolutely required by God's Law?) and by the problematical granting of absolution in a general or communal manner. The latter seems to make the sacrament more into a grace offered a community than precisely the reincorporation of a repentant sinner into this worshipping community.

A second effort at renewal of ecclesial penance is the effort to bring charismatic prayer for healing into close conjunction with absolution from guilt. This requires a personalized and more leisurely confession of sin, a sensitive effort at spiritual discernment by both penitent and confessor, and the readiness to approach God with audacious confidence in begging him to pour out his healing grace upon a penitent seeking a new wholeness in his service. This renewal effort has, of course, the great advantage of making ecclesial penance more clearly the continuation of Jesus' ministry of healing and forgiveness. Special effort, however, is needed to accentuate the impact of healing precisely upon relationships with others and so to prevent penance from becoming again a sacrament of introverted individual consolation.

6. How is sacramental penance being reformed in our day?

Recent historical and theological work has prepared the way for a reform of the rite of penance that will enrich considerably the experience of penitential conversion and reconciliation in the lives of Catholics.

History has revealed the variety of forms used over the ages in this sacrament. We know that the public and communal aspects of ancient Christian penance were less to shame the repentant sinner than to highlight the intercessory prayer and other helps by which the community was supporting the conversion of a member from sin. Penance occurred within a network of helpful human relationships.

Theology has pondered the place of reconciliation in the work of Christ. Those who celebrate the Eucharist together are persons reconciled with each other (Mt 5:23f). The people gathered by Christ in the church are the sign and instrument of coming reconciliation throughout all humanity. Christ came to carry out God's plan for the reconciliation of mankind with himself (2 Cor 5: 18–20). Hence, sacramental forgiveness of sin should be experienced above all as the healing and renewal of one's personal relation with God through reincorporation into the full life of the people of God.

The new rite of penance promulgated in early 1974 is now being introduced in the different language-areas of the world. The setting for individual confession and reconciliation is to be an uncluttered and unconfined room with sufficient light for the reading of Scripture.

There should be space to allow the penitent the option of sitting or kneeling, whether anonymously behind a screen or in a more open, face-to-face dialogue with the priest. The decor is to create an atmosphere of warmth and welcome.

Individual reconciliation has six steps. (1) The penitent is received by the priest with encouraging words, such as, "May the grace of the Holy Spirit fill your heart with light, that you may confess your sins with loving trust and come to know that God is merciful." (2) A passage of Scripture may then be read to foster the penitent's awareness of his sinfulness and of God's merciful call to conversion and reconciliation. (3) The penitent then confesses his sins and accepts the priest's advice and proposed action of penitential satisfaction. (4) The priest invites the penitent to a prayerful expression in his own words of sorrow for sin and desire of reconciliation with God. (5) The prayer of absolution is given by the priest with hands extended over the penitent's head. "God, the Father of mercies, through the death and resurrection of his Son has reconcilied the world to himself and sent the Holy Spirit among us for the forgiveness of sins; through the ministry of the Church may God give you pardon and peace, and I absolve you from your sins in the name of the Father, and of the Son, and of the Holy Spirit." (6) The rite concludes with an expression of praise of God and of encouragement, in words such as these, "The Lord has freed you from sin. May he bring you safely to his kingdom in heaven. Glory to him forever."

In addition, to this individual reconciliation, provision is made for the celebration of penance in the setting of a liturgical assembly, with song, prayer, Scripture and homily, self-examination (especially of one's relationships with others), communal prayers of sorrow and repentance, and praise of God's merciful forgiveness. If practicable, individual confession and absolution may be included in the service, or it may take place immediately after the conclusion of the communal celebration. In another form of communal service, a general confession can be made and absolution can be given to a group of penitents, with later individual confession of serious sins. It remains to be seen whether this third form of reconciliation will be restricted in use to extraordinary occasions or will become a regular part of the ministry of reconciliation in the Church.

7. What, then, is the fundamental meaning of sacramental penance?

The sacrament of penance is a key moment in the life of continued conversion and transformation that is imperative on members of the church. The believer is always in passage from the old to the new, from self-concern to selfless service, from sin to greater intimacy with Father, Son, and Holy Spirit. This process of conversion, or "life-penance," must be to the fore, so that the sacrament becomes embedded among the deepest concerns of serious Christians.

In the process of conversion, receiving the sacrament is a sharply focused expression of the needs of persons called to growth and renewal. If one has fallen into a sinfulness creating a serious distance from God, the need of reinsertion into the sphere of God's mercy and love will be to the fore. Penance will be the arduous way of renewal of one's baptismal dedication. But if a person has not sinned in a decisive way, the emphasis will be on expressing one's longing for healing and a more thorough integration of all one's attitudes, desires, and tendencies into the central orientation of one's heart to God. The penitential renewal of one's bond with the priestly people is an important means of this growth and integration.

In administering penance and absolution, the church articulates incisively the gospel of Christ to its members. For those who have broken with God in a fundamental way, the church makes manifest the merciful readiness of Christ to once more welcome a sinner into table fellowship. Here the church engages itself in support of the arduous work of conversion and expresses with solemn assurance God's acceptance of the repentant sinner. For those living in communion with God's love, but concerned to gradually overcome the foothold sin may have in them, sacramental penance expresses the church's engaged support of a healing work of God's Spirit.

Penance, therefore, is both a sacrament of reconciliation and of healing. Its reconciliation heals the fractured relationships with God's people and with God himself. The healing grace it confers transforms hearts for living a reconciled life. In both aspects the life of God's priestly people becomes visibly expressive of the mercy and love of God for sinners and for those plagued by the impact of sinfulness upon themselves. In both aspects the people of God manifest themselves in the world as mediators of God's Spirit of peace and charity.

8. Is sacramental penance the only way sins committed after baptism are forgiven?

Penance is a most important way in which God's forgiveness is extended to us, but it is not the sole means for this. We must recall that the essential point in forgiveness is the passage, or movement of heart, away from self-regard, self-affirmation above the affirmation of God and others and the many forms of self-seeking. Forgiveness is identical with submission to God and the beginning or deepening of our love for God. God's grace is a transforming gift and it becomes truly ours only as we freely surrender ourselves to God.

Therefore, whatever engages a person in this movement of love is a way to bring about the forgiveness of sins. Meaningful celebration of the Eucharist engages us with the Lord whose blood was poured out for the forgiveness of sins. In communion we deliver ourselves over to the influence of the Lamb of God whose death has taken away the sins of the world. A heartfelt prayer to God expressing sorrow for sin and submissive love for him is an important way toward growth and forgiveness. We should experience something of this through the penitential rite at the beginning of the Eucharist. There are, as well, the works of penance by which we turn against those self-assertive or self-indulgent tendencies that drag us down into sin.

When a person has made a decisive shift of personal direction away from God (mortal sin), then conversion back to God is not brought about lightly. A sharp change of course is needed to bring one's heart back under the gentle sway of God's presence and grace. Here the sacrament of penance has a primary role, by setting us in dialogue with another person, by engaging the church on our behalf, and by articulating our submission to God in submission to a forgiving person representing the Lord. Therefore, even if one has moved from serious sin to a wholehearted and loving sorrow outside the sacrament, there remains an obligation to submit one's serious sin to a confessor. This saves us from self-deception and leads us to articulate the fact that the forgiveness attained was not from ourselves but from God who touched our heart. We must come out of our anonymity to seek reconciliation with the priestly people whose mission our sin has damaged.

ANOINTING OF THE SICK

9. How did sacramental anointing of the sick originate and develop in the church?

The gospels repeatedly tell of Jesus' compassionate approach to those afflicted with sickness. Healing the sick was a demonstrative sign of the new era his preaching inaugurated. The evil powers were

being put to rout and God's new reign made its presence felt as
cramped, weakened, and broken lives were restored under the loving
impact of Jesus' touch and prayer.

The gospels also record that when Jesus' disciples went out to
preach the repentance of the kingdom the same dramatic events occurred. "They cast out many demons and anointed with oil many that
were sick and healed them" (Mk 6:13). The practice of anointing with
curative oil in this ministry to the sick then reappeared in the principal
New Testament text witnessing to sacramental anointing: "Is any
among you sick? Let him call for the presbyters of the church, and
let them pray over him, anointing him with oil in the name of the
Lord; and the prayer of faith will save the sick man, and the Lord will
raise him up; and if he has committed sins, he will be forgiven." (Jas
5:14–15).

James values highly a sacred anointing with oil in the name of the
Lord by pastoral officials. This will save and raise up the sick person
in victory over the power of sin. Evidently the power of the risen
Christ was being felt among his newly gathered people precisely in its
impact on sick people. We can see here a continuation of the healings
recorded in the gospels, a work now carried out under the influence
of the redemptive death of Christ. One benefit of his death is to
strengthen and renew his people when they are weakened or struck
down by illness.

10. What do the first centuries of Christian history tell us of this sacrament?

For many reasons the first centuries of Christian history offer little
evidence of the anointing of the sick. It was not as central to the life
of the church as baptism and the Eucharist, not as public as penance
and ordination, and its New Testament basis was not located in a
work as important as the gospels or the letters of Paul.

The earliest references to anointing are in the liturgical rites of
blessing the oil of the sick. The first instruction on anointing came
from a fifth century pope. What is clear, however, from these early
references is that anointing is closely conjoined with healing the sick
of their physical, mental and spiritual debilities.

Only in the ninth century did a gradual shift begin, leading to the
conception of anointing as the sacrament of the dying. In the twelfth
century the name "last anointing" (extreme unction) was adopted,
and medieval theologians discussed it as the sacramental preparation

for the final passage into glory. As a sacrament of Christ, it had to affect the soul of man and so bring inner graces, such as the forgiveness of venial sins or preparation for the final spiritual struggle before death. The idea gained ground that it was best to put off reception of the sacrament until the last possible moment of one's life.

This notion of the sacrament of the dying, for which there was scant if any biblical or patristic evidence, was countered by historical theologians in the mid-twentieth century. The sacrament is now officially called "anointing of the sick," and can be administered to those suffering from any serious sickness or injury, or simply from the general debilities of old age. Death need not be imminent and certain, for the sacrament relates to the cramping effect of illness on one's spiritual vigor in living in union with Christ.

The sacrament is conferred by anointing the sick person on the forehead and the hands, while saying, "Through this holy anointing may the Lord in his love and mercy help you with the grace of the Holy Spirit. May the Lord who frees you from sin save you and raise you up."

11. What is the fundamental meaning of sacramental anointing?

Anointing of the sick is a celebration of Christ's loving concern for a member of the church afflicted with illness. It is not simply an offer of relief and consolation, but the conferral of a grace that heals at the deepest level of our physical afflictions.

As human persons we are not simply composites of body and soul in juxtaposition. A person is before all else *one,* and his physical, emotional, mental, and spiritual experiences are tightly intertwined with one another. The presence of evil, disorder, or weakness, at any level of the person is sure to affect the whole. Thus, when a person is physically ill, whether by sickness, injury, or gradual debility, his outlook on life, on his fellow men, and on God is affected. We know from experience how illness fills us with self-regard, distracts from prayer, and generally narrows the horizon of our conscious life.

Therefore, the risen Christ is greatly concerned that illness not turn members of his priestly people away from their sharing in his redemptive mission. He wants them to have peace of heart and a vigorous confidence in God, so they can turn to God in worshipful submission and praise. They need the help of his healing grace, that they may suffer in union with Christ and pass with him into new life—whether still in this world or beyond death.

Therefore anointing is the sacrament of the seriously ill which offers a grace of healing, so that the members of the priestly people may grow through their sickness. Anointing consecrates them for suffering in a dedicated manner with Christ and offers restorative graces that counteract the myriad debilities of sickness. To receive sacramental anointing is a striking act of faith in the risen Christ, who became "a life-giving spirit" (1 Cor 15:45), and continues his redemptive and compassionate service of men and women in need.

Ordination

1. What does the New Testament relate concerning ordination to the church's ministry?

A number of New Testament passages refer to the act of appointing persons to ministry within the church by laying on hands with prayer (Acts 6:6, 13:3; 1 Tm 4:14; 4:22; 2 Tm 1:6). The gesture of imposing hands is traditional biblical sign of blessing and consecration, by which the early church conferred the gifts of the Holy Spirit. The letters to Timothy make clear reference to the grace given the minister to fit him for the task committed to him: "Do not neglect the gift you have, which was given you by prophetic utterance when the elders laid hands upon you" (1 Tm 4:14; also 2 Tm 1:6). The rite of laying on hands is therefore a key moment in the continuity of office and mission within the church. But as such it is not merely done to insure validity and administrative effectiveness. In Acts, Paul's farewell to those in charge of the church at Ephesus links their appointment to the Holy Spirit's continuing concern for those saved by Christ: "Take heed to yourselves and to all the flock, in which the Holy Spirit has made you guardians, to feed the church of the Lord which he obtained by his own blood" (Acts 20:28).

These passages, however, are from relatively late books of the New Testament, and as such must be seen as one strand in a complicated development. The variety of ministries stands out in the primitive church. The Spirit issued different calls and consequently different responsibilities were borne by the twelve, by apostles, by prophets and teachers, by overseers ("bishops"), by elders ("presbyters"), and by deacons. Only gradually did a firmly fixed pattern take hold. The titles and forms of service in the church were at first quite fluid and went through considerable evolution in the years mirrored in the New Testament.

One point, however, the New Testament makes quite clear: the men bearing these responsibilities were not called "priests" and their roles were never defined as ritual or cultic service (sanctuary maintenance, sacrifice, blessing). Jesus Christ is the one priest of the New Covenant which was sealed by his martyr's blood poured out. Christ lives to make intercession in God's presence for his people. This priestly work of Christ does not rule out special offices in his church, but it does mean that they radically differ from the services rendered by the pagan or Jewish priestly caste. The New Testament ministry is a "ministry of reconciliation" (2 Cor 5:18) by men set apart, not for cult, but for the gospel of God to bring men together in the obedience of faith (Rom 1:1–6). The New Testament minister is one sent out to gather dispersed mankind in faith and fellowship around the table of the Lord that they might be more fully incorporated into the new man, Jesus Christ.

2. How are apostles described in the New Testament?

Jesus' public life in Galilee and Jerusalem was marked out by the presence with him of *the Twelve.* These were the men he chose to be his personal companions—an inner circle in the larger group of disciples. After Easter, the Twelve witnessed to the risen Christ (1 Cor 15:5) and as a group they played an important role in the first years of the Jerusalem church. Since the Twelve do not appear to have played a major role as missionaries, their service is best understood as symbolic or representational. The fact that there was a group of twelve is more important than what they did. By simply being with Jesus and then being in the church, they gave graphic expression to Jesus' claim to be initiating the kingdom of God. As Israel was built on twelve tribes, so the new people of God began with a group of twelve men chosen by Jesus. Just by being twelve, these chosen disciples gave witness to the beginning of a new order.

Doubtlessly, the dominant figures in earliest Christianity were the *apostles.* These missionary preachers spoke the decisive words which feed the faith of all other Christians. The vocation of an apostle began with his commission by the risen Christ to go forth and make disciples by preaching on his behalf. His initial work is the founding of churches by gathering together those who prove responsive to his message. In St. Paul's letters, especially those to the Corinthians, we see an apostle (Paul) carrying out his further responsibilities to a church he has founded: answering questions, making rulings concerning worship, applying the Gospel message to problems of daily life, and urging the requirements of community discipline on lax or weak members. In these early days, even though the apostle continued his missionary journeys, he remained "in charge" of the church founded by his preaching.

3. What is the New Testament role of prophets, teachers and overseers?

At Corinth and in other churches founded by Paul, an important and active group were the *prophets and teachers*. Paul listed them immediately after apostles among those appointed by God and endowed by the Spirit for service in the church (1 Cor 12:28). Paul speaks appreciatively of the value of prophecy for consoling, encouraging, and building up the life of faith (1 Cor 14:1–5). These ministries of the word were a charismatic or non-institutional service in the early church, and in some places they were valued far above the administrative offices which served the continuity of church life.

The word *overseer* ("bishop") appears in the New Testament, but it is not used in the modern sense of the single chief pastor of the church in a given locale. The word most frequently occurs in the plural, referring to a collegial body leading a local church. The best evidence is that in the New Testament "overseers" is an alternate manner of referring to the men more frequently called elders or presbyters.

4. What does the New Testament say of elders or presbyters?

The office of *elder* or *presbyter* is attested widely in the books of the New Testament. In Jerusalem the elders were linked with the apostles (Acts 15:2) and with James (21:18), with whom they formed a collegial ruling body over the community. In the mission field, Paul is said to have appointed elders in the churches he founded (Acts 14:23). However, there are no references to such an office in the letters certainly written by Paul. Paul did urge the Thessalonians to respect those who were "over them in the Lord" (1 Thes 5:12). Paul also addressed a group of "overseers" in Philippi (Phil 1:1). These local officials were clearly subordinate to the travelling apostle, and only gradually did they come to bear the main pastoral responsibility for their church.

Later New Testament works, like the letters to Timothy and Titus, 1 Peter, Jude, and James, show the elders holding a firmly established office. As the apostles passed from the early Christian scene and as the charismatic ministry failed to develop, groups of elders emerged to take over the direction of the churches, to hand on the apostolic message, to defend against error and deviation, and to lead their communities in prayer. They are the men inducted into office by the laying on of hands and prayer, whose appointment is ultimately an act of grace under the lead of the Holy Spirit. In the immediately post-apostolic times the elders of the various churches held the critical responsibilities for the continuance and growth of the church. The initial and foundational service rendered by the apostles passed on to elders who were charged as follows: "Preach the word, be urgent in season and out of season, convince, rebuke and exhort, be unfailing in patience and in teaching. . . . Always be steady, endure suffering, do the work of an evangelist, fulfil your ministry" (2 Tim 4:2.5).

5. Who were the deacons of the New Testament?

The earliest written reference to *deacons* is in the greeting affixed to the letter to the Philippians. A later passage lays down these requirements: "Deacons must be serious, not double-tongued, not addicted to much wine, not greedy for gain; they must hold the mystery of the faith with a clear conscience. . . . Let deacons be the husband of one wife, and let them manage their children and their households well" (1 Tim 3:8–12). But neither of these passages using the term "deacon" gives an account of the responsibilities they were fulfilling or of the way they were inducted into office. The Jerusalem church did appoint seven men to an office of special service by the laying on of hands and prayer (Acts 6:1–6). An initial indication was given that they were deputed to serve at table so the apostles could preach the word. But two of the seven, Stephen and Philip, appear almost immediately as men of the word in confronting the Jews and announcing Christ. Consequently, the diaconate did not receive its definitive definition in Scripture, but remained open to development.

Ordination by laying on hands with prayer is, therefore, firmly established in the later books of the New Testament. Earlier calls to the service of the church came by a direct encounter with Christ or the Spirit. But with the passing of the first generation of believers, roles became more fixed, responsibilities were modified, and the pattern of leadership was established by which local churches were shepherded by a group of elders or presbyters assisted by deacons. Ordination was the expressive rite that joined new presbyters to these groups by laying on hands with confident prayer that God would endow the man called with gifts of power, love, and self-control in the service of the Gospel (2 Tim 1:7).

6. How has ordination to the episcopal and priestly ministry been understood in the past ages of Christian history?

In every age, the understanding of ordination has been deeply affected by the predominant notion of the ministry serving the church.

One of the earliest developments was the emergence, at the end of the first century, of individual leaders from the local colleges of presbyters. Very soon each local church was under the guidance of a *single chief pastor,* or *bishop.* The college of presbyters did not disappear, but remained as the senate or council sharing responsibility with the bishop for teaching, worship, and guidance in the church. However, the predominant importance of the bishop was unmistakable. He insured continuity with the authentic preaching of the apostles; his liturgical presiding focused the unity of the church; his directives called for obedient submission by all. By the early third century, St. Cyprian saw the apostles as the first bishops and claimed that the church is one through the one bishop in each locale, who insures that there is one altar, one priesthood, and one chair of authority. "You should understand that the bishop is in the church and the church in the bishop and that whoever is not with the bishop is not in the church." Catholic unity depends on unity with the bishop and on the unity or communion of the bishops among themselves.

HIGH PRIEST

A second early development of great importance is clear in the early third century ordination rites. A man ordained as bishop is installed in the pastoral office of feeding the flock and the exercise of a *high-priestly service.* A growing emphasis on priestly service came with the new self-understanding of Christianity as the new Israel. The old temple and the old sacrifices have passed and been replaced by the Christian people and their sacrifice, the Eucharist, over which the bishop presides. At first, only the bishop is called "priest," but it was not long before the presbyters assisting and advising him came to be assimilated to his priesthood. The common baptismal priesthood of the whole Christian people faded from awareness and a growing distinction appeared between priesthood and laity. This further development from ministry to sacral priesthood was already visible in the third century prayer of episcopal ordination: ". . . that he might serve blamelessly by night and day, that he might unceasingly behold and propitiate your countenance and offer to you the gifts of the holy church, and that by the high priestly spirit he may have authority to forgive sins according to your command, to assign offices according to your bidding, and to loose every bond according to the authority you gave to your apostles."

The theme of priestly service in the church gave ancient Christian writers ample opportunity to insist on the high *moral demands* of the priestly office based on prescriptions of ritual purity found in the Old Testament. Priests must be separated from the world, and their marital life came under gradual restrictions and eventual prohibition. Roman law came to confer privileges upon the Christian clergy and the people were urged to support their priests by tithing. Consequently, ordination came to be more and more a rite of consecration and induction into a sacerdotal, celibate, and hierarchically distinct group within an emerging Christian society.

COLLEGIATE MINISTRY

A third element in the early Christian understanding of ordination derives from the *collegiate* or *corporative* understanding of the church's ministry. One was never bishop, presbyter, or deacon alone, but always with others. The solidarity of the ancient episcopate is clear from the lively correspondence of bishops with each other, from the frequent synods or councils, and from the presence of other bishops to impose hands when a new bishop joins their ranks. In the local church the presbyters formed with the bishop a collegial body. Presbyters ("priests") were not isolated individuals each with his own charge, but were part of a group (or "order") with a collective responsibility. The ancient bishop was no absolute monarch, but rather the chief member in the local presbyterate. In the earliest centuries the advisory function of presbyters was more to the fore, while the bishop was the sole presiding priest at the liturgy. But with the growth of the church presbyters came to be more active presiding on their own in the liturgy as well. Some presbyters even became rural pastors. But ordination to the presbyterate or priesthood retained its strong corporate emphasis. The imposition of hands in ordination is above all an act of incorporation into the responsibilities borne by the presbyters in the local church. By ordination the new priest was received into the group, or order, assisting the bishop in his pastoral care and liturgical leadership of the church.

RE-ORDINATIONS

A significant change in the understanding of the ministry was triggered by the Donatist controversy over re-ordination in the 4th and 5th centuries. The Donatists were North African schismatics who refused to deal with priests ordained by bishops who had cooperated with Roman authorities during the last persecutions. The Donatist position was that this failure invalidated the ordinations performed subsequently by these bishops. The orthodox defense naturally came to state emphatically that as a sacramental act ordination (here, to the episcopate) conferred a power on the person ordained which he could then exercise even if he became a sinner or went into schism from the church. This stress on the objective character of sacraments rests ultimately on the conviction that it is Christ who confers grace through the ritual act he uses instrumentally. But the view of ordination that came to prevail in the church's consciousness was that of a conferral of sacral powers upon the individual ordained. Thus anti-Donatist polemic ushered in the classical medieval view that ordination is the conferral of the priestly power to consecrate the Eucharist and absolve from sins.

MEDIEVAL VIEWS

Another factor in forming the medieval synthesis was the increasing number of ordinations in monastic communities. Here, monk-priests would often have few pastoral responsibilities and so their ordination was easily interpreted as the empowerment for a eucharistic consecration, an act which was increasingly separated from the public liturgies in which the Eucharist is clearly expressive of the unity of the church. The unity of the church was seen less as arising from the Eucharist and more as coming from hierarchical subordination to bishop and pope.

Another important shift of focus in the middle ages was the denial of the sacramental character of episcopal consecration. If the primary meaning of ordination is the conferal of power to consecrate the Eucharist, there is no real ordination beyond that of the ordinary priest. The bishop would be distinguished by a higher jurisdiction, not by a further sacramental reality. Underlying this development was the failure to see ordination as entry into the many duties of pastoral leadership: preaching, instruction, liturgy, reconciliation, consolation, guidance, and discipline. Worst of all, the Eucharist was no longer seen as the focal point of all this activity, but rather as a miraculous act of consecrating earthly elements as the Christ of sacrifice, adoration, and individual communion.

REFORMATION

This one-sided view of the ministry came under heavy fire in the Reformation of the sixteenth century. The Protestant reformers were one in affirming that among the duties of the ordained the preaching of the gospel was by far the most important. A man was ordained to make God's word a living reality in the lives of his people. By ordination he was designated a preacher of God's consoling words of forgiveness.

Another Reformation emphasis was on the priesthood of every believer. Luther proclaimed this initially with the German princes in view to try to arouse them to reform the church. But the argument that faith and baptism made one a Christian priest soon led to the denial that ordination to the ministry was a sacrament constituting a distinct rank of persons in the church. Ordination, in the Protestant tradition, is rather an act of appointment which, for purpose of good order, delegates a person to do that for which his baptism has already empowered him. The baptismal priesthood thus became a weapon of anti-hierarchical polemic and the basis for declaring all Christians of equal rights and powers.

Against this Reformation view the Council of Trent affirmed the sacramental character of ordination to the priesthood. The common priesthood of the faithful was not denied, but the ministerial priesthood was declared to be distinctive in the powers it conferred for the exercise of a sacramental ministry of the Eucharist and the forgiveness of sins. Other efforts of reform brought about a remarkable revival of preaching and pastoral care by Catholic bishops and priests in the post-reformation era. But ordination itself continued to be seen as the conferral of sacral power for the miraculous changes of Eucharistic consecration and the forgiveness of sins.

7. How is the understanding of episcopal and priestly ordination developing in our day?

The declaration by the Second Vatican Council that episcopal consecration is a sacramental act is leading to considerable modification of the Catholic understanding of ordination. The rite must be seen as conferring much more than certain sacral powers that mark out a man as a cultic mediator. Often ordination is presented as induction into a threefold ministry, that of word, sacrament, and direction, in imitation of Christ, who was prophet, priest, and king. But more emphasis is being placed on the unity of the pastoral office of leadership in the church. Central to this leadership is the Word of God which the ordained must preach, apply to the lives of believers, and bring to its fullest reality in the eucharistic liturgy. There is a single service of leadership in the church that nourishes the life of faith, instructs in Christian living, leads in prayer and worship, and seeks in everything to reconcile men with each other and with God. Episcopal ordination confers this responsibility in a full and comprehensive way. Priestly and diaconate ordination confer a limited and subordinate responsibility in this same service of leadership.

Another development is the recapture of the theme of the priestly character of the people of God as a whole. All the baptized are consecrated and deputed to serve as holy mediators between God and the whole of humanity. They make up a priestly people marked out to celebrate God's reconciling presence in the world. They came before God, especially in the Eucharist, as spokes-people for the human race, to offer God homage and address him as the Father of needy mankind. As a result of this enriched view of the church as a whole, the ordained ministry is seen less as priestly in its own rite and more in the context of its service of building up and leading the priestly people *for whom* ordination creates prophetic and sacramental leaders.

8. What are the issues being discussed today?

A lively series of contemporary discussions are less concerned with the nature of ordination than with calling in question the "clerical culture" that has grown up around the priestly ministry in the church. Cannot some of the early Christian flexibility be reintroduced into the church's ministry by the inclusion of married men in this service of the people of God? Must all those who carry out this service be marked out or set apart by special garb, a peculiar education, and the absence of an occupation in the world? Perhaps most urgent of all is the question whether this ministry is to be borne exclusively by males? All of these questions are calling for change and flexibility in practices that have long traditions behind them. It is not clear at present that these traditions express essential or substantial aspects of ordination and ministry in the church. Much that we have associated with our male, celibate, clerical ministry may well prove to be open to change as the service given to the people of God is adapted to their changing needs.

9. How has the diaconate developed in the church?

All through the Christian world of the first eight centuries ordained deacons played important roles assisting bishops in their ministry. Deacons cared for orphans, widows, the poor, the sick, and prisoners. They often coordinated the hospitality extended by the local church to fellow Christian visitors. Deacons frequently had charge of the catechumens and aided their teachers. Their liturgical roles were varied: seating the congregation, taking the collection, reading from the Scripture, distributing Communion, assisting at Baptisms. In many areas deacons were in charge of rural communities which the bishop or a priest could visit only sporadically. Thus deacons fulfilled important responsibilities for charity, liturgy and administration.

In late antiquity this third part of the church's ordained ministry began to decline. First, it was narrowed to exclusively liturgical roles and then became little more than a ceremonial step on the way to priestly ordination. Christian medieval society had a place for bishop and priest in the clerical class endowed with supernatural powers and authority, having no secular profession, and supported by benefices. But a deacon did not fit, since he was so clearly ordained to serve, not to rule.

In our own day the importance of the ordained diaconate is becoming clear again and is being restored as a permanent calling in the church. The theme of serving the people of God is the master idea in contemporary thinking about the ordained ministry. The church sees herself as servant of mankind. It is urgent therefore to express this in a sector of the ministry unequivocally dedicated to service.

In a church where priests frequently serve alone as pastors of communities, the diaconate is needed to keep the sole pastor from a spirit of domination and from absorption in peripheral matters of administration which a deacon can well perform. Liturgical scholarship has shown that the most worthy way to celebrate the Eucharist is with a single presiding priest assisted by a deacon. Most of all, the many non-liturgical responsibilities of deacons make it quite clear that the ordained person is not one set aside simply for cultic purposes. Ordination, rather, marks a man for the complex work of building up the church as God's elect people and a reconciling presence in the world. Only one part of this service is fulfilled by liturgical presiding. It is most significant, therefore, that the first level of the ministry is one given over to the full range of other services needed by the priestly people.

10. What is the fundamental meaning of sacramental ordination?

Ordination to the church's ministry is an event where many processes converge. Therefore, the meaning of ordination can only be grasped through a series of different aspects.

Before a man is ordained, a work of the Holy Spirit must precede, by which he is endowed with a *vocation* to ministerial service. Certain fitting dispositions and talents mark a person out for this calling. Then there is the grace, or charism, by which a person senses an attraction to priestly service of the people of God. This call does not overpower a person, but leaves him free to accept or decline. The final acceptance of such a call from God comes in ordination itself when the ordinand responds, "I am ready and willing." The sacramental act then places the seal of the Spirit on the call that has been experienced. The grace of vocation makes it clear that ministry is not just a job one chooses to take on, but arises from the call of Christ providing pastors for his people.

Another preliminary aspect of ordination is the *approval* of the people of God. Principally this is done by the bishop or religious superiors of men approaching ordination. As St. Paul counselled Timothy, one should not be hasty in laying on hands (1 Tim 5:22). The normal signs of a genuine vocation must be discerned, especially one's growth in love of the word of God and in willingness and capability for serving God's people. The ancient church made the testing of ministerial candidates an affair of the whole people, and a remnant of this remains in the present rite of ordination where the bishop asks the people to express their approval of those about to be ordained to serve them.

INCORPORATION

A central aspect of ordination itself is *incorporation* into the body of those holding ministerial responsibility and authority in the church.

Ministry is not a personal gift held by solitary individuals, but rather one's share in a collegial responsibility held by a group. Ordination inserts a new member in the order, or rank, of those dedicated to this leadership and service in the church. Episcopal ordination incorporates a man into the universal college of pastors who lead the universal church. Priestly ordination places one in the presbyterate assisting the bishop in his pastoral service of the people of a given locale. The ordination of a deacon marks one out for sharing in a range of services under the bishop and in collaboration with priests. The communal dimension of these different ministries points to the deepest reality of ecclesial service, the service of unity, or communion, in the church. The universal church is the communion, or sacramental network, of many churches—in a unity expressed and fostered by the college of bishops. A parish or smaller gathering of the people is placed "in communion" with other parishes or gatherings because their pastors are members of one and the same presbyterate.

DESIGNATION AND CONSECRATION

Ordination is also an act of *designation* and *consecration* for a leadership role in the church. By the sacrament a person becomes linked in a new way to the prophetic and priestly mission of Christ. Ordination marks one out to live in service of the word of God and to become a man of the gospel, which is "the power of God for salvation to everyone who has faith" (Rom 1:16). All the ordained, bishops, priests, and deacons, become primarily responsible for evangelization, preaching, instructing, encouraging, and all the other ways the mystery of Christ is communicated in our world. Bishops and priests are commissioned to speak and act in the person of Christ as they preside at the Eucharist and impart absolution. As a consequence of their service of word and sacrament the ordained bear authority to foster right order in the church and to make explicit the directives flowing from the gospel. A person does not assume such responsibilities on his own, but only by reason of the sacramental consecration assimilating him in a special way to Christ for the continuance of Christ's mission.

Finally, ordination is an act of *sanctification* by which a person is endowed with the light and strength to live a life of dedicated service in the church. The deepest meaning of the gesture of laying on hands is the imparting of the Holy Spirit as the divine Consoler to undergird the mission being taken on (1 Tim 4:14; 2 Tim 1:6). Thus, ordination touches a person in the core of his humanity to make him capable— if he cooperates—of effectively building up the body of Christ not only through word and sacrament, but also through his very identity and presence amid God's people.

11. What is the meaning of ordination performed outside the unity of the Catholic Church?

Ordinations in the separated churches are often thought to be defective because *apostolic succession* has not been maintained in these churches. Many of them do not have bishops at all, and among those which do only the Eastern Orthodox and Anglican communions have maintained episcopal continuity by the successive laying on of hands.

However, it would be wrong to understand apostolic succession simply as a physical reality. In the primitive church, the manner of transmitting office was at first quite fluid. There is no evidence that prophets and teachers were ordained by the imposition of hands, and they may well have presided at the Eucharist in Corinth. Furthermore, our reflection on the meaning of ordination has shown that the pastoral ministry depends not simply upon a clear line of transmission but upon the Holy Spirit endowing a person with charisms of spiritual leadership.

Also, we must recognize that the communities and churches separated from Catholic unity are far from being devoid of Christian significance. In them the word of God is treasured, baptism is properly administered, and God is worshipped in hymn and prayer. The work of the Holy Spirit becomes manifest in the dedication to holiness, love, and service which these churches foster in their members.

Consequently, we must affirm a true significance in the act by which a separated church designates a person for the pastoral ministry of speaking and acting in Christ's name in their midst. There is a true conferral of office and pastoral responsibility. However, because of the separation of such a body from the universal episcopal college, such an ordination is to some extent deficient in sacramental meaning. This fact is further complicated by the widespread denial among Protestants that ordination is a sacramental act conferring a share in a distinctive pastoral office in the church.

Consequently, while the Catholic Church cannot fully guarantee the sacramental acts of Protestant ministers, it does acknowledge their call to serve the word of God and work for the building up of the people of God in their community.

Marriage

1. How does the Old Testament present marriage?

The Bible reflects a notable evolution in the Jewish and Christian understanding of marriage. We can trace marriage from a time when early Israel hardly differed from her pagan neighbors down to the momentous connection made in the letter to the Ephesians between marital love and Christ's self-sacrificing love for those he has redeemed.

Jesus himself commented how the ancient laws were adapted to Israel's "hardness of heart" (Mt 19:8). Polygamy was tolerated (e.g., 1 Sm 1:2); certain marriages between in-laws were even required in order to perpetuate physical descent (Dt 5:5–10); and the husband could repudiate his wife for a number of defects (Dt 24:1–4). The earliest meaning of the commandment, "Thou shalt not commit adultery," was that a man should not violate the proprietary rights a husband held over his wife. The husband did not sin by intercourse outside marriage, unless he laid with the wife of another man and so violated the other husband's rights—the notion of a double standard has a long history.

Later portions of the Old Testament reflect a growing purification of Israel's ideals concerning marriage. The second account of creation (Gn 2) indicates that marriage is not just an arrangement for procreation, but that man and woman are made to support each other in intimate companionship. Each completes the other as they live together and become one flesh. Marriage is a partnership intended by God in spite of the elements of pain introduced by the couple's sin.

In spite of the Law's provisions for divorce by repudiation, the writer of Proverbs urged men to live in loving fidelity to the wife of their youth (5:15–20). The prophet Malachi inveighed against divorce as a practice the Lord hates (2:15), and took the significant step of calling marriage a covenant witnessed by the Lord (2:14). If marriage is a covenant, then suddenly a wealth of religious meaning—mutual trust, sacred commitment, God's own fidelity—clusters around the relation between husband and wife. The covenant theme was the powerful purifying force that brought forth the full Christian ideal of marriage in the Lord. Almost on the eve of the Christian era, the Book of Tobit presented a highly spiritual picture of a couple living before God in prayer and fidelity, dedicated to the ideal of a life-long and godly marriage (especially Tb 8:5–8).

2. What did Jesus think of marriage?

Jesus stood in the reforming tradition mirrored in Malachi and Tobit when he laid down the unqualified principle, "What God has joined together, let no man put asunder" (Mt 19:6). Jesus made obligatory for his followers the ideal of the Lord's covenant with Israel, in which the Lord remains faithful even when Israel wanders off in sin. In the Gospel of Mark, Jesus stated the revolutionary principle that the wife too has rights in marriage that are violated by her husband's infidelity: "Whoever divorces his wife and marries another commits adultery against her" (Mk 10:11). According to Matthew, Jesus harkened back to God's original intention in making man and woman to live not as two but as one in a union consecrated by God himself.

3. Where else in the New Testament are his views reflected?

Along with these insistent words of Jesus we must take account of the quality of loving dedication he manifested as he went to death on behalf of sinful mankind. Jesus' love for those he redeems is the true foundation of Christian married love. The New Testament, in fact, came to refer to the redeemed as the body Christ loves as his own bride (2 Cor 11:2; Rev 19:7; 21:9).

In an early letter, St. Paul gave Jesus' teaching on lifelong obligation of both husband and wife within marriage (1 Cor 7:10–11). Paul made quite explicit the full parity of husband and wife within marriage—a dramatic, though unappreciated blow for feminine equality: "the wife does not rule over her own body, but the husband does; likewise the husband does not rule over his own body, but the wife does" (1 Cor 7:4).

Then in the later letter to the Ephesians (ch. 5) we come to the climactic biblical passage on marriage. The context is the extended exhortation that Christians, as those chosen and reborn by God's grace, walk worthy of the vocation to which they are called (4:1). We should "walk in love, as Christ loved us and gave himself up for us, a fragrant offering and sacrifice of God" (5:2). Within marriage, this Christ-like love is to transform the relation between husband and wife (5:21–23). But there is more here than ethical injunction. The two-in-one relation intended by God from the beginning is a great mystery that expresses Christ's relation to the redeemed (5:32). Marriage itself can image forth Christ's own loving fidelity and thus be a sign or sacrament of Christ the redeemer who gave himself up for sinful mankind.

We have clearly travelled a long distance from the mentality reflected in the ancient laws of Israel. The meaning of marriage has grown in richness, depth, and beauty. When one looks around himself in the Western world of the mid 1970's, the thought arises that many of us Christians need to retrace this path. We need urgently to recapture the vision of marriage as a sacred covenant, witnessed by God, that links husband and wife for life-long companionship in a love mirroring Christ's self-sacrificing love for those he redeemed.

4. How was marriage viewed in the first centuries of Christian tradition?

Writers of the first generations after the apostles made only fleeting references to marriage, but even in these we sense that Christian marriages are different. Christ's redemptive love is the norm; marriage is a concern of the bishop; the civil laws allowing divorce are merely human laws that do not apply to Christians.

Some spiritualist movements of early Christianity—more inspired by Plato and Stoicism than by Scripture—came to look down on the bodily aspect of human existence. The notion that the body is the hostile prison of the soul led to suspicions that marriage was gross and carnal. In spite of the exalted blessings with which the church "sealed" Christian marriages, Christian thinking was infected with a preference for the purer asceticism of virginity. A teacher like St. Augustine knew and cited the verses of Ephesians on the Christlike love and fidelity of the married, but at the same time he believed that original sin had so deeply wounded human sexuality that marital intercourse was always infected with some evil. Only the procreative purpose could override this evil and make marital intercourse morally tolerable.

In late antiquity an important development took place in the areas of the Eastern Roman Empire ruled from Constantinople. As the church came more and more under the influence of imperial authority a spirit of accomodation led to modifications in the rigorous stance previously taken by the church against divorce and remarriage. Churchmen of the East came to cite the words of Jesus in Matthew (5:32; 19:9) that appear to introduce an exception to the rule against divorce. i.e., "except on the ground of unchastity." Civil law allowed remarriage after adultery, and the Eastern Christian tradition came to tolerate the remarriage of the "innocent party" after a first marriage collapsed on the rocks of infidelity. Thus, in contemporary Orthodox Christianity there is a special liturgy for a second marriage, however, a liturgy punctuated with penitential prayers for pardon and cleansing.

5. What development occurred during the Middle Ages?

The most important development in the West in the Middle Ages was not the inclusion of marriage in the definitive list of the seven sacraments. Rather, it was the entry of a legal and contractual mentality into Christian thinking about marriage. By the late middle ages, references to marriage as a sacred covenant of fidelity had become rare, and marriage was more often seen as a contract formed by mutual consent exchanging exclusive rights over each other's body for procreative acts. The language of contract made it possible to speak of marriage with amazing clarity, but at the cost of reducing it to an almost commercial exchange of goods and services. Echoing Augustine, the medieval tradition also reiterated the primacy of the procreative purpose in marital love.

As canon law grew in extent and refinement, the Western medieval church developed wide-ranging stipulations about the legal requirements of a proper marriage contract, especially concerning the "impediments" hindering certain kinds of marriages.

6. What was the Reformation problem and the Catholic response?

The Protestant reformers of the sixteenth century launched a fierce attack on the competence of papal and episcopal authority to lay down binding stipulations concerning marriage. The Reformation view of a sacrament as a word and sign promising the forgiveness of sins made it impossible for most Protestants to see marriage as a sacrament of Christ and the church. The Protestant tradition holds rather that marriage is an ordinance of creation, a unique human relationship instituted by God but not included integrally in the dispensation of redemption through Christ. Marriage remains basically a secular reality. The church can clarify God's mandate and exhort couples to live in fidelity, but Christian marriage itself is not an articulation of the mystery of Christ's redemptive love.

In responding to the Reformation, the Council of Trent reaffirmed that marriage between Christians is a sacrament of Christ, a teaching said to be indicated in the letter to the Ephesians. The Council rejected the notion that the church had exceeded her competence both in developing a marriage law and in insisting on the life-long character of Christian marriage. Trent was careful not to condemn outright the Eastern church's tolerance toward divorce with remarriage, but it showed no readiness to admit this into the Catholic tradition.

In recent times, this Catholic tradition was remarkable for its impressive rigor and consistency concerning marriage. Every marriage between two baptized persons is viewed as a sacramental union enduring until death. No compromise was admitted on divorce, except where it turned out that a first marriage was in fact no marriage in the sacramental sense. Within marriage the prime purpose was the procreation of children, a purpose that had to be respected in every expression of love through marital intercourse. In the very recent past this Catholic tradition has been subjected to questioning from a number of sides. Consequently, Catholics are today traversing the biblical road of pilgrimage in quest of new depth and clarity concerning marriage in the Lord.

7. In what sense is marriage indissoluble?

We single out this question for treatment prior to stating the fundamental meaning of sacramental marriage. A reflective approach to the life-long character of *some* marriages is the best way to mark out the precise area where one can speak of the meaning of marriage in the perspective of a Christian vision of our life on earth.

Many today wish to interpret Jesus' prohibition of divorce as the statement of a high ideal toward which Christians must strive, but which in fact cannot be attained. Matthew placed this prohibition in the Sermon on the Mount, beside the ethical commands to love our enemies and to turn the other cheek. These are goals to seek, but hardly norms we can make legally binding. Does not considerable "hardness of heart" still continue in the Christian era? Therefore, there would seem to be warrant in Scripture for coming to terms with an ordered practice of divorce and remarriage in our imperfect world.

In considering this argument for tolerating the solubility of marriages, a number of important points have to be made. Centrally, we question whether it is enough to simply treat divorce as an ethical question. The New Testament has more to say about marriage than is recorded in the Gospels. The idealism taught by Jesus is more than a simple imperative imposed as law on his followers. We have a wider and richer vision of marriage given us by Scriptures and church teaching. If the marriage of two baptized believers is in fact a covenant witnessed and guarded by God, and if such a marriage images forth Christ's love for the redeemed, then a truly Christian marriage is a reality that simply does not waste away and become negligible, whatever the subsequent change in the persons involved.

INSTANCES OF MODERATION

But while we ponder the lifelong character of a covenant marriage, we must take careful note of the many instances of moderation in the church's treatment of divorced persons. A patristic writer like Origen (died 254) relates, albeit unapprovingly, that some bishops permit women to remarry during the lifetime of their husbands. We saw that the Eastern Church chose to accomodate itself to the Roman law of divorce. In the troubled days of the early medieval West, the penitential books allowed remarriage in certain cases after the collapse or destruction of a couple's life together. Although the late medieval church refused to dissolve sacramental marriages, the many canonical impediments provided ways of subsequently determining that a broken marriage was no marriage at all. Canon law often worked to free people for a new marriage. In recent centuries, popes have exercised competence to declare dissolved many marriages in which one or both of the parties was not baptized. Parallel with this latter practice is the "Pauline privilege" granting freedom to remarry to a convert to Christianity, if the non-baptized spouse does not wish to continue the marriage (1 Cor 7:15).

TOLERANT CONCERN

We find in these practices a long tradition of tolerant concern for persons involved in broken marriages. There are two elements in this concern. (1) The full Christian view of marriage as a life-long covenant is not verified in every kind of marriage. Some marriages, as among the unbaptized, are in fact *not* marriages in the Lord. These marriages are thus not indissoluble in the strict sense—however much we must lament the deep wounds in the lives of couples and children caught in divorces and broken homes. (2) Even when a first marriage appears to have been a sacramental dedication of believing Christians, there are signs that at times the church has tolerated a second marriage to avoid worse evils. Frequently, the church has been quite rigorous in refusing the blessings of full communion to persons in such a union. Many have seen such second marriages as little more than organized adultery. But this rigor is not the whole story. The church has never completely forgotten her mission of healing to her members still weakened by sin.

Because there are such elements in our tradition, and because the tragedies of broken Christian marriages surround us, there is an increased urgency to the question about the church's ministry to her members in intolerable marriage situations. The signs are clear all around us that the rigor toward those in second marriages is abating and that the channels for forgiveness are opening. This is not to call for the solemn celebration of second marriages as covenantal unions in Christ, but it is a development in the direction of restoring to a fuller sacramental life those Christians living in stable second marriages.

8. What is the fundamental meaning of Christian marriage?

A couple enter a Christian marriage by their pledge of lifelong love and fidelity. They do not merely exchange rights and duties, but rather confer themselves in a total way. Each takes on a new identity for the other. Under the influence of Scripture, we are constrained to see this pledge of love as the sealing of a covenant before God. As the Lord selected Israel from the other nations to live in a covenant relation, so also the spouses select each other, forsaking and excluding all others for the rest of their lives. As a covenant, such a marriage has God as its author and witness. Because the new husband and wife are members of the priestly people, God is the guarantor and guard of their union.

The biblical strictures against divorce bring out a central aspect of marriage in the Lord. However, they only have complete meaning if such marriages are in fact godly covenants. If these marriages are contracts, then they can be broken by mutual agreement, lack of compliance, or civil intervention. But covenants are not broken by anyone. Rather, they are violated by a breach of the fidelity promised. Scripture insists on God's fidelity even when Israel turned to alien gods. Such fidelity belongs to the covenant pledge of couples entering Christian marriages.

Clearly not everyone is capable of such loving dedication to life together. No little maturity is required for a person to enter such a life partnership. Beyond a certain psychological development and stability, this maturity must include a real vision of faith if a couple are to call upon God to witness and seal their pledge to each other. The mere fact of baptism does not insure this. Today, not a few apparently Christian marriages are in fact the union of baptized "unbelievers" and should not be treated as covenants in the Lord.

COVENANT LOVE

Such a pledge—and the life together that ensues—is a sacrament of Christ because of what the husband and wife articulate to each other. This is so because their pledge of covenant love can only arise out of the deepest levels of their freedom. Such a dedication can only be an engagement made in the power of a transformed identity under the Holy Spirit. Marital love is sacramental when it is vowed by persons assimilated to Christ and consecrated by him in his priestly people. Each partner expresses to the other the self-forgetting and redemptive love that Christ manifested in going to death on our behalf. Because their love is such an engagement of their persons, it is sanctifying and enriching for a lifetime—as the partners prove responsive to each other's sacred commitment.

The full expression of self-giving in Christian marriage does not occur in the ceremonial words of the wedding. Such words give a marriage a public visibility that enriches both the church and the wider society. But the covenant love of a married couple is preeminently articulated in the intensely personal interchange of sexual union. Here their mutual gift of self and their new identity for the other find a language of deeper engagement and fuller personal dedication. Again, the assimilation of the couple's love to Christ's dedication issues in a requirement, that of openness to the creation of new life. As Christ's love bears fruit in the conferral of life and more abundant life (Jn 10:10), so the conjugal love of those pledged to each other must be oriented to the gift of and growth of life. In their children, the partners of a Christian marriage find that their mutual pledge to each other has issued in new persons expressive of and responsive to their parents' dedicated giving.

The grace of married love is thus enriching for the couple whose love is sealed, deepened, and strengthened by the Spirit. Within the priestly people married couples offer a forceful articulation of the loving fidelity to which all are called. But the ultimate service they render is not to the church, but to the whole of humanity as they image forth in their love the one foundation of a fulfilling life in this world. For life—whether in marriage or outside it—only unfolds its riches when we overcome egotism and self-regard to become persons for others.

Eucharist

1. What do the synoptic gospels tell us about the Eucharist?

Each of the first three gospels relates how at supper on the night before his death Jesus took bread and wine and offered them to his disciples saying as he did this, "This is my body which is given for you. This cup is the new covenant in my blood poured out for you. Do this as a memorial of me" (Lk 22:19–20; Mk 14:22–24; Mt 26:26–28). The three gospel accounts of the supper differ slightly in their reports of the words of Jesus, a fact ordinarily attributed to the use of the words over and over again in the earliest Christian celebrations of the Eucharist. When the gospel writers finally wrote down their narratives, the accounts of the supper already showed how certain communities are coming to slightly different understandings of the action Jesus left them as the great memorial of the last hours of his life.

In the Gospel of Mark, the words over the cup are quite direct, "This is my blood of the covenant" (Mk 14:24). This is a nearly perfect echo of the words of Moses (Ex 24:8), when he ritually sealed the Lord's covenant with Israel by sprinkling the blood of sacrificed animals over the altar and over the people assembled at Sinai. This suggests that Mark wrote in a community which understood the eucharistic cup as part of a sacrifice ratifying the covenant between God and the new Israel. Thus the Eucharist brings the fulfilment of Old Testament sacrifice and is the act in which the new people of God are gathered and newly dedicated to life under God's covenant love.

The account in Luke's Gospel places more emphasis on the *new* covenant and highlights the redemptive significance of Jesus' body and blood ("... given *for you* ... poured out *for you*"). This tendency in Luke places the Eucharist against the background of the great redemptive message proclaimed in chapter 40–55 of the prophet Isaiah. A chosen servant is to establish God's new covenant with men (Is 42:6; 49:8; 54:10), and the blessings of this new relationship are closely connected with the servant's suffering and death as a martyr on behalf of his people (Is 53). Hence, the tradition standing behind the Gospel of Luke sees in the Eucharist an expression of Jesus' readiness to give himself over to death for mankind. The words and gestures with the bread and wine are expressive of the basic mentality of Jesus: "I have come not to be served, but to serve, and to give my life as a ransom for many" (Mk 10:45). What he did with the bread and wine at the supper was a dramatic enactment of the meaning of the violent death he met the next afternoon. On the cross his body was broken and his blood was poured out for others, so that they might come to live amid the blessings of God's mercy and predilection in a new covenant.

A further light is shed on the Eucharist by Jesus' mandate, "Do this as a memorial of me." Again, a great biblical theme is sounded both by the words themselves and by the celebration of the supper in the week of Israel's Passover feast. The paschal meal was the family celebration in which the Jews commemorated their deliverance from Egypt and captivity. They ate the pasch each year in the conviction that they, the Israelites of later generations, were thereby included in the loving regard God continued to show his elect people. The paschal supper was an occasion for recalling and dwelling on Israel's liberation from bondage. But it was more, for the Jews saw in it a rite that recapitulated the Lord's great deed of mercy and brought it to bear on the lives of later generations.

Consequently, the church's repeated celebrations of the Eucharist memorialize the final events of Jesus' life on earth, expecially his death on behalf of others. The words and gestures are dramatic expressions of the significance of his death to found a new covenant. Consequently, we must see in the Eucharist our great sacrament of covenant renewal, by which Jesus' death on our behalf is set before us so that we might share more fully in the covenant blessings of God's nearness and predilection.

2. What does the Gospel of John teach about the Eucharist?

The fourth gospel makes frequent references to the "signs" worked by Jesus (e.g., Jn 2:11; 20:30). These were primarily his miracles, such as changing water to wine at Cana and healing a man afflicted with blindness from birth. But the signs were also the great images Jesus used to illustrate his message, such as a new birth (3:3–8), living water (4:10–15), light (9:5), and the good shepherd (10:11–15). The sign most intimately connected with the Eucharist is "the bread of life," of which Jesus spoke in John 6, after he fed more than five thousand persons on the lakeshore.

In the first part of his discourse (6:35–50), Jesus only hints at the Eucharist, since his main purpose is to show that his words and teaching are the new manna with which God is feeding his people. He chides their unbelief, since they are depriving themselves of life-giving nourishment. "He who comes to me shall not hunger, and he who believes in me shall never thirst" (6:35). Verse 51 opens the second part of the discourse, where the "bread of life" is now his flesh given for the life of the world. The focus has shifted to Jesus's own body, which he is to offer in death to unleash on the world a new gift of unending life. The words that follow then explain two precious aspects of the Eucharist.

Receiving the Eucharist, that is, eating his body and blood, imparts the gift of intimate sharing with the living Christ. "My flesh is food indeed, and my blood is drink indeed. He who eats my flesh and drinks my blood abides in me, and I in him" (6:55f). There is a gift of life, that is clear, but life in mutual nearness and intimacy with Christ. It is not a momentary gift, but enduring; not a one-sided relation, but mutual; not simply physical, but personal and spiritual. We are reminded of Jesus' declaration, "I have come that they may have life, and have it abundantly" (Jn 10:10). Thus, the fourth gospel takes us to the center of the eucharistic mystery, to a place where our explanations fall far short of the reality and we are left to ponder and pray over Jesus' words about the life he shares with us through the Eucharist.

Another important perspective is opened by the words, "He who eats my flesh and drinks my blood has eternal life, and I will raise him up on the last day" (6:54). The Eucharist has significance reaching beyond death to our resurrection unto everlasting life. It is a pledge or token of a future, fuller gift of life yet to come. A seed of life is planted now, to be harvested in our risen and renewed lives with God in eternity. Consequently, Christians have always found their eucharistic meetings with Jesus to be profound sources of deepened and renewed hope. In celebrating and receiving the Eucharist, the Christian people are shaped as a people of hope who gaze into the future with the steady eye of positive expectation. Death, the ultimate enemy, will be overcome. The Eucharist offers us an element of security rooted in Christ and can free us from the frantic concern to root our security in the possessions and achievements we might accumulate in this world.

3. What does St. Paul teach about the Eucharist?

In two passages in First Corinthians, St. Paul responds to problems arising among the Corinthian Christians by urging them to see their Christian obligations in the light of what they do in the Eucharist.

In chapter 10, Paul develops an incisive argument that Christians should take no part in the worship of idols (10:14), nor in pagan sacrificial meals. The problem arose from the cult of the goddess Aphrodite then flourishing in Corinth. Paul stated categorically that this is incompatible with the Christian Eucharist. "You cannot drink the cup of the Lord and the cup of the demons. You cannot partake of the table of the Lord and the table of demons" (10:21). The root of this argument is that these are mutually exclusive loyalties that cannot go together. In a striking formula, Paul reminded his readers that the Eucharist brought them into a relation of intimate sharing with our Lord: "The cup of blessing which we bless, is it not a sharing in the blood of Christ? The bread which we break, is it not a sharing in the body of Christ?" (10:16). Partaking in Christ's body and blood is, consequently, an act of allegiance to him that admits of no compromise in the public arena of the city in which they live.

In the next chapter, St. Paul turned to treat a serious problem of factiousness and disregard for the poor of the community. To show how wrong this was, Paul recited the traditional account of Jesus' words and gestures at the last supper. The Corinthians knew this account well, since they heard it each time they celebrated the Eucharist. Paul wanted them to ponder it in connection with their own cliquishness and lack of charity. They should examine themselves (11:28) and see that they are eating and drinking unworthily (11:27).

The reason for their unworthy reception is not a lack of faith in Christ's presence, but their lack of agreement with the mind of Christ which is expressed in the Eucharist. What a clash between their spirit and the attitude Christ demonstrated in giving his body over for them and pouring out his blood for them! Paul sees the Eucharist in the closest possible relation to Jesus' death: "As often as you eat this bread and drink this cup, you proclaim the Lord's death until he comes" (11:26). This sacrament that places Jesus' death in that midst of the Corinthian community life is not without consequences. The attitude of Jesus, the dedicated servant of the Lord, is expressed in the

Eucharist in a way calling for Christians to become conformed to his unselfish gift of himself. If they resist this call by persisting in factious unkindness, they celebrate unworthily. Their unity is rooted in the Eucharist: "Because there is one bread, we the many are one body, for we all partake of the one bread" (10:17). But they must maintain and foster their oneness by growing more like the expression of Jesus' attitude they find confronting them in this same Eucharist.

4. What have the eras of Christian history contributed to our understanding of the Eucharist?

Because the resurrection has transformed the humanity of Christ to make him "a life-giving spirit," early Christians quite easily thought of him as present and active in their midst. They often spoke of the Eucharist as a festive meal in which Christ was among them as the host serving and caring for his guests. Christ is the "Lord of the Supper" who gathers his guests from the highways and byways so that they might enjoy the hospitality and nourishment he offers.

Since the Christ of glory remained fully human, he could represent the whole of humanity in offering prayer and homage before God. Thus, the central person in the early Eucharist was Christ the High Priest, who mediates the Christian offering of thanks and glorification to the father.

Beyond this presence of Christ acting as Lord and High Priest, the earliest Christians knew of a change in the bread and wine through the prayer of blessing recited in the Eucharist. There was, however, little extended discussion or argumentation about Christ's presence as the food of the eucharistic meal. St. John Chrysostom, a fourth century bishop of Constantinople, moved quickly from the fact of Christ's presence to stress the result of receiving the Eucharist. "For what is the bread? The body of Christ. And what do they become who partake of it? The body of Christ, that is, not many bodies, but one body. . . . He gave it to all to partake, so that being nourished by this flesh and laying aside the old dead material, we might be blended together into that which is living and eternal."

In late antiquity, Christians lost much of their sense of the glorified humanity of Christ and centered almost exclusively on the fact that he was God the Eternal Word become incarnate. Gradually attention shifted from the activity of Christ in the Eucharist to the fact of his divine presence. In the eleventh century, controversies broke out about how the body and blood of Christ are present as food. The subsequent teaching of the church accentuated the reality of the change, or conversion, of the bread and wine, and this spurred medieval theologians on to draw up intricate explanations of the presence of Christ.

REFORMATION

During the Reformation in the sixteenth century, bitter arguments broke out over the established practice of allowing lay people to receive Communion only under the form of bread. Luther charged that in doing this the church was daring to change a practice instituted by Christ, who commanded that we eat and drink. Luther also attacked the Catholic understanding that the Eucharist was an action in which those celebrating are active in offering sacrifice, Christ's sacrifice and their own, to God. Luther's great concern was for people to recapture an experience of God's grace and forgiveness as this is extended to them in the Eucharist. They should not work or offer, but rather listen in trusting faith to the words in which Christ approaches them and offers the forgiveness of sins gained by the sacrifice of his body and blood on the cross.

Also in the Reformation, Zwingli and Calvin argued against any transformation of bread and wine into Christ's real body and blood. Both of them stressed rather the spiritual presence of Christ in the hearts of those who ate and drank in a vivid act of faith in Jesus' redemptive work. Luther, though, was an adamant defender of the real presence of Christ.

The Catholic response to the Reformation covered the three points of the leading Reformers. Communion under one form, it was taught, is fully communion, because Christ is fully present, whether under one or both forms. Also, the church spoke with conviction that it had authority from Christ to regulate the mode of receiving the Eucharist as well as the other sacraments.

The Council of Trent defined as a central truth of faith that in the Eucharist Christ's unique and all-sufficient sacrifice is made present again in his church. What was offered in a bloody manner on Calvary is present in the form of an unbloody offering in the Eucharist.

In response to Zwingli and Calvin, Trent defined that the bread and wine are marvelously transformed into the true body and blood of Christ. Hence the consecrated elements may be venerated and even adored. Also, after the celebration the body of Christ may be kept in the tabernacle so that Communion can be brought to the sick and the faithful may pray in the presence of the eucharistic Christ.

In our own century the bitterness of Reformation argumentation is dying down and the great scandal of division over the sacrament of unity is gradually being allayed. Catholic teaching on the Eucharist is expanding from stress on the dogmas of real presence and sacrifice to recapture the many splendors of the Eucharist that are revealed by Scripture and a renewed theology.

5. How then is Christ present in the Eucharist?

We begin from the conviction that Christ has been raised to a life of imperishable glory. By his resurrection, his humanity has been endowed with a new ability to be near to us. "It is sown in weakness, it is raised in power. It is sown a physical body, it is raised a spiritual body. . . . The last Adam (Christ) became a life-giving spirit" (1 Cor 15:43–45). The resurrection, by God's power, leads to a manifold mystery of Christ's presence and communication with his people.

In the Eucharist, Christ is thus present and exerting influence in the word addressed to us through Scripture and preaching. Christ is present in the presiding priest to gather us, lead us in prayer, and bring our homage to God. Christ is present in the whole community brought together in his name. Through Christ this community of the people of God approaches God to speak the loving word learned from Jesus, "Father." Thus, much as the early Christians, we too profess a many-sided "actual presence" of Christ as Lord and High Priest in the eucharistic celebration. He it is who gathers us; he it is who assimilates us to his sacrificial death set before us in living memorial.

Within the movement of this actual presence of Christ, there is the "somatic" or "substantial" presence of Christ as the food offered to us. This conviction rests on the forceful words, "My flesh is food indeed, and my blood is drink indeed" (John 6:55), and on the startling implication drawn by St. Paul, "Whoever eats the bread or drinks the cup of the Lord unworthily will be guilty of profaning the body and blood of the Lord" (1 Cor 11:27). Within the eucharistic action, the risen Christ takes the elements of bread and wine into personal identity with himself and makes them from that moment onward the expressive means of conferring on his followers the gift of his martyr's body and his blood shed for us. The purpose and reality of the bread and wine is changed; by Christ's words and gestures the elements henceforth have a new meaning and identity: Christ, who is totally *for us* in loving and intimate nearness.

Consequently, Christ is present in the spiritual power of his risen existence, both actually and somatically, in the eucharistic action and gifts.

6. What kind of action takes place in the Eucharist?

The central action of the Eucharist is above all the memorial of Jesus' redemptive death on our behalf. As Israel's pasch celebrated the passage of a people from bondage to freedom, so the Christian Eucharist celebrates Jesus' passage into the new life of his resurrection.

This memorial, however, is not simply the act of our thinking and pondering about what Jesus did. His mandate was that we do this, in living enactment of what he did at the supper. At the heart of the Eucharist is a dramatic gesture strikingly expressive of his death on our behalf. We do not memorialize the supper, but the giving of his body and the shedding of his blood in death on our behalf. Consequently the memorial action carried out is an expression in our midst of the self-sacrifice of Jesus. The living Christ is in our midst to unleash in our lives the great event of his death.

The dynamic force of this eucharistic memorial is to draw us into the same attitude of offering and selfless dedication to God. We saw how this was implied in St. Paul's argument in First Corinthians. Christians proclaim his death and their community lifestyle should be made like to the death of Christ on behalf of others.

In the Eucharist, Christ seeks to assimilate his body, the church, to the offering he the head made on the cross. It is this work of assimilation that ultimately determines our style of prayer in the eucharistic celebration.

7. How does the church pray in the Eucharist?

The central prayer of the eucharistic liturgy is the great prayer of "blessing" that begins with the invitation, "Let us give thanks to the Lord our God," and continues to the climactic offering through, with, and in Christ of all honor and glory to God the Father. The blessing prayer, or Eucharistic Prayer, has developed from the solemn chants that accompanied parts of Israel's paschal supper. The leader blessed God in thankful remembrance of the mercies showered on his people. Thus, much of the blessing prayer was narrative in character as it recited exultantly the great events of Israel's history.

The Christian Eucharistic Prayer offers thanks and praise to the Father for his mercies, which reached their highpoint in the coming of Christ. The climactic moment is the recital of Jesus' words and deeds at the Last Supper, in which he expressed the meaning and significance of his imminent death. This is no mournful eulogy of a fallen leader, but an exultent celebration of Jesus' passage through death into the glory of the resurrection. Most Eucharistic Prayers even glance ahead to express our longing for the completion of the work of Christ that will come when he appears at the end of our days.

Thus the form of our prayer gives the Eucharist a steady orientation toward God the Father, whom we approach and to whom we offer our grateful acknowledgement. Christ is our mediator with the Father, and we strive to associate ourselves with the spirit of dedication with which he offered himself to God.

The Eucharistic Prayer conforms closely to the memorial of Jesus' death and exaltation. It gives concrete form to the offering Christians make of themselves in assimilation to Christ's offering. Thus, the Eucharistic Prayer is the form in which the sacrifice of Christ makes itself present and visible in the liturgy of God's priestly people who are called "to declare the wonderful deed of him who called you out of darkness into his wonderful light" (1 Pt 2:9).

Within the Eucharistic Prayer, a further prayer of great importance is the *epiclesis,* or invocation of the Holy Spirit upon the elements of bread and wine. The church prays that the same Spirit who acted in creation (Gen 1:1) would act to transform the bread and wine into the body and blood of Christ. Different forms of this prayer also invoke the Spirit upon the assembled people, so that they might become what they profess, "a living sacrifice holy and acceptable to God" (Rom 12:1). For, in the last analysis, we celebrate the Eucharist "in the Holy Spirit," that is, as people baptized by one Spirit into one body (1 Cor 12:13) and by this same Spirit empowered to approach and say "Abba! Father!" (Rom 8:15).

8. Why is the Sunday Eucharist of special importance?

The regular keeping of a "day of rest" corresponds to deep physical and personal needs of every adult. We need to depart from the constant round of practical planning and calculated pursuit of short-range goals. Sunday is a day of heightened sensitivity to deeper levels of reality, to a reality which we cannot control, but only receive as a pure gift of presence and freely given enrichment. Sunday is the day of personal focus on the silent otherness out of which God approaches us and calls us to listen, to ponder, and to take hold of his gifts of freedom, vocation, and new life.

The first day of the week is such a day, because on it Jesus came forth from the dead as the first-born of the new creation. Each Sunday is a "little Easter," a day that bathes our lives in the light of Jesus' risen glory. The risen Christ is the deeper but personal reality on whom Christians focus and from whom they strive to take nourishment on Sunday.

Sunday is preeminently the day of eucharistic commemoration, in exultant celebration of the passage of Jesus through death to his new life of glory. Since this passage is God's deed and action, we must approach it receptively and gratefully. We cannot generate a substitute or alternate center of the Christian faith. God's new creation began with the raising of his Son who had passed through an obedient death on our behalf. Hence the central focus of the Christian Sunday is the arrival of the final purpose of God's work in the new life of glory which Jesus now has and now radiates into his people for the world.

Finally, Sunday is a day on which we glimpse for a moment the ultimate future on which our hope rests. Sharing the Eucharist grants us a foretaste of that ultimate union with God which the prophet described as a feast on the mountain of the Lord (Is 26:6–8). Jesus spoke of final salvation as "sitting at table with Abraham, Isaac, and Jacob in the kingdom of heaven" (Mt 8:11). Thus our eucharistic meal with the Lord is a gift of God that anticipates a final and totally satisfying communion with God in eternity.

Christians have from the beginning celebrated the death of the Lord "until he comes" (1 Cor 11:26). The Eucharist at one time often gave rise to prayers of longing, "Come, Lord!" Our gaze is not fixed backward, but on the grand movement of history, as we follow the arc extended from Jesus' resurrection to his final manifestation as Lord and Judge. Thus we grasp how all human history will one day converge with the personal history of Jesus Christ, and our Eucharistic Prayer issues in longing that this be fulfilled. In a Sunday of rest and worship, we seek to savor and fix our hope more fully on this coming triumpth of Christ.

Sunday, therefore, is the day of our ever renewed beginning in the light of the resurrection of Christ. We celebrate the memorial of his death; we share in his body and blood that we may have life and have it abundantly; we nourish our hope of a fuller and final life with him when he returns in glory. All this began on the Sunday of his resurrection.

PART THREE

Principles of Morality

The Moral Law
Fundamental Moral Theology—1

1. Did Jesus come to teach morality?

Jesus came to save us. "God so loved the world that he gave his only-begotten Son that those who believe in him may not perish, but may have life everlasting" (Jn. 3:16). It would be a fundamental misunderstanding of the gospel to interpret the mission of Christ moralistically, as if Jesus came primarily to teach men a moral code and to help them to live good lives. Jesus did teach us that we must respond to God's love by doing his will and living moral lives. But Jesus' moral teaching was secondary. Jesus did not come as an ethical teacher but as our redeemer. He did not bring us a new morality but a new reality. His primary mission was to remake men into sons of God who have a new life in him. "God's love for us was revealed when God sent into the world his only Son so that we could have life through him; this is the love I mean: not our love for God, but God's love for us when he sent his Son to be the sacrifice that takes our sins away" (1 Jn. 4:9–10).

2. What is a Christian life?

A Christian life is a life "in Christ." As the Son of God has become a sharer in our humanity, so we have become sharers in his divinity. Through our redemption we have become sons of God and participators with Jesus in the divine life of grace. Therefore our morally good actions are not merely the acts of good men but of adopted sons of God; they are the vital activity of the new divine life we now share in Christ Jesus. It is not enough therefore that a Christian life be moral. It must also be a life in Christ, that is, a life lived in grace which is a participation in the life of Christ and his relationship to the Father.

[169]

3. What is meant by "the following of Christ"?

The following of Christ means more than the mere moral imitation of him. It means the acceptance of Jesus as the center and purpose of our lives and our personal union with him.

4. Is Christ the norm of morality?

The norm of morality is ultimately more than an impersonal law which is sanctioned by God. The person of Jesus Christ is our norm of morality. It is important to get the meaning of this clear.

When theologians say that Christ is our norm of morality, they do not mean merely that he is an example for us to imitate. Jesus was a unique person with his unique role and vocation in history. He could not and did not leave us an example to imitate except in a very general way. God does not want us to be carbon copies of Christ. He wants us to live out our unique roles according to his special plans for us.

Theologians mean that Christ is our norm of morality in a profound metaphysical and theological sense. As the prologue of St. John's gospel tells us, all things were created in him. He is the prime exemplar, the exemplary cause, of all created reality. Since Christ is the exemplar of all reality, he is the exemplar of all goodness. Therefore whenever one conforms to the objective moral good in any situation, he is in fact conforming to Christ its exemplar.

5. What is the Old Law?

The Old Testament itself is sometimes referred to as the Old Law. But frequently the expression is used to designate those precepts—moral, ceremonial and judicial—which Israel was obliged to observe. Specifically, *the Old Law* is often used to mean the law of Moses and in particular the decalogue or ten commandments.

The first three commandments reflect Yahweh's covenant with Israel, and the last seven reflect the mores and ethical standards which were common in the Near East at the time. The whole decalogue was seen and read in the context of God's covenant with Israel, but those commandments dealing with a man's relationship with his neighbor were not unique in Israel, nor were they any better or more moral than the law of many of Israel's neighbors.

Israel's law was culture bound, limited in its moral insightfulness, and reflected a particular moment in history. For instance, in its original form the fourth commandment was simply: "Do not curse your father or mother." The fifth commandment did not forbid killing or murder but rather any illegal killing which was harmful to the community, even if it was accidental. The sixth commandment prohibited sexual intercourse with a woman who was the property of another man but said nothing about a married man copulating with an unmarried woman. Originally the seventh commandment was meant to outlaw the kidnapping of a free Israelite man; and the ninth and tenth forbade the stealing of dependent persons like women, children and salves as well as property, but said nothing about mental coveting. And the eighth commandment excluded false witness in a court of law but said nothing about lying.

6. What is the New Law?

It is a common mistake to describe the New Law as the law of love. The New Law is much more than any external precept, even the precept to love God above all things and one's neighbor as oneself. The New Law is primarily an inner law: it is the grace of the Holy Spirit. Any external law, including the precept of charity, is only secondary.

It is primarily the grace of the Holy Spirit that is normative for the actions of Christians. This is true of both habitual and actual grace. Habitual or sanctifying grace is the ultimate perfection of a Christian man, and therefore he is to act in accordance with this new nature. As his human nature is normative of behaviour to the extent that a man is morally obliged to live in accordance with it and realize its perfection, so too is his new life of grace: since he has been made a son he ought to live as a son. Actual grace also is normative for a Christian, since it directs his mind and will in doing God's will. For as everyone knows, except Pelagians, our good actions are the actions of God's Holy Spirit in us.

The inner law of grace therefore is the primary element in the New Law. External precepts and rules are only secondary and are totally in the service of the primary element. Primacy in the New Law does not belong to the sermon on the mount or to the law of love. It belongs to the grace of the Holy Spirit. Grace justifies and saves, not external rules and precepts, not even the precept of love. Apart from the law of grace and the charity *given* with grace even Jesus' great commandment of love is deadly, in fact the most deadly of all. Without the power of the grace of the Holy Spirit the moral precepts of the New Testament are no better than the moral precepts of the Old Testament. Not only are they not salutary; they are as deadly as the Mosaic law. Without the healing power of grace, St. Thomas tells us, the letter of the gospel would kill. Apart from the inner law of grace, the external law of love is lethal, and all that St. Paul wrote about the Mosaic law would have to be said of it.

7. What is the importance of external laws and rules?

Universal laws and rules are the external formulation of the internal direction of the grace of the Holy Spirit. External precepts serve to explicate in a legal way what the Spirit moves us toward internally. Charity is the primary work of the Holy Spirit within us, and external laws explain what human acts are or are not valid expressions and mediations of Christian love. Since in our present state we are still in danger of rationalization and misinterpretation of the inner motion of the Spirit, the external precepts are useful to oppose such falsifications.

8. What is meant by "the freedom wherewith Christ has made us free" (Gal. 4:31).

The freedom wherewith Christ has made us free is the freedom that belongs to the sons of God. Through the grace of Christ we are set free from the moral necessity of breaking the law and are now free to accomplish the justice of the law. Christian freedom does not imply license or absence of restraint. It is freedom under a new law—a law which replaces slavery to sin with slavery to God. (1 Pet. 2:16).

9. What is natural law?

Historically there have been many different theories of natural law developed by philosophers and theologians (e.g., Aristotle, St. Thomas, Locke, Pufendorf). The doctrine of natural law which controlled Catholic ethics in the recent past understood natural law as a body of immutable precepts which are grounded in the immutable essence or nature of man (rational animal).

The contemporary Catholic theory of natural law has returned to the more dynamic theory of St. Thomas Aquinas. Natural law is first of all the objective moral order to which man's behaviour ought to conform. The foundation of natural law precepts is not the abstract metaphysical nature of man but the concrete nature of man as it actually exists.

This doctrine of natural law affirms an objective moral order and is primarily concerned to exclude legal positivism and subjectivism in ethical theory. Its basic assertion is that moral good and evil are objective realities. Man does not create or arbitrarily decide what is right or wrong. Rather he discovers what is truly good or bad in the objective moral order.

10. Is the natural law the law of Christ?

Since God de facto created man's nature in a supernatural order and with a supernatural destiny, natural law is and always has been supernatural law. But more than this, natural law is specifically the law of Christ. As we noted under question 4, all things were created in him (cf. Jn. 1:3). Christ, the God-man, is the exemplar of all creation; all things were created in his image. The natural law, therefore, was created in Christ. Hence, to conform to the natural law is in fact to conform to Christ its exemplar.

11. Does natural law change?

Late nineteenth and early twentieth century theologians argued that the natural law does not change because human nature does not change. St. Thomas Aquinas, on the other hand, argued that the natural law changes because human nature changes (cf. *Suppl.* 41, 1, ad 3; 50, 1, ad 4; II–II 57, 2 ad 2; *De Malo* 2, 4, and 13). The nineteenth and early twentieth century theologians grounded natural law precepts in the abstract metaphysical nature of man (rational animal) which is unchanging through history. Contemporary theologians ground natural law precepts in the metaphysical nature of man as it is concretely realized in the various stages and situations of history. Therefore, like St. Thomas, contemporary theologians recognize the important effects that accidental changes in man's nature can have on the natural law.

12. Do the universal precepts of the natural law oblige absolutely, ie. without any exceptions?

Some precepts of natural law are transcendental, that is, very general norms having no specific material content, for instance, "Do good and avoid evil," "Love your fellow man," "Give every man his just due." Other precepts are tautological, for instance, "Do not commit murder," "Do not steal," "Do not lie." These rules forbid us to do an illicit killing, to take what we have no right to, to tell an illicit untruth. But they do not specify which killings are murder, which appropriations are thefts, which false statements are lies.

Finally, there are concrete rules which do designate specific pieces of human behaviour and declare them morally good or bad. For instance, the prohibition of adultery, abortion, premarital sex, contraception, sterilization, masturbation, etc., are concrete moral norms. In the past Catholic moral theologians described these actions as intrinsically evil, immoral in themselves, and therefore always forbidden under any circumstances. Today, however, many Catholic moralists argue that concrete moral norms are not absolutely binding. They say that these actions are morally wrong in general but not in all possible circumstances. Concrete moral norms, therefore, are usually and presumably binding. In fact, in some cases it may be difficult to imagine any practical circumstances in which they are not binding. But one cannot exclude a priori the possibility that the generally forbidden actions may be morally permissible in some circumstances. It is possible that the value protected by the universal law may be outweighed by another value in some situations.

13. In addition to universal norms are there also singular existential imperatives of the natural law?

A situation ethics which rejects all universal norms is caught up in the error that each person is in all respect unique, that there is nothing at all common in human beings, and that it is impossible for man to have any universal knowledge which represents and applies to objective reality. There are certainly common elements in human nature that ground moral principles which are universally binding. But there is also a unique element in the spiritual person that cannot be reduced to any general principle. It seems arbitrary to say that the only basis of moral decision or formation of conscience is that part of reality which is abstracted in universal concepts and that the unique and ineffable part of the same reality makes no ethical difference. It seems only consistent to say that as the common elements can found universal laws, so the unique, singular elements of the individual person and the concrete situation can ground concrete imperatives which are valid and normative in the existing situation.

In other words, a deductive, syllogistic ethics, which applies a general norm to a more particular (but still general) case or even to an existing situation may not be sufficient to disclose a moral imperative that in fact represents God's will binding an individual's conscience in a concrete situation. Take as an example a young girl faced with a decision about her special vocation in life. Universal norms applied to her situation will reveal to her that she may not become, for instance, a prostitute or an extortionist. But after applying the universal norms to her situation, she is still left with a number of options: for instance, she may become a teacher, go to graduate school, enter the convent or marry one of three eligible suitors. From the fact that these choices are morally indifferent in the abstract it does not follow that they are all morally indifferent for her in the concrete, so that she may do as she pleases in so far as God is concerned as long as she does not violate some universal rule. It is difficult to believe that what she actually does in these important areas is a matter of indifference to a personal God who is not just concerned about mankind in general but calls each one of us by name.

The most practical and difficult problem with this theory concerns the way of knowing the individual ethical imperative. Karl Rahner suggests that there is a function of conscience which grasps the concrete imperative arising out of the existential situation. The fact that we do not possess a developed theory or clear reflex knowledge of the formal structures and basic nature of perceiving the existential moral imperative is no proof that all ethics is essentialist and deductive. Just as there was logical thought before the development of formal logic, so there can be existential ethical decision without a formal doctrine of existential ethics.

14. What is situation ethics?

Situation ethics is not a univocal term designating a worked out system of ethical thought. It is a vague expression that is applied to certain philosophical and theological tendencies, strains of thought and efforts at generalizations.

15. What is the most extreme form of situation ethics?

The most extreme form of situation ethics is that of certain French existentialists like Sartre and Simon de Beauvoir. Rooted in atheism and actualistic personalism, it is professedly antinomian. It is described by Sartre as a "morality of authenticity." Reality is altogether discontinuous. Each person, action, and situation is new, unique and unrepeatable. No ethical norms can come from God, since there is no God. Nor can they come from man's nature, since man is not a nature but freedom. The freedom of man is unlimited and the only genuine value. The only moral demand on man is the development and actualization of his personal freedom.

16. What is Protestant situation ethics?

Protestant situation ethics takes many forms. A handy summary of these can be found in the June, 1967 issue of *Theological Studies.* But even a lengthy survey finds it difficult to do justice to the numerous strains of situationism among both European and American Protestant theologians. In very general terms we might say that it considers universal norms of morality useful and indicative of God's will but not as absolutely and unexceptionally binding. As a consequence, each person must decide for himself what God's will is for him here and now, for ultimately God's will for man is found in the concrete situation, not in abstract laws. Historically at least, the theological roots of Protestant situationism probably has been the Lutheran conception of original sin and its destructive effects on human nature; and in many instances its philosophical roots lie in nominalism.

17. Has the Church's magisterium condemned situation ethics?

A 1956 instruction of the Holy Office condemned the ethical teaching of certain unnamed Catholic theologians who held an "Ethics of the Situation." The instruction points out that these theologians held that the ultimate ethical decision of man is not an application of the objective moral law to a concrete situation according to the rules of prudence. Rather it is the immediate internal judgment of the individual through which he knows what is to be done in the present situation. Moreover, the instruction says, these writers hold that while there are perhaps a few absolute principles deriving from metaphysical human nature, for the most part the precepts of natural law are based on existing human nature and so are relative, changeable, and can always be adapted to any situation. As a consequence, each person has to make his own ethical decisions according to his own subjective conscience by means of its individual lights and personal intuition rather than in accord with objective laws.

Accordingly, the instruction of the Holy Office did not condemn every form of situation ethics. It condemned that form which has as its ultimate norm some interior personal judgment or subjective persuasion which is not based on and measured by an objective standard or norm existing outside of man's mind. This objective standard, the instruction says, is *esse.*

18. Are Catholic ethics situational?

In a broad sense of the term even the scholastic ethics of the nineteenth and early twentieth century could be called situational, since it held that concrete circumstances can alter the morality of an act. Nonetheless, it also held that some actions are morally evil *ex objecto* or of their very nature, so that no circumstances or good intention could ever make them morally good.

As we pointed out under question 12, many contemporary Catholic theologians no longer hold this view. They argue that the morality of an act cannot be finally determined from the physical structure of the act alone. It must be morally evaluated together with its purpose and in all its circumstances. Like the Holy Office, these theologians reject subjectivism and insist on the objectivity of the moral order. That is precisely why they admit the possibility of exceptions to universal moral norms. For objectivity and universality are not the same thing. If there is a conflict between the universal law and the objective moral good, a man is bound to the objective good not to the universal law.

19. What is the principle of double effect?

The principle of double effect is an attempt made by scholastic theologians to deal with the moral ambiguity that exists in almost every human action. It rests on the common sense perception that man as agent is responsible not only for his actions and omissions but also to some degree for their consequences.

The principle of double effect is generally enunciated in the scholastic manuals something like this: It is licit to place an action which has two forseen effects, one good and one bad, if four conditions are all verified: (1) the action itself is good or indifferent, (2) the good effect is not produced by means of the bad effect, (3) only the good effect and not the bad effect is directly intended, (4) there is a proportionate reason for placing the action and permitting the bad effect.

Few human actions are totally good or totally bad. Most, if not all, have both good and bad consequences, for instance, smoking a cigarette, driving a car, stealing, giving an alms, lying, telling the truth, sleeping, taking medicine, eating food, aborting a fetus. The principle of double effect assumes that there is a significant moral difference between doing evil and permitting it as a side effect of a good action. It asserts two things: (1) for a sufficient reason we may permit unintended evil consequences of our acts, and (2) we may never purposefully do evil even for a good reason.

20. Do contemporary Catholic theologians have any problem with the principle of double effect?

Yes, they do. The second assertion of the principle causes the main problem. Is there really a moral difference between doing evil for a good reason and permitting evil for a good reason? Is it true, as the principle asserts, that one may never do evil that good may come of it? In other words, can a good end ever justify a bad means?

21. How did traditional scholastic ethics answer this question?

Traditional scholastic ethics answered: We may never do evil that good may come of it. We are responsible for our behaviour as well as for the consequences of our behaviour. There are certain human actions which are morally evil in themselves, no matter what the circumstances or ultimate purpose or result. To will moral evil with a direct intention as a means to a good end is to will it in itself if not for itself, and to will moral evil in itself is always wrong.

22. How do contemporary Catholic theologians respond?

An increasing number of contemporary moralists argue that the physical structure of an act is not enough to determine its moral significance. Concrete ends and means interpenetrate one another to establish the human meaning and moral significance of an act. The means-end categories expose one to the risk of ignoring this fact and making the mistake of deciding the goodness or badness of a human act prematurely, considering only the physical structure of the act and ignoring its human meaning.

Contemporary theologians argue that there are two kinds of moral norms—very general formal norms which are absolute and without any thinkable exceptions and concrete material norms which are directive of our behavior in the world with other men. The concrete norms apply in normal but not all imaginable circumstances. They are affirmations of certain specific and limited values, and the realization of these values in the concrete situation may run into conflict with ather values so that not all the values can be achieved at the same time.

Traditional Catholic theology always has recognized that most concrete rules are liable to exceptions. But in a few instances, e.g. the rule prohibiting the direct killing of an innocent person, it saw the rule as absolute. It maintained that only God, the Lord and giver of life, could allow exceptions to be made. Contemporary theology questions this. It is true that the life of an innocent man generally deserves preference over other values. But is there actually no good thinkable that could come into conflict with the life of an innocent man and deserve preference over it? Physical life is fundamental, but it is

THE MORAL LAW [179]

neither an absolute value or the highest one. Man therefore should be willing and able to make responsible judgments of preference even in such basic areas.

In other words, contemporary theologians believe that concrete rules are governed by a more general principle. This preference principle has been formulated both positively and negatively. Stated negatively it reads: "Put in a position where he will unavoidably cause evil man must discover which is the worst evil and avoid it." Stated positively it says: "Put before two concurring but mutually exclusive values, man should discover which merits preference and act accordingly."

23. Does this mean that the end justifies the means?

It does not mean that a good end justifies an immoral or sinful means. But it does mean that a good end can justify a means that is evil in a physical or premoral sense. We may never do moral evil, that is, sin, that good may come of it. But sometimes it will be permissible, in fact morally obligatory, to do physical or premoral evil that good may come of it.

24. Do human laws oblige a Christian?

In general both civil and ecclesiastical laws oblige the Christian, since they reflect and enjoin a genuine moral good. The binding force of a human law, of course, supposes that it is made by legitimate authority, that it does in fact command what is good not evil, that it is a just and fair law, that it is necessary or useful for the common good, and that it is morally possible (i.e. not excessively difficult) for an individual to observe.

25. Are some civil laws merely penal?

This is a disputed question among Catholic theologians. Some think that the deliberate violation of some civil laws is not sinful. They argue that in the modern secular State the infraction of some civil fault does not constitute a moral fault but only a juridical or civil fault which is punishable by the State. According to this theory of the merely penal law, a citizen does not have a moral obligation to obey the law; he only has a moral obligation not to use unjust means to escape the penalty if he is caught. Theologians who support this theory argue that the modern secular State does not intend to oblige its subjects under sin but only under civil or legal fault to which a determined penalty is attached. Merely penal laws, they say, are fairer to all and are sufficient means for the State to achieve its goal of providing for the common good. A growing number of contemporary theologians, on the other hand, reject the theory of the merely penal law, arguing that all just laws are usually morally as well as legally binding, because they generally reflect and enjoin a genuine moral good or proscribe a genuine moral evil.

26. What is the virtue of epikeia?

Following the lead of Suarez many of the early twentieth century moralists understood epikeia as the benign interpretation of the mind of the legislator who is presumed in a particular case not to wish to urge the observance of his law because of special circumstances. From epikeia they distinguished excusing causes due to moral impossibility or serious inconvenience. They applied epikeia to the cases in which the legislator did not wish to urge the obligation and excusing causes to the cases in which the legislator was not able to oblige.

Contemporary theologians are returning to the explanation of St. Thomas, who did not regard epikeia merely as a reasonable restrictive interpretation of the law but rather as the moral virtue controlling the correct application of the law in a way that is contrary to its literal sense. For the positive law simply affirms what is normative in general and so binds in many instances. But it does not and cannot assert the true moral good for every instance and in every situation. The virtue of epikeia, which is part (*pars potior,* Thomas says) of legal justice, finds the true moral good in the concrete situation in a way that is opposed to the words of the law.

Epikeia therefore is not just a loophole or a way out of moral obligation. It is a true Christian virtue, and not to practice it when it obliges is a sinful act. For we are obliged to seek out and practice the true moral good in our existential situations, not merely to observe the letter of positive laws. When there is a conflict between the good and the law, a Christian is bound to the good not to the law.

According to this explanation there is no need to distinguish epikeia from excusing causes or moral impossibility. If there is a disproportion between fulfilling the law as it is expressed on the one hand and the inconvenience or harm connected with the fulfilling of the law on the other, the virtue of epikeia will correctly apply the law to the situation in a way that contradicts the words of the law.

Personal Conscience
Fundamental Moral Theology—2

1. What is Christian moral theology or Christian ethics?

Moral theology is the scientific study of the behavioral implications of being a Christian, therefore, of the behavioral implications of Christian beliefs about man—his origins, his destiny and his world. Though a theoretical distinction can be made, and an operational one sometimes is, between moral theology and Christian Ethics, increasingly the terms are used interchangeably. Over the centuries Catholic moral theology became highly juridicized and case-oriented due largely to the preoccupation of the discipline with practical confessional solutions and pastoral care. Recent developments in the world and the Church (ecumenism, pluralism of thought, the biblical renewal, a new historical consciousness, rethinking of natural law, the autonomy of the secular, the limitation of the juridical order, a renewed social consciousness) have broadened the concerns of moral theology and deepened its roots. This accords with the mandate of Vatican II which, after noting that the scientific exposition of moral theology should be more thoroughly nourished by scriptural teaching, stated that this discipline "should show the nobility of the Christian vocation of the faithful, and their obligation to bring forth fruit in charity for the life of the world." (W. Abbot, S.J., *Optatam Totius*, n. 16, p. 452).

2. What are some of the practical emphases implied in this renewal of moral theology?

Some of the emphases that are present in moral theology are the following: a rejection of legalism, a new awareness of the depth and complexity of the moral-spiritual life (especially a recovery of the notion of fundamental or basic liberty and its implications), the centrality of the person in the understanding of the meaning and limits of moral norms (in contrast to an analysis tied somewhat too closely to a

[181]

restrictive faculty-finality analysis), the legitimacy and meaning of dissent within the magisterial process of the Church, a more positive pedagogy in the communication of moral values, a more sensitive awareness of the tentativeness and culturally conditioned character of some earlier moral formulations, the dominance of the social in the moral concerns of Christians, a new awareness of the place and importance of personal conscience in the decision-making process, a shift in emphasis from act-orientation to value-orientation, a new willingness to explore and question in contrast to a preoccupation with certainties.

3. Are there dangers in such changes in moral theology?

Yes, clearly. The danger is one of over-reaction. Thus, in abandoning legalism, there is the danger of undervaluing the place of law in the moral life. In abandoning authoritarianism there is the danger of moral anarchy. In abandoning paternalism in conscience formation, there is the real danger of individualism and isolationism. In abandoning an other-worldly supernaturalism there is the danger of pagan secularism. The history of theology reveals a constant struggle to avoid the traps of onesidedness.

4. Is there a distinctively Christian or Catholic ethics?

This question has its origins in many currents but especially in the contemporary attempt of Catholics to relate to and better understand the non-Catholic Christian world, and of Christians to relate to and better understand the non-Christian world. Though the matter is still a subject of discussion among theologians, the answer would build around a proper understanding of the term "ethics." If the term "ethics" is restricted to an essentialist ethic (norms that are applicable to all men, where one's behavior is but an instance of a general, essential norm), there is growing agreement that human morality (natural law) and Christian morality are *materially* identical in the sense that Christian sources add no material content (prescriptions, proscriptions) foreign to and beyond the human and in principle unavailable to sound reasoning processes. However, since Christ is the archetype and exemplar of human perfection, the Christian community is a privileged place for the discovery of what is humanly promotive and humanly destructive. Thus Vatican II noted: "But only God, who created man to His own image and ransomed him from sin, provides a fully adequate answer to these questions. This He does through what He has revealed in Christ His Son, who became man.

Whoever follows after Christ, the perfect man, *becomes himself more of a man*" (W. Abbott, S.J., *Gaudium et Spes,* n. 41, p. 240).

However, there is more to the term "ethics" than essentialist ethics. Three further meanings are suggested by the term. First, there is the choice of the good that the individual should realize (existential ethics). Secondly, there are those ethical decisions a Christian must make precisely because he belongs to a community to which the non-Christian does not belong (essential Christian ethics, e.g., to receive the sacrament of penance). Finally there are decisions that the Christian as individual must make (existential Christian ethics, e.g., the choice to enter religious life). Therefore, before the relationship between Christian and non-Christian, Catholic and non-Catholic ethics can be clarified, the term "ethics" must be carefully distinguished. For Christian ethics seems obviously distinctive in the last three senses of the term.

5. How does a Christian know what is morally good or bad?

The Christian knows what is morally good "in the light of the gospel and human experience" (Vatican II). The light of the gospel furnishes the Christian with a knowledge of man's integral vocation. Thus it is that "faith . . . directs the mind to solutions that are fully human." The light of the gospel is mediated to the Christian by the Holy Spirit in a variety of ways: tradition, the magisterium of the Church, personal reflection and prayer, reflection and discussion with other Christians and even non-Christians (e.g. Catholic with non-Catholic Christians), theological scholarship. These sources of moral knowledge are not mutually exclusive; they are complementary. For the Christian moral knowledge (the new mind in Christ) is always and above all shared or communal knowledge—a knowledge mediated to him by the community of believers. Thus it is that the magisterium ought to enjoy such high esteem in the believing community; for it is the authentic vehicle for the delineation of this knowledge.

However, if the Christian's knowledge of the morally good and bad is to take concrete meaningful form, it must also draw upon and integrate the insights and experience of a variety of disciplines that study the world and provide the context of decision and choice: economics, medicine, psychology and psychiatry, sociology, law, cultural anthropology, etc. Thus the light of the gospel in confrontation with human experience will be the source of ever fresh insights into the meaning and challenge of being a Christian in the modern world.

6. What is conscience?

In its narrowest and most precise sense, conscience is judgment about the moral licitness or illicitness of an individual's concrete action. In this sense it is the subjective norm of morality. Whereas an objective norm provides general information about the moral character of human actions (objective morality), conscience mediates this task for the morality of an individual's personal, concrete conduct (subjective morality). Conscience has its roots in the depths of the person where a person is innately inclined to the good, to the love of God and neighbor. This inclination takes more concrete form in general moral knowledge and becomes utterly concrete and personal when a person judges about the loving or unloving, selfish or unselfish —briefly, about the moral quality—of his own action. While in no way denying that conscience is a dictate about personal concrete action, contemporary theologians are returning to an appropriate stress on the profound personal roots of conscience judgments and the knowledge and self-awareness surrounding these roots.

7. What is meant by formation of conscience?

In its broadest sense, formation of conscience includes attention to all those factors which have an influence on the ultimate judgment of conscience. For instance, the practice of virtue, prayer, sensitivity to the Spirit, consultation, cultural and familial ambience, etc. More narrowly, the formation of conscience refers to the personal appropriation of moral knowledge, those more or less general principles that are the more immediate sources of conscience judgments.

8. Is the moral teaching of the magisterium binding on the Catholic conscience?

The practical moral teachings of the magisterium have a very important place in the formation of conscience. It is generally agreed that when the authentic magisterium makes moral pronouncements, such teachings pertain to the noninfallible magisterium. Traditionally the response to such teachings was said to be internal religious assent. That is, an assent that is sincere and internal (external conformity and respectful silence are insufficient), religious in character (motivated by belief that the Pope and the bishops with the Pope have received from Christ authority to teach). This assent was said to be morally (not absolutely) certain; that is, it does not exclude the possibility of error. Therefore, it is conditional, the conditions being variously expressed:

"unless a grave suspicion should arise that the presumption is not verified," "so long as it is not clear that these teachings are wrong."

The Second Vatican Council repeated this teaching when it said that "the faithful are to accept their [the bishops'] teaching and adhere to it with a religious assent of soul. This religious submission of will and of mind must be shown in a special way to the authentic teaching authority of the Roman Pontiff, even when he is not speaking ex cathedra."

This "religious assent" and this "submission of will and of mind" must not, however, be understood in such a way that study, discussion, personal reflection are foreclosed and ruled out of order. In the past decades this was too often the case. Just as the Church was conceptualized along highly juridical lines, so its teaching function was interpreted within such perspectives. "Submission of will and of mind" was too easily read to mean unquestioning, uncritical obedience.

With a change in several of the variables that influence the notion of Church and therefore the notion of the teaching Church, the proper response to the magisterium's authentic but noninfallible utterances ("submission of will and of mind") has undergone qualification. This response (on the part of those with sufficient competence) is said to be docility of mind and will, a cast of mind and bent of will open, ready and eager to assimilate the teaching, to make the wisdom of the teacher one's own. Such openness and readiness will translate into respect for the teacher and his office, a willingness to reassess one's own position, reluctance to conclude error on the part of the teacher, behavior in the public sphere which fosters respect for the teacher. If one brings these qualities to the noninfallible teachings of the magisterium, he has responded proportionately to the authority of the teacher. It is in this sense that the ethical teaching of the magisterium can be said to be binding on the Catholic conscience.

9. Does this mean that dissent is possible?

Yes, and this has always been provided for even in traditional theology, though it was not often emphasized.

10. When may a Catholic legitimately dissent from the moral teaching of the magisterium?

Assent may be withheld, indeed must be, when it is reasonably clear that the magisterium has inadequately formulated its teaching or even positively erred. It will be reasonably clear (not absolutely clear because such clarity eludes us in moral matters) when a competent individual, after arduous study, prayer and consultation, arrives at genuinely persuasive reasons and arguments against the teaching. This conclusion would be strengthened if other competent individuals arrived independently at the same conclusion. Such a phenomenon should be and will be a relatively rare happening if the magisterium is functioning in a healthy and fully collegiate way. But it can occur. As the Belgian bishops noted in their declaration on *Humanae Vitae:* "If someone competent in the matter and capable of forming a well-founded judgment—which necessarily supposes sufficient information —after serious investigation, before God, reaches different conclusions on certain points, he has the right to follow his convictions in this matter, provided that he remains disposed to continue his investigation."

11. Is public dissent ever legitimate?

The basic duty of one who believes that the magisterium has erred is to attempt to get the error corrected, unless this very attempt would carry with it greater evils. For delay in retracting or revising such a decision could easily undermine the credibility of the magisterium in the long run. The manner of attempted correction depends very much on the circumstances. But in circumstances where a teaching applies to very many, is widely publicized, and involves widespread and agonizing conflicts of conscience, public discussion can easily be the best, perhaps the only, means of resolving the problem. This means that public dissent, respectful and reverential, is not in principle illegitimate.

12. What is the proper relationship between the magisterium and moral theologians?

The relationship must be like that of all theologians and the magisterium, one of harmonious cooperation. For the teaching function of the Church involves at least the following processes: (1) the search for new understanding by asking fresh questions, hypothesizing, testing old formulations, attempting new ones; (2) the discovery of the action of the Spirit in the Church by eliciting the insights of all competences, encouraging communication and dialogue among Christians, supporting individual charisms; (3) the determination of the identifiable dimensions of Christian faith in our times by bringing the wisdom, reflection, experience of the entire Church to authoritative expression, either infallibly or in guidelines less than infallible; (4) the publication and circulation of this expression in an effective way through the various communications media. It is the interplay of these processes that constitute the teaching function of the Church. The experience of Vatican II provides a model of the relationship of theologians to the magisterium. The great documents of this council could not have been produced without the research and writing of the council's outstanding theologians. Yet these documents became authentic magisterial expressions only through acceptance by the college of bishops in union with the Roman Pontiff. It is recognition of the limits of one's own competence (whether he be bishop or theologian) and subsequent cooperation that prevents the existence of competitive magisteria in the Church.

13. How is one to weigh the opinion of theologians in the formation of one's conscience when this opinion is at variance with the official formulation of the magisterium?

This remains a debated question. Some theologians contend that the official position of the magisterium must take precedence over the opinions of theologians in the formation of conscience. Others, viewing Church teaching in more processive terms, view the response of theologians and other well informed persons in the Church as an integral part of the teaching-learning process within the Church. In this perspective, when there is widespread and presumably responsible theological dissent in the Church on a certain point, these theologians assert that a person may legitimately take account of such dissent in the formation of his conscience. For when such dissent originates with reputable and responsible theologians it reflects the inherently probable or tenable character of their positions.

14. Is such a conclusion a use of probabilism?

At the practical level of conscience-formation it is. However, the problem is much broader than that. It concerns ecclesiology above all especially how the magisterium of the Church should be conceived, how its pronouncements relate to the individual conscience, how it must be compared with other sources of enlightenment available to Christians in the formation of their conscience. When these larger questions are in a state of transition or are the subject of disagreement, the individual should not be held to a conclusion which presupposes a single view of these broader issues.

15. When a Christian is in doubt about the moral goodness of an action, what should he do?

Since it is immoral to act with a conscience uncertain about the morality of the action in question, the doubt should be resolved. Traditionally, three steps have been proposed for the resolution of practical doubts and there is nothing in contemporary theology to undermine the validity of this approach. First, one should attempt to solve the doubt directly, that is, the morality of the act in itself should be considered by weighing the evidence and arguments, by consulting experts or books that give reasonable certainity about the moral character of the action in question. Secondly, when the first step fails and one cannot discover the moral character of the act from direct evidence, then sources other than a consideration of the action in itself can give certainty. These are known technically as "proximate reflex principles." One such is the following: in choosing a necessary means to attain a necessary end, the safer means must be chosen. For instance, one may not rest satisfied with a baptism that is only doubtfully valid when one that is certainly valid is possible. There are several such proximate reflex principles. Finally, if neither the first nor second step succeeds in removing the doubt, one may have recourse to the remote reflex principle of probabilism. This principle asserts that even though a doubt remains about the inherent morality of the action to be placed, one is morally free to choose that course for which there are solidly probable reasons. This principle has had an honored if turbulent place in the history of moral theology.

16. But is probabilism still useful and valid in an era when moral theology is purifying itself from an excessive preoccupation with casuistry? What are the limitations of the principle of probabilism?

No purification or renewal of Christian morals can do away with the fact and urgency of concrete decisions. As long as these decisions are to be made and as long as uncertainty adheres to some of them, some such reflex principle is essential for the achievement of certainty of conscience. In broader perspective, probabilism—by whatever name it is called—remains a tribute to the claims of human freedom against all systems or ideologies that would attempt unduly to restrict this freedom. Furthermore, it has indirectly benefitted the science of moral theology itself by preventing premature closure of difficult moral questions.

However, probabilism is not without its difficulties, difficulties inseparable from modifications in other areas of theology. It is often difficult to determine what is a genuinely probably opinion, who is a reputable theological authority, what weight is to be given to past and even present magisterial pronouncements. Furthermore, the very notion of a probable opinion on moral questions seems associated with an epistemology overly preoccupied with and confident of the achievement of a type of certainty that is frequently impossible. Chastened by history most reputable theologians have a renewed awareness of the depth and complexity of moral questions and prefer to grope, explore and question in an attempt to enlighten rather than to elaborate positions recognizable as "probable."

17. What is mortal sin?

Mortal sin is an act of fundamental liberty by which a man disposes of himself before God who is calling him through grace. It is therefore a fundamental option, in which an individual turns in rejection from the charity of Christ whether Christ is thematically known or not. It is the rupture of a covenant relationship with the God of salvation and therefore also with his People, the Church. Since mortal sin is a denial of charity, it bespeaks the death of the life of friendship with God. If such a mortal illness becomes one's final option, it effects eternal death. But as long as it is not final and definitive, conversion is possible, but only with the grace of Christ.

18. How should we understand fundamental liberty, a fundamental option?

The term "a fundamental option" or "the fundamental option" is very misleading. It suggests an action separate from and independent of concrete human activity. More accurately, fundamental liberty is an aspect or dimension of concrete human activity. It is the free determination of oneself with regard to the totality of existence, a fundamental self-determination or choice between love or selfishness, between the self and the God of salvation. Such self-determination can only occur in and as an aspect of concrete human choice. It is only when such self-determination does occur that we may speak of a serious moral act, whether good or bad. Such radical self-disposition is conscious, but very obscure since it pertains to a form of self-knowledge profoundly identified with the person himself and his mystery.

19. Is the use of such fundamental liberty frequent in our activity? In other words, are serious moral acts of frequent occurrence?

Choices originating out of the core of one's being, concerned as they are with acceptance or rejection of God's enabling grace and salvation, have unique dimensions and intensity. This excludes the possibility of frequent and repeated transitions between spiritual life and death. As St. Thomas noted: "Although grace is lost by a single act of mortal sin, it is not, however, easily lost. For the person in grace does not find it easy to perform such an act (mortally sinful) because of a contrary inclination." (De Ver., q97, a.l., ad 9). This suggests that truly serious moral acts are not as of frequent occurrence as catalogues of serious matter would suggest.

20. What is venial sin?

Venial sin is not an act of fundamental or core liberty. It is not a person's disposition of himself as a whole, or from the personal center of his being. It is rather a relatively superficial act involving only peripheral or slight freedom. Venial sin, committed as it is at a less central level of the person, is compatible with love of God (charity) alive in the depths of the soul. But it undermines the fervor of charity and, over a period of time, can dispose one for the commission of mortal sin.

21. When is a person capable of a serious moral act (mortal sin or act of charity)?

A person is capable of serious moral acts when that person is, at least in the depths of his person, in possession of his total self and capable of disposing of himself in a free manner. This will vary from person to person depending on circumstantial factors such as personality traits, parental influence, formal education, cultural variants. But it is generally agreed that sufficient moral maturity for the performance of serious moral acts is reached at a considerably later date than was earlier supposed. For instance it is generally agreed that children prior to adolescence are incapable of mortal sin.

22. How does the notion of fundamental liberty affect our notion of the moral-spiritual life?

It suggests above all that the moral life should be thought of as a continuous and dynamic growth process rather than a series of fragmented observances and avoidances. The moral-spiritual life is a gradual unfolding (or drying up) of our personal beings as Christians. The Holy Spirit within us is inviting to a progressive deepening, stabilizing, rendering more facile and dominant of our charity, building a growing likeness to the person of Christ, strengthening the biblical "*adhere Deo.*"

23. What is the meaning of serious matter where mortal sin is concerned?

Serious matter is that concrete human disorder likely to provoke an individual to the use of basic freedom in rejection of God. It is that peak moment in which a person can embody and seal a disintegrating relationship with the God of salvation. Whether an individual actually does sever his relationship with God (commit mortal sin), we generally cannot say with certainty.

24. Should we not distinguish three types of sin: mortal, serious, and venial?

This is a matter of debate and discussion at present. Some theologians, using the very helpful analogy of a marriage relationship, argue that there are incidents or actions within marriage which are not slight, but neither do they break up the marriage. They are serious but not deadly to the marriage. Similarly with the relationship to God. Others call attention to the fact that the basic difference between mortal and venial sin is the quality of liberty involved in the action (in the first instance, core or fundamental freedom; in the second slight or peripheral freedom). Thus if there are many degrees of peripheral freedom, some very slight, others quite serious and intense, and therefore if the term "venial" is not taken to be equivalent to "unimportant," then the threefold distinction seems unnecessary. But the fact remains that many people understand the term "venial" to mean "not important." The threefold division of sin is a practical way of calling attention to the inaccuracy and great danger of such an equation. But it can lead to unnecessary confusion.

25. Traditionally it was said that there are three requirements for serious sin: serious matter, full knowledge, full consent (these last two could combine into sufficiently full liberty). Does the notion of fundamental or core freedom add anything to, or modify that traditional presentation?

Yes, in two ways. First, though most people would not respond with core freedom where the matter involved is not perceived to be serious, still it is possible (though probably quite rare) that a self-disposing option could occur in slight matter. Secondly, and more importantly, when traditional theology and catechetics spoke of full freedom as required for the commission of mortal sin, it seems that this freedom was understood of and restricted to freedom of choice. This freedom has to do with the absence of the standard impediments (fear, force, passion, ignorance). It is utterly essential to the performance of serious moral acts. But it is not sufficient. Beyond this absence of impediments to object-choices there is also required the use of fundamental freedom, the self-disposition of a person in acceptance or rejection of the God of salvation. This dimension of moral activity, not new but newly recovered, seems to have been overlooked in the traditional understanding of "full liberty." For decades moral theologians spoke of "a fully free venial sin" *(peccatum veniale plene deliberatum)*. Strictly speaking this is a contradiction in terms. For if a sin is venial, only peripheral freedom is involved. If it is fully free, then fundamental or core freedom is involved. Hence by saying that an action was both venial and yet fully free, the freedom understood could have meant only freedom of choice, not fundamental freedom.

26. Can an individual act be a mortal sin?

A significant number of authors have begun to deny this. They argue that human freedom (core or fundamental freedom) is such that it can be realized only in a series or pattern of acts. Thus they see mortal sin as a process no single act of which need be or even can be "the mortal sin." Rather mortal sin is committed over a period of time. It is the undoing of a relationship and relationships disintegrate over a period of time, through growing infidelity and unconcern. This perspective represents a healthy reaction against an excessively act-oriented and fragmented notion of sin. Yet it may well be an overreaction. For it can be argued that if a single act (e.g., adultery, serious injustice) is properly understood it can embody the rupture of a relationship with God, and be mortally sinful. Properly understood, the individual action is not an abstract, atomized occurrence that happens in a five or ten minute span. It is the culmination of an experience involving doubts, vacillations, thought, desires, deliberations over a period of time. When the individual act is placed in a fuller, more realistic context, it seems that it can be mortally sinful.

Here the marriage relationship can be instructive. Marriages break up over a period of time, by daily neglect, unkindness, insensitivity. This is infidelity in the making. Adultery must be seen as the culmination of this process—an action wherein one embodies an accumulating unconcern and rejection. All serious matter should be viewed in this way, as a moment wherein a deteriorating relationship with God can be summed up, intensified and sealed—broken.

27. Can the violation of ecclesiastical law be mortally sinful?

If the matter is inherently serious, it could be the occasion of an existential break in one's relationship with God (serious matter to be understood in the realistic and processive sense indicated above). But what is inherently serious needs careful qualification. Ecclesiastical laws which prescribe a single act (e.g., observance of form for marriage) are much more easily vehicles for a serious moral response than those which prescribe repeated actions (e.g., observance of Sunday observance). For violations of such single important prescriptions can easily and perhaps often do include rejection of, or contempt for, the whole value-structure behind the prescription. On the other hand, where frequently prescribed actions are concerned, it is only substantial violation (which is gathered from one's habitual conduct) that is apt to occasion a serious moral response.

Faith, Hope and Charity

1. What is a virtue?
A virtue is a good habit, i.e., a habit that perfects a person's capacity for human or personal activity by disposing him to act rightly.

2. Is man alone the subject of virtues?
In this world, only man is the subject of virtues. For virtue perfects a being precisely as a person.

3. How does virtue perfect man as a person?
Personhood or being a person is constituted by transcendence, the openness to the Absolute and Infinite that enables a being to determine or "dispose of" himself in relationship to the Absolute, his fellow men and the rest of reality. This "self-disponibility" *vis-à-vis* the totality of reality is freedom in the sense of a capacity. Virtue perfects freedom by establishing man in the state of a right and good personal relationship to the rest of reality and by disposing him, consequently, to act in ways that express and deepen this relationship.

4. What kinds of virtue are there?
Besides moral virtues, which perfect the will, St. Thomas Aquinas, following Aristotle, recognized also intellectual virtues such as art and theoretical wisdom. But the latter type are virtues only in certain respect *(secundum quid)* because they make a person good only in a limited way and not precisely as a person, e.g., a good musician or metaphysician. Because they do not establish an individual in a right personal relationship with the Absolute, his fellow men and the rest of reality, the so-called intellectual virtues are not virtues in the full sense of the word. However, in addition to the moral virtues there are others, and these are theological virtues.

5. Why are some virtues called theological?
Some virtues are called theological because, as their name suggests,

they primarily establish an individual in a right personal relationship to God himself in his true personal identity and thus dispose the individual to acts that express and deepen this interpersonal relationship with God.

6. What are the theological virtues?

The theological virtues are faith, hope and charity.

7. Are the theological virtues supernatural?

The theological virtues are supernatural. Christian tradition has expressed this truth also by saying that they are infused into the soul directly by God. Although all creation is from God, a person's being in personal relation to God as he is in himself is a special gift, coming from God as gratuitously revealing and communicating himself to his creatures. Man's own part consists only in a Yes to God acting in him.

8. What is the relationship between the theological virtues and sanctifying grace?

This has always been a disputed question in theology. Some theologians have seen sanctifying grace as a substantive habit and virtues as operative habits. On this view, grace inheres in the substance of the soul, perfecting it in the order of existence, while virtues inhere in the operative faculties of the soul, perfecting them in relation to their acts. Other theologians, however, have maintained that sanctifying grace and the virtue of charity are identical.

Contemporary theology seems more inclined toward the latter understanding. The personalism that characterises much recent philosophy and theology makes it more difficult to conceive of charity, in the way of the past, as basically an act of the will. Love, on a personalist view, is the act of a person precisely as person. It is the act by which one person, in his personal individuality, relates himself to another in his unique identity and, in so doing, is related personally also to God, at least anonymously. This interpersonal relation, moreover, is understood as the apex of being, rather than as a mere "accident," which is by definition the lowest category of being. With love understood as the fulfillment or totality of personhood, it is hard to conceive of sanctifying grace as really distinct from the virtue of charity.

9. Are theological virtues the only supernatural virtues?

Although the common opinion of theologians in the past was said to be that there are supernatural, infused moral virtues, this does not seem to be the theological consensus today. Due to the work of Henri de Lubac, Karl Rahner and others, the supernatural order is now seen as more closely linked with nature than it previously seemed to be. In light of a better grasp of the intimate bond between grace and nature, the fact that charity is the form of all other virtues (q. 36) seems to render superfluous the postulate of infused moral virtues that reduplicate their acquired counterparts. Nevertheless, besides the theological virtues, there are certainly other supernatural gifts of God.

10. Are the theological virtues three different realities?

This question is somewhat connected with that concerning the relation between the theological virtues and sanctifying grace (q. 8). In a holistic view, faith, hope and charity together name the one ideal state of man or the state of perfection. Collectively the three virtues designate the state of a person existing (in this world) in the perfect kind of personal relationship primarily with God and secondarily with his fellow men and the rest of reality. From this standpoint it is already partially clear why Scripture can sometimes use only one word, e.g., "faith," to designate the same state that is named also "faith, hope and charity."

There is, however, a more basic reason for this biblical use of terms. Although there are really distinct and even separable aspects of the one state of perfection, the theological virtues, as we shall see when treating them individually, are only partially distinct from one another.

11. What is the relationship between the Church and the theological virtues?

The Church is the community that God has created by his gift of faith, hope and charity. This community is called by God to live the life that flows from this ideal state and thus to witness to the coming reign of God.

12. Are there theological virtues outside the Church?

The Church is not simply an either-or reality: either something is perfectly the Church or it is not the Church at all. The Second Vatican Council acknowledged churches of separated brethren while seeing them also as lacking the "fullness" or "total reality" of the Church. Something of the Church exists where its fullness is missing.

Similarly, the state of perfection is not an either-or reality: either something is perfectly the state of faith, hope and charity or it is not this state at all. Because of God's universal salvific will, Christ died for all men, and his grace is offered to everyone. Without explicit faith and hope, there can be charity. In this case a person participates in the one state of perfection, although its fullness is wanting. Rahner has aptly called such persons "anonymous Christians."

13. What is the virtue of faith?

In the past the act of faith was often defined as a firm intellectual assent to the truths revealed by God, based on the authority of God revealing them. The virtue of faith was defined as the habit by which man is disposed toward this act. However, this view of faith does not exhaust the riches of the biblical notion of faith. Rather, it expresses an essential aspect of faith.

We saw that "faith" in Scripture can bear the same meaning as "faith, hope and charity." But this meaning of "faith" is not a mere figure of speech in which a part stands for the whole. For faith is man's acceptance of God's revelation. And this revelation is not only a disclosure of information. It is primarily God's disclosure of himself, a disclosure culminating in the Person of Christ. Christ himself is the revelation par excellence. Hence the acceptance of revelation is not simply an assent to divinely revealed information; it is, above all, an acceptance of the Person of Christ, through whom man has access to the Father. Thus, in Rahner's words, faith is "primarily the ordination of the whole human person to God, since the act of faith totally concerns and engages the whole man."

Moreover, of the essence of faith is its communal character. Faith is, first of all, the faith of the People of God, and the individual Christian possesses this gift of God inasmuch as God has enabled him to share the faith of the Church.

14. What is the role of intellectual assent in faith?

Faith is the acceptance of the divine communication. Interpersonal communication, however, is not primarily the transferring of information, even information about oneself, from one person to another. Rather, it is a person's communication of *himself,* making himself known, to another. Although it is not completely identical with providing or manifesting facts about oneself, interpersonal communication includes this. Conversely, knowing another person, although not identical with knowing about him, does include such knowing.

Through faith man accepts and knows Christ himself and, in him, the Father. But in order to know Christ, one must know about him, i.e., intellectually assent to truths about him and his Father which are contained in the gospel. Thus faith comes from hearing the gospel preached (Rom. 10:17).

15. What is the special duty regarding faith incumbent on the magisterium of the Church?

Since faith includes intellectual assent to truths about God and his self-communication to man, the magisterium guards and preserves the authenticity of the Church's faith by determining and upholding the truths to which intellectual assent should be given and by rejecting notions incompatible with these truths.

16. Can faith be lost?

Although the faith of the Church, through promised divine assistance, cannot fail, any individual can lose faith. Inasmuch as faith is an intellectual assent based, not on compelling evidence, but on the influence of a person's own will (q. 13), the believer remains always capable of inclining himself away from this assent, just as he allows himself to be inclined toward it. And inasmuch as faith is a commitment to God that engages the whole person, it is love and authentic or realized freedom. But in this life no individual's hold on love and freedom is absolute; it is possible for anyone to slip into the bondage of sin.

17. Is the loss of faith always a mortal sin?

Since, in addition to grave matter, other conditions are necessary for mortal sin, viz. "sufficient reflection and full consent of the will," one may not designate any gravely wrong behavior (e.g., blasphemy) as mortal sin without further ado. However, faith, in the sense of a personal acceptance of and commitment to Christ is not simply a kind of external behavior. It is an interior state. Since God is always faithful, it is not possible for a person to reject the Lord whom he had accepted without sinning mortally. Indeed, this rejection is the epitome of mortal sin.

However, faith in the sense of personal commitment to Christ presupposes religious maturity, which may or may not be present with physical or emotional maturity. Long before he has achieved "the use of reason"—not to mention the use of "self-disponibility" (q. 3)—a child can and does assent to religious truths that he is taught. But he cannot realize faith in the full sense of the term. Thus, it is possible that an older person, e.g., a college student, mature in other ways but religiously immature, can reject his faith in the sense of intellectual beliefs without sinning mortally. This case is to some extent comparable with the situation of a person, baptized in infancy but never taught the truths of faith. In both cases the person has never arrived at faith in the full sense.

18. Why is the loss of faith as personal commitment the epitome of mortal sin?

The quintessence of mortal sin is the rejection of God and a personal relationship with him. In turning deliberately against his neighbor, a person turns also against God. But in the loss or refusal of faith, a person directly and explicitly turns away from God himself.

19. Is the virtue of faith lost by any mortal sin?

Yes, the *virtue* of faith is lost by mortal sin. As St. Thomas taught, the faith that is not informed by charity is not a virtue.

Faith as the commitment of oneself to God communicating himself is not really distinct from love and authentic freedom (q. 16), i.e., from charity. It is faith in this sense that is obviously lost by the breaking of one's relationship with God, which is mortal sin.

Faith as a state of intellectual assent is not necessarily lost by mortal sin. But faith in this sense is not the virtue of faith. As such it is basically an "intellectual virtue" and thus not virtue in the full sense of the word (q. 4). For it makes an individual only a "good believer" and not a good person. Moreover, even the intellectual assent of faith is based on the will, and the motive for willing assent is the authority of God revealing (q. 13). Hence the turning away from God that is mortal sin cannot but weaken one's very motive for assent and thus render even the intellectual assent of *fides informis* more precarious than that of *fides formata*.

20. Are there degrees of faith?

The state of perfection or ideal state of man that is faith, hope and charity is not an either-or reality, either complete and perfect or altogether missing (q. 12). And being in this state of perfection is not the same as being perfect in this state, just as the notion that religious life is the state of perfection never implied that the individual religious was perfect.

Moreover, an individual can realize faith as intellectual assent earlier in life than he can realize it as a personal acceptance of the Lord that involves his own total person. There are, then, degrees of faith, and man should grow in it.

21. What is the relation between divine revelation and growth in faith?

God's self-revelation is an historical process of many centuries which reached its climax in Jesus Christ. The life, death and resurrection of Christ and his sending of the Holy Spirit are themselves so many cumulative phases in the historical process of revelation. Just as God's revelation to the human race is a gradual process spread out in history, so also this revelation comes to the individual gradually and extended in time. The response of the individual, which is faith, should develop and mature as God's self-revelation comes to him ever more fully.

22. What is the virtue of hope?

Hope has traditionally been defined as the supernatural habit by which man is disposed to trust with certainty that God will grant him eternal life and the means necessary to attain it. Here again, however, a theological virtue is seen from a very narrow perspective while Scripture offers a larger view, in which hope is not entirely distinct from faith. For to trust that God will bring to completion the saving work that he has begun in man is not totally different from the faith by which man wholly accepts the God who reveals himself as man's loving Savior.

The serious inadequacy of the traditional definition is that hope appears self-centered: an individual trusts that he himself will be granted beatitude by God. But the true object of Christian hope is primarily God's glory, the universal reign of God, through which all creation will be definitively liberated from sin. For hope is the virtue by which a Christian, in the words of the Eucharistic Liturgy, waits in joyful hope for the coming of our Savior, Jesus Christ.

23. Is the virtue of hope lost by any mortal sin?

Like the virtue of faith (q. 19), the virtue of hope is lost by mortal sin. For without charity there can be no true virtue.

Understanding hope, in the traditional way, as the expectation of one's own beatitude from God, St. Thomas asked whether a person can hope for beatitude also for someone else. His answer was that hope is ordered indirectly, not absolutely, to the eternal happiness of others. This means that it is love that orders an individual directly to others, and only through it does he hope for their beatitude. Thus, even according to the traditional view, the loss of charity that is mortal sin must reduce hope to more than hope for one's own beatitude from God. But this self-centered expectation is, to say the least, not the fullness of the virtue of Christian hope.

24. Can a person in mortal sin hope?

Note must be taken here of the fact that the theology of sin is currently maturing. In recent years emerged the conviction that there are fewer mortal sins committed than previously supposed. This opinion arose in conjunction with the view that mortal sin consists much more in rejecting a personal relationship with God than in the commission or omission of a single act—a view that does not necessarily deny that an individual act can embody this rejection of God. At present, moreover, this view is evolving into the theological opinion that sin is inadequately divided into only two catergories, mortal and venial. Between these two divisions some theologians now introduce a third: serious sin. Serious sin, distinct from mortal sin, is seen as acts that express evil trends in a person's heart without bringing about a radical rejection of God.

It remains to be seen how this new theology will be further refined and whether it will eventually win general acceptance. But, if we assume it here, it becomes clearer than it was in the past that the hope of the person in the state of mortal sin is the disordered hope called presumption. For the person in mortal sin lacks the charity that would enable him to hope for the universal salvation of others (q. 23). Moreover, he has turned himself away from God in the depths of his being. With no love or concern for God, a person expecting God to save him is egotistical and rash. To the extent, however, that the sinner begins to desire in some way to be converted himself, his hope ceases to be inordinate, and he is already responding to God's uninterrupted offer of grace, calling him to be converted from sin to God.

25. What is despair?

Like presumption, despair is an abuse of hope, but an opposite one. It has traditionally been defined as the loss of confidence in obtaining from God one's beatitude and the means to arrive at it.

While the virtue of hope is a state of hope primarily for all creation (q. 22), despair is contrary to hope as hope for oneself. To lose hope for mankind is not really distinct from losing faith in the God who has revealed himself as the universal Savior. And to retain faith while losing hope only for oneself seems to be, besides a distortion of faith itself, more a psychological and emotional crisis, perhaps generated by past sins, than a mortal sin in itself. Obviously, despair is a grievous matter. But it is very difficult to conceive how a person who despairs could fulfill in this act the other conditions requisite for mortal sin. It is particularly difficult to believe that a person who despairs does so with full consent of the will or in a radically free act. Theology therefore must be careful not to create an exaggerated notion of what presumption and despair have in common.

26. What is the virtue of charity?

Charity is the love of God poured forth into our hearts. Specifically as a virtue, charity is the transformation of the creature's heart that is brought about by the outpouring of God's personal love, which is God himself. Through this transformation of his heart, man participates in the divine Love that is Life and is enabled to love God and his neighbor as God loves.

27. What is love?

In the pre-personalist thinking of the past, man was seen primarily as the rational animal rather than as a person in relation to other persons. Love was defined, in the manner of "faculty psychology," around the central notion of appetite. It was seen as an act of the intellectual appetite or will. With this wide understanding of "love," one could speak, for example, of a love for football and beer as well as of love for another person.

More adequately understood, however, love is a person's relating himself as one to another. It is the opening of oneself to another person, the personal giving of oneself to another and the personal acceptance of him as the person he is.

28. Are charity and love the same?

If love is defined, on the basis of appetite or desire, as the inclining of the will toward a real or apparent good, charity and love are not identical. But if love is understood as a person's unselfish giving of himself to another and the receiving of the other into his own life, charity and love are identical.

29. Can there be charity without faith?

Because God wills the salvation of all mankind, his outpouring of grace is not confined to the Church. The love of God is poured forth into the hearts of others besides those professing the Christian faith. However, in the case of these "anonymous Christians" it is not idle to speak of a transcendental or implicit faith based on divine transcendental revelation. In our order of salvation God offers himself personally to everyone. This self-offer of God that comes to each person by reason of his existing in the order of salvation has been called by Rahner man's "supernatural existential." Looked at from God's side, it is his transcendental self-revelation, and man's acceptance of it is transcendental or implicit faith. Although the idea of transcendental faith is not easily conceived, it will appear less strange and contrived if we recall that faith is not primarily an intellectual assent but an involvement of the whole person with the Mystery that is God (q. 13).

30. What is the relation between charity and the natural law?

The Church has always held that the life of charity in man is eternal, supernatural life in its inchoative form, and that man cannot, in Pelagian fashion, raise himself to it. Furthermore, as long as the Church has seen morality as based on the natural law, it has taught that man cannot live his life according to the natural law, i.e., in substantial accord with it, without supernatural help from God.

In light of a clearer perception of the intimate bond between nature and grace (q. 9), one must now add that the natural law is the law of charity. This conclusion, however, does not imply that nature is grace or charity or that the natural is the supernatural.

The natural law is the design or law of man's being as a person, and a person is designed for interpersonal, not solipsistic, existence. By the very design of his being a person can be "completed" or fulfilled only in the interpersonal reality of love and, ultimately, only in that universal love in which all persons are fully united. Only in the infinite and universal Love that is God himself can all mankind be gathered together to achieve the fullness of their own interpersonal nature.

The basic reason, then, for man's inability to live in accord with the natural law without a supernatural gift from God is that the natural law is the law of love, and true love is charity.

31. How is love supernatural?

God is love, and love is the personal life of God as he is in himself.

True human love is a participation in the life of God as he is in himself and is therefore supernatural. For authentic love is the selfless giving of oneself and accepting of the other into one's own existence, just as the Father communicates his being to the Son, and the Son lives by and for the Father.

To live a moral life is to live a life based on love. But in order to live a life based on love, a person must first accept Love into his heart as the Absolute in his life. This acceptance into one's own soul of Love as Absolute is in fact the acceptance of God's supernatural self-offer to oneself, God's gift of himself as he is in himself.

32. What is the law of charity?

The law of charity is the twofold law of love taught by Jesus. The first commandment is, " '. . . you shall love the Lord with all your heart . . .'. This is the second, 'You shall love your neighbor as your-self' " (Mk. 12:30–31).

33. Does the law of charity require a person to love himself?

Love, in the proper sense of the term, is an interpersonal act; by its very nature it is unitive, bringing one person into personal relationship with another (q. 27). Since love is really the outgoing reality in which a person gives himself to another and accepts the other as he is, the disposition or attitude called "self-love" would be better designated by another name, e.g., self-affirmation or self-esteem. In any case, it is of the utmost importance to recognize the *essential* difference between the interpersonal, unitive state of real love and the self-centered disposition called "self-love."

The New Testament clearly presents the law of charity as a twofold, not a threefold, commandment: the duty to love God and the duty to love one's neighbor. In the Synoptics' accounts of the public life of Jesus, he is seen preaching the second duty, like the first, as it was taught from of old: "You shall love your neighbor as yourself" (Lev. 18:19). But Jesus taught this duty also in the form of the golden rule, "Treat others the way you would have them treat you." Thus, he saw this rule as summing up the law and the prophets (Mt. 7:12), just as he saw the law of love as this same summary (Mt. 22:40), and just as St. Paul would see the Leviticus commandment as the summary of the law (Rom. 13:8). Neither the Leviticus commandment nor the golden rule expresses any other duty than that of loving one's neighbor. Finally, at the Last Supper, in St. John's Gospel, Jesus teaches his disciples the second commandment in its perfect form, "a new commandment": "Such as my love has been for you, so must your love be for each other" (Jn. 13:34). The measure of a disciple's second duty is no longer seen as his disposition toward himself; it is Christ's love for him.

34. Why has theology in the past seen the law of charity as a threefold, rather than a twofold, commandment?

Theology saw a threefold commandment, adding a commandment to love oneself, where Scripture sees only a twofold commandment because theology adopted Hellenistic philosophical views. In Greek philosophy, love was defined on the basis of the notion of appetite (q. 27). Thus, love was not seen to be essentially an interpersonal giving of oneself, and a self-centered understanding of love came into Christian thought.

35. Besides his duties toward God and his neighbor, does a person have duties regarding himself?

A person has many duties regarding himself. However, these duties are not based on a supposed law of charity that commands him to love himself. Jesus is, as the contemporary phrase aptly asserts, the man for others, and the law of charity is that everyone else should be like him. Each person has been called by God into the midst of mankind and has been given a vocation to build up this community toward the kingdom of God. A person's duty toward God, who has called him, and his duty toward the community, into whose midst he has been called, are the basis of an individual's duty regarding himself. In short, God's glory, his kingdom, and not a supposed law to love oneself, are the foundation of any individual's duties toward himself.

36. How is charity the form of all other virtues?

We have already seen that without charity neither faith (q. 19) nor hope (q. 23) are true virtues. Hence here we must consider only the relation between charity and moral virtues. But charity itself is a moral virtue and not only a theological virtue. For by this one virtue a person is oriented, not only to God in himself, but also to his neighbor in himself.

That charity is both a theological and moral virtue indicates that it is a unique kind of moral virtue and that it holds the primacy among moral virtues.

Agere sequitur esse. It could be said that charity is the virtue of being (i.e., of *being* in relation to others), and the other moral virtues are virtues of doing. Or, charity is the virtue of caring, and all authentic moral activity presupposes this caring. Charity is the virtue by which a person is predisposed to enter into, to *exist* in, personal relationship with whomever he can. Before the Good Samaritan could *act* virtuously toward the man lying by the wayside, he had to *care*. He had to care about this man as a person, i.e., he had to allow himself to be affected by this other so that the other's existence became entwined with his own. In other words, the Good Samaritan had first to relate himself personally to the other, allowing him room in his own life. The priest and the Levite, on the other hand, exercised neither compassion nor generosity nor any other moral virtue because they did not care. They did not allow their own personal lives to be touched or affected by the man whom they passed by.

Charity, then, is that fundamental virtue of the moral order by which a person is disposed to allow himself to be affected by others and to care about them and, consequently, to act toward them according to their different needs in varying situations. Every other moral virtue is a specific disposition toward a particular kind of moral activity that responds to certain needs of people in some situations. But charity is the universal virtue of caring that responds to the universal need of all men in every situation.

Thus, charity, unlike the other moral virtues, is not ordered to a particular kind of deed. Rather, it is ordered, through the particular moral virtues, to the deeds of all of them. It is the deeds of these other moral virtues that are the works of charity. Further, a habit can be a virtue only through charity, i.e., only if it is based upon the caring that is charity. Thus, the numerous deeds commanded by the law are all summed up in those two prescriptions of the law that constitute the law of love.

PART FOUR

Living the Christian Life

Religion and Piety
*The First Four Commandments**

A DIALOGUE BETWEEN GOD AND MAN

1. Why are the first four commandments of the decalogue brought together under one title?

The decalogue is not a collection of unrelated statements. It is a group of commandments which try to describe man's responsibilities to God, to himself, and to his neighbor. The first four commandments can be considered a dialogue between God and man.

The first commandment has two parts: "I am the Lord your God," and "you shall have no other gods before me." The first sentence is, as it were, an all-embracing statement which gives meaning and direction to all the subsequent commandments by stating the unique position of God as the origin and goal of all that exists. In the light of this statement man must relate to God as well as to his fellowman. The second sentence points out that this unique honor which belongs to the creator cannot be given to any other being. It would be offensive to God and detrimental to man himself to do so.

The second commandment which forbids the irreverent use of the Lord's name points essentially to the same thing. In the Old Testament, much more than in our time, the knowledge and the use of a person's name was an indication that one was acquainted with the inner depth of this person. The Jews were not allowed to mention the

*There are at least four different systems of numbering the Ten Commandments, or the Decalogue, widely used in the United States: that used by Western Roman Catholics and one used by Lutherans, differing only in the last two commandments; and the traditional Jewish numbering and the Eastern Christian system, followed also by most English-speaking Protestants, dividing what we call the First Commandment into two so that what are numbered Second to Eighth in this catechism are Third to Ninth for them. Cf. *Catholic Biblical Encyclopedia, Old Testament,* "Decalogue."

name of Jahweh because his person could never be fully understood by man. He could only be referred to as the God and the source of being. To misuse his name would mean to reduce God to the level of a creature.

The third commandment points out that it is necessary for man to express the deeper meaning of his life in visible human terms. Individually as well as in society, man needs to set time aside to express his dependence on God through visible acts of worship.

The fourth commandment seems to refer to an interhuman relationship rather than to a relationship between God and men. However, it gives us also a concrete form in which the creative, life-giving self-extension of God is in dialogue with responsible human self-unfolding. This dialogue is expressed in the interaction and mutual responsibilities between parent and child, and between individual and society.

In these four commandments God seems to reveal himself to men and he asks from men a concrete human response.

MAN CAN ADORE ONLY ONE GOD

2. What does it mean that man can adore only one God?

This means that God must be the goal of human life. Man is created in the image of God. The fullness of "being human" asks that man express that his life is a mystery of the manifestation of God's presence and God's love. Consequently, the more the human potential is constructively developed and activated, the more does man make God's presence and goodness a visible reality on earth. The concrete human reality, however, demands also that man express in visible terms his complete dependence on God. The acts through which this complete dependence on God and the deeper meaning of human life are made visible are called acts of worship.

3. Which elements are required before a human action is really an act of worship?

Before an action can really be called an act of worship there are several requirements. First, the action must express in some symbolic way man's recognition of God as the master of human life. Second, it must express man's willingness to accept this authority of God. And third, it must somehow express that the individual precisely as a member of a community recognizes God's authority. Every human being finds his fullness only in a human community in which he becomes more deeply human through interaction with others. This element of his being must also enter into his dialogue with God.

4. Which are the more important acts of worship in the Christian faith?

The most important act of worship in the Christian faith is the self-giving of Christ to the Father. The total life of Christ was one continuous expression of complete dedication to the Father. This dedication culminated in the death upon the cross. In the eucharistic celebration Christ continues this self-giving to the Father in a manner which is simultaneously symbolic and real. The actual participation in this act of worship is for the Christian community the most fundamental expression of the deepest meaning of human life. However, St. Augustine admonishes us that "the sacrifice on the altar stone is meaningless if it is not accompanied by the sacrifice on the altar of the heart." Therefore, acts of worship must be integrated into daily life. Worship and morality cannot be separated.

There are many other human activities which can properly be called acts of worship. Perhaps the more important among them is the vow.

5. What is the meaning and the religious value of a vow?

A vow is an act designed to make one's every day human living an act of worship. A person does this by making a special promise to perform a specific act (such as prayer, pilgrimage, working for the poor) or to live in a particular life (such as the priesthood, the religious life, etc.) so that the action or the way of living itself expresses a special dedication to God. Although in everyday life man honors God by his human activity, in a vow he takes on an extra obligation and responsibility to make his life itself an act of worship.

6. Does that mean that every promise one makes to God is a vow?

No, the promises one makes to God are usually not vows. Such promises express the individual's intention to show his gratitude or respect for God in a special way, but they do not have the particular strength of a vow. A vow adds to the promise the responsibility that if one does not live according to the vow one commits a special sin. Therefore, a vow is rare and demands more serious thought, deliberation and preparation than is necessary in a spontaneous promise. Vows can be either public or private.

7. When is a vow "private"?

A vow is private when it is made by an individual alone. This means that he does not make it as a member of an organization or as a member of the Church. Nor does he inform any authority of his having made it. It is a matter only between God and himself. For instance, an individual can make a vow to work for the poor without pay for one month. This is a commitment that he as an individual makes before God.

Obviously, such a vow cannot be valid unless the person knows quite well what he is doing. He also must be free to make such a vow, and the work that he promises must be within his abilities. Therefore a vow is a very serious matter since it is a special form of worship-through-life which demands full human involvement.

8. When is a vow "public"?

A vow is public when it includes also a special responsibility to the Christian community and a recognition by the ecclesiastical authorities as a special responsibility to God in the Church. The more common examples of such public vows are those taken in religious orders, and, although it is not usually called a vow, the promise of celibacy as required of priests. These vows are made to God within the community for the sake of the community.

In the vow of obedience we see a readiness to put one's abilities at the service of the community at places where these services are most needed. In that of poverty the person makes a deliberate effort to place material possessions at the service of God's concern for mankind. In celibacy there is a dedication of one's own personality to extend God's loving concern to all of humanity.

In these vows there is a definite effort to make human life an act of worship to God. This life style contains a kind of representation of all of mankind before God. Consequently, it is necessary that the authority of the Church accept them, otherwise they cannot be valid.

9. Since there is such a close relationship between daily life and worship, there might be more service of God in "apostolic" labor than in prayer.

It has always been the Church's teaching that prayer which does not somehow induce service to others is sterile and meaningless. Genuine interhuman concern is a true form of worship (cf. James 1:27). The human condition, however, makes it necessary to express the spiritual meaning of life in visible terms. The orientation to God must become visible precisely as orientation to God. This means that a certain form of prayer is necessary. Moreover, because the human being is present in this world in and through the material existence, he tends to focus on the material existence. In daily human existence we may safely say that human activity is prayer only when human life is a life of prayer.

10. Is is possible that certain actions are intended to be acts of worship, but in fact they are offensive to God?

Yes, this is possible and it even may be fairly common among certain people. It occurs mostly in superstitious practices.

11. What are superstitious practices?

Superstition has a different meaning for different persons. Some actions which are seemingly the same can be expressions of a deep faith for one person while they are superstitious acts for another person. One should be very careful in making a judgment in this matter.

The ultimately decisive factor determining whether an action is superstitious or not is when a specific spiritual effect is inappropriately and with too high a degree of causality related to the performance of a specific religious expression.

Superstition distorts man's view on the absolute sovereignty of God. It is inspired by the idea that man can, by his own expert ritual words and actions, propitiate God or the heavenly forces on which he feels that his own mysterious existence depends. In the final analysis, in superstitious practices man makes God dependent on man's own ritual words and actions.

12. Aren't superstitious practices a thing of the past?

Not really, for they may be more common than many people care to admit. Either jokingly or in a serious vein many people believe in the magical power of certain words, actions or objects; some may be very hesitant to make any important decisions on Friday the thirteenth; others will consult their horoscope before they make any important decision, or they consult "spirits" to find out the course of their lives. Even people who claim to have no religion at all may still adhere to superstitious practices.

13. Is there any difference between superstition and magic?

There is a difference. Magic is always superstition, but superstition is not always magic. In superstition man believes that he can propitiate God or the heavenly forces by his own ritual words or actions. The power actually remains God's power. In magic man believes that supra-human powers are either localized in certain rituals or objects, or that they can be controlled and manipulated by certain ritual words or actions. The "divine" or heavenly powers come literally under human control. For instance the power of protection is contained in the good-luck charm in the car.

14. Isn't then the use of medals, crucifix, etc. a form of superstition or magic?

Only when medals, crucifix, etc. are *misused* can their use become superstition or magic. The decisive difference between "magic" and "other actions" is situated in this, that the "other actions" are placed entirely in the service of God and are inspired by prayer. Their whole structure is, as it were, a dialogue with God. These actions are prayerful expressions of petition, of gratitude or of respect, while man hopes to receive God's blessings because of this. In "magic" the structure of the action is manipulation or control over the supra-human powers. Thus, the use of a medal (e.g. St. Christopher) may be a humble prayer for protection in honor of this saint; it may also be a manipulative gesture to control powers beyond one's own.

15. Is it superstition to believe in one's horoscope?

Belief in one's horoscope can mean several things. It can mean to accept that certain conditions of climate or season, or certain stellar constellations exercise a certain influence or create a specific predisposition in human beings without controlling human life. This is not readily superstition. Such influences may or may not be real but whatever, the human being retains his freedom. If, however, belief in one's horoscope means that climate and season and constellations exercise a direct power over man, and that man can control this power by certain ritual words or actions or abstension from such actions, then the expressions become a form of superstition. In such circumstances man begins to accept "super" human powers where there are none and then he tries to gain control over these super-human powers by unrelated actions.

16. What is spiritism?

Spiritism, in the strict sense of the word, is the practice of entering into communication with spirits, usually with spirits of defunct persons. Such communications are usually established in a special ceremony via a "medium."

Spiritism is very different from Extra Sensory Perception (ESP). Scientists debate (many accept, many reject,) the possibility of ESP. People who believe in ESP speak about interhuman communication through psychic energy which as yet can not be explained. There is no question of control of superhuman powers.

In spiritism, however, there is supposed to be a direct communication between the human and the world of spirits. The world of spirits is made subject to and is controlled by human formulas. Since human power cannot reach beyond its own way of being, spiritism claims to control the intervention of either divine powers or the powers of the devil. In both instances man would appropriate to himself these spiritual powers in defiance of God.

GOD DEMANDS RESPECT FOR HIS PERSON

17. How is respect for God's person primarily expressed in human life?

In general, respect for God's person is primarily expressed though a human life which is truly lived in the image of God. This means a human life that is lived in interhuman concern and in worship. More particularly, however, respect for God's person is expressed when respect is shown to his name, to persons who represent him, and to objects that are set aside for his service. Respect for his name is primarily shown in the taking of an oath. Respect for persons and objects dedicated to his service is expressed in behavioral patterns, too many to enumerate. Frequently, such behavioral patterns become more clear by a study of their major opposites which more frequently occur for instance, sacrilege, blasphemy and simony.

18. How does an oath express a special respect for God's person?

An oath is an act in which one calls upon God to witness to the truth of a statement that one makes. For a person who believes he is created in the image of God, and who accepts that God is the source of all existence and the origin of all truth, an oath is the strongest possible affirmation of truthfulness that he can make.

The oath is an explicit recognition of God's authority and majesty. A person who takes the oath expresses explicitly that he accepts God's majesty and that he declares his statement to be as true as God is true. The human community in front of whom the oath is taken accepts the truth of the statement as they accept the truth of God.

Because of its deeply religious nature an oath is a very important human expression. Consequently, it is necessary that it be taken only for significant reasons. The American regulations to add an oath to a great variety of official documents may tend to reduce the oath to a routine matter. This custom can easily cheapen the oath and obscure its religious value. The person who takes the oath must know what he is doing since the oath includes a personal dedication to God in the matter of truth. The statements for which the oath is taken must be true, or at least the person who takes the oath must be honestly convinced of their truth and accuracy. Finally, the oath must be taken in a formula that can be recognized and accepted by the community as a special form of reverence to God.

Because of the deeply religious nature of an oath and because of its importance in the society it is obvious that perjury in any form or degree is highly offensive to God, to oneself and to the human community.

19. How is a sacrilege offensive to the person of God?

A sacrilege is an irreverence for a person, an object or a place precisely in so far as this person, object and place are sacred because of their dedication to God.

It is true that God is present everywhere and that every existing being belongs to God. However, God cannot be seen by men. Therefore, in all human dealings with God, particularly in the relationship of the community with God, persons, places and objects are set aside specifically for the relationship between the community and the divine. They receive a special task and meaning which put them in a different category than other persons, places or objects. They are in this different category, not because of any personal or material superiority, but because they represent the divine with men as well as representing the community before God. The reverence given them reflects the reverence that individuals and a community have for God. On the other hand, the irreverence expressed to them also reflects the individual's or community's lack or respect for the divine.

20. What kind of irreverence constitutes a sacrilege?

The special reverence which is given to persons, places, and objects is not due to any personal or material superiority but exclusively to their dedication to the service of the community. Consequently, the irreverence which constitutes a sacrilege would be the kind of irreverence which counteracts this special dedication. For persons this irreverence would be shown in an unjust physical attack upon the persons or in an unjust slanderous attack upon their personality, but not, for instance in arguing with them or in a just, physical defense against him.

Another form of sacrilege which perhaps occurs more frequently is the irreverence towards sacraments, particularly by the reception of sacraments when one knows that their reception would be invalid or illicit. Since the sacraments are the signs and reality of God's presence with men, irreverence toward them is particularly serious.

For places it would mean using such places for purposes which are either offensive to God or which would suggest that the community's relationship to God is not above material values. For instance if a church were used as a recreation center without any necessity.

Concerning objects, especially vessels and vestments, it would become an irreverence to use them for profane usages without any special reason. There are no strict guidelines one can follow since reverence and respect are subject to cultural values and changes.

21. Can persons, places and objects lose their character of sacredness?

Yes, this happens rather frequently. Churches become delapidated or are not any more needed for other reasons. Vessels and vestments become worn out, and so forth. Frequently so-called sacred objects are destroyed when they cannot be used any more. Churches can be converted into other uses with permission and by decree of competent authorities. Religious authorities who established such places as sacred also can bring them back to profane daily use.

Persons too, can lose their "sacredness" by relinquishing the representative functions they had. A religious can be dispensed from his/her vows, a priest can leave the active ministry. As soon as they have left the specific state or function which makes them representative of the religious bond between God and mankind they also lose the characteristic which would make grave irreverence against a sacrilege.

22. What is the meaning of blasphemy?

Blasphemy is intentionally insulting or denying the goodness of God. It is, therefore, directly opposed to the reverence and respect which is due to God as a person. Blasphemy can occur in various forms. It can be immediately directed against God when, for instance, one would express the wish that God didn't exist, or one accuses God of injustice or cruelty. It also may be directed against a fellowman when one would ask God to act contrary to his goodness and justice by destroying another person.

Blasphemy does not occur frequently. In many instances the verbal expressions which sound blasphemous are said in anger and not at all or only partially intended. This is particularly the case in profane language which usually is only an emotionally release although it does express a disrespect for God and for one's fellowmen.

23. What is simony?

Simony is the deliberate design of selling or buying something spiritual or something that is annexed to the spiritual. This means that one would try to put a monetary value on something which is spiritual. In final analysis this would place God in the same value category as material things. Simony can be the direct design to "buy" something spiritual, such as the graces of the sacraments, or to buy spiritual power by buying certain ecclesiastical (spiritual) functions, or to exchange one function for another. Respect for the person of God demands abstention from all trading of the spiritual.

Frequently payment is offered for eucharistic celebrations and other spiritual functions. Such payments are not simony, but remunerations for the physical labor and materials involved, and for the sustenance of the ministry. Because of their external similarity with simony, however, many places prefer to provide the minister with an adequate salary and to discontinue such payments on occasions of spiritual functions.

MAN'S RECOGNITION OF GOD IN EXTERNAL RESPONSE

24. Why is the "day of the Lord" such an important issue?

The day of the Lord has always been an important factor in the history of religions. In the Old Testament the expression was mostly understood in two different ways. Sometimes it meant a moment or period in history in which the presence of God was particularly evident either in blessing or in punishment. Usually, however, it referred to the Sabbath. The Sabbath was the gift of God to man so that man could rest from his manual labor and come to a greater awareness of the spiritual meaning of his life.

Theologically the "day of the Lord" seems to be a demand of human existence. Created in the image of God the human existence has two dimensions, the (physical) existence in time and space and the spiritual reality. Since man experiences his well-being through his presence in the physical world, he is also inclined to be exclusively preoccupied with the physical. The balance of the human totality demands that men set time aside to keep the awareness of his spiritual dimension alive and to express this dimension in visible terms. The total integration of human existence asks for the "day of the Lord."

From earliest Christian history the Sunday has been accepted as this day of the Lord. Sunday was the day of Christ's resurrection, the day of his victory over death and sin, the day of the completion of our redemption. No other day of the week can be better suited to reflect upon the spiritual meaning of human life and existence, and to place our human material existence in the light of God's calling.

25. Why is the celebration of the Eucharist required on Sunday?

The eucharistic celebration is not mentioned in the decalogue. It is the Church's explanation and application of the commandment to keep the day of the Lord. The purpose of the eucharistic celebration and the purpose of the day of the Lord coincide almost completely. As is mentioned above, the day of the Lord is a demand of the spiritual need of the human individual as well as of the human society. Man is in need of spiritual self-realization not only as an individual, but also as a member of the human community.

The eucharistic celebration is precisely the celebration of man's redemption, since it is the renewal of the mystery of Christ's life, death and resurrection. It would seem, therefore, that the celebration of the Eucharist on Sunday as a communal celebration is not the result of random pietism. It is rather the concurrence of a basic spiritual need in man and the participation in Christ's redemptive mystery. In this mystery Christ reaches out to man while man reaches out to Christ and to his fellowman.

26. What is the meaning of the prohibition to do "servile work" on Sunday?

Even in the Old Testament there were certain days dedicated to God on which "no sort of work" was allowed (Lev. 23:7). Such days were intended to express exclusively that man belonged to God before he belonged to himself. The prohibition to perform servile work on Sunday is of a rather late origin (6th century) and was originally a reaction against the landlords who forbade their "serfs" to take time off for participation in the eucharistic celebration of the Christian community on Sundays.

The prohibition to do servile work on Sunday is, therefore, not actually directed against a specific type of activity. Its purpose is to indicate and to safeguard that the human being will distance himself at certain times from material preoccupations in order to have time to reflect upon the spiritual dimension and spiritual meaning of his life. Furthermore, it is a human need, not only to work with others, but also to relax with others. Thus man can build up a human community in which the spiritual dimensions of human existence blend with the aspects of friendship and concern.

GOD'S CONCERN IN HUMAN INTERACTION

27. How is the dialogue between God and man expressed in certain human conditions?

The dialogue between God and man is visible in every constructive human and interhuman activity, but it is in a very specific manner expressed in a parent-child relationship. This specific relationship is a concrete realization of a creative, life-giving self-extension and of the growth toward a mature, personal responsibility. The fourth commandment speaks about "obedience to parents" but this obedience must coincide with the growth of personal responsibility. This means, it is an obedience that leads to independence.

This specific nature of obedience gives also a special direction to parental authority whose task it is not to mold them, but to develop individual personalities.

28. Parental authority: creative self-extension and personal growth.

The parental task is the transmission of human life. This task does not only include the physical procreation, it extends itself in no lesser way to the communication of such a degree of intellectual and emotional development that this person can assume a personal responsibility before God and before the human society. Parental authority, therefore, covers a variety of responsibilities.

The financial responsibility asks that the parents do what is within the reasonable limits of their financial abilities to take care of the needs of their children. This includes a concern for their health, their lodging and their clothing. It is impossible to draw accurate dividing lines between the various areas of responsibility. The concern for education is partly financial, partly social. It is the parents' responsibility to provide such an education which is in accordance with their own social status and with the interest and abilities of the child.

In many instances the child is able to assume partly a personal responsibility for the financial aspects of his schooling. Frequently the participation of the child in these matters can have important educational and formative advantages.

The more important dimension of parental authority, however, is the formation of the personality. Such a formation can not take place according to pre-established rules. As a basic principle there is much truth in the saying that the greatest love a parent can give to his child is the love he gives to his marriage partner. The formation of a personality does primarily take place through experience. Whenever the child experiences true love between the parents, the child can learn how to love. Whenever the child experiences antagonism it will learn to be continuously on the defensive and be mistrustful of other people.

Parents have the authority in the family, but it is an authority whose proper goal is not to demand submission, but to be a guidance toward independence. This asks for a constant alertness for the degree in which a child can assume responsibility. It demands in the parents a special prudence and courage to allow the child to take reasonable risks and to experience personal responsibility. It may demand that the parents allow the child to make mistakes, and that they be ready to forgive and to guide when the child comes back in search for assistance. Genuine education and formation is the conveyance of values which are deeply embedded in the person of the educator. This conveyance, however, takes place in such a manner that there is no imposition of values but rather an activation of the potential in the young person.

Genuine parental authority is a balance between protective concern, dynamic self-extension and creative permissiveness. In this extremely delicate balance the parents grow toward a high degree of true and unselfish love, and become in the deepest sense of the word co-creators with God of a new humanity.

29. Obedience to parents—requisite for personality development.

Children owe their parents respect and obedience. It is necessary to repeat what has been said before, the goal of obedience to parents is not primarily submission but the formation of responsible independence. Such a formation is a long and slow process in which the child himself plays an important role. Gradually the young person must take on more and more responsibility for his own formation. The major problem, however, is that he has no experience and that, because of his lack of experience he is little qualified to evaluate possibilities and dangers.

Although obedience to parents is not primarily a matter of submission to authority figures, it includes a large degree of dependence. Perhaps it is more accurate to say that obedience to the parents is primarily a respectful searching under parental guidance for the most complete self-expression of which a young person is capable at this moment of his development. It is the search for the delicate balance between submission and independence.

In many other ways the child owes the parents respect and gratitude. Many of these factors are culturally determined, but in their deeper meaning they center around the concept that people usually value their origin to the degree that they value themselves.

In the parent-child relationship one encounters the deepest human expression of self-extension and of personal growth. Parent and child reach out to each other in a gesture of mutual giving and receiving. In this gesture each one creates and is being created in the image of God.

Human Life
The Fifth Commandment

1. What is the source of the moral demands of the fifth commandment?

Respect for life or the sanctity of life in the Christian perspective comes from the fact that life is a gift from God the Creator. The creator has called us all into being; we have not brought ourselves into existence. Life is a precious gift that we have received from the hand of the creator. As human beings we do not have total control over our life or the lives of other humans. Every person exists because of the gracious love of God and is called by God to share in the fullness of his life and love. The theological tradition has expressed this reality by saying that the Christian does not have full dominion over life, even one's own life, but rather has stewardship or imperfect dominion. In this way the value of human life illustrates the Christian understanding of all existence with the primary emphasis on the gift of God but with the need for human beings to respond positively and thus share in the life-giving action of God. The fact that life is a gift from God does not mean that human beings are merely passive recipients of the gift of life, but we have the vocation to nourish, protect, and defend and improve human life.

2. To what is this Christian understanding opposed?

Such a Christian understanding of the value of human life as a gracious gift of God is opposed to the value that is often attached to human life by many people including Christians in our contemporary society. Too often we attribute value to human life only in terms of what one makes, does, accomplishes or possesses; but in the Christian perspective the dignity of human life does not rest primarily on one's works or accomplishments.

3. What are the practical implications of this?

The different theoretical bases for the dignity of human life have enormous practical consequences. Too often it seems that people today want to forget about those who are not contributing to society or who are not successful in terms of acquiring material goods, reputation or power. Christian love can never be selfishly directed just to one's own advantage for Christian love pays great attention to the needs of the neighbor. In fact, there is always a Christian bias or prejudice in favor of the poor, the weak and the oppressed. The value of human life can never depend primarily on the wealth one accumulates, the position of power that one obtains or even the good works that one does for others. The Christian gospel stands opposed to such understanding, since it proposes as a criterion of our love for God, our love for the poor, the naked, the hungry, the thirsty and the prisoner.

Responsible and creative Christians must incarnate this understanding of the value of Christian life in contemporary society. Our respect for life must bear witness to this basic biblical injunction in today's world. Unfortunately, there are many people in the world today who are hungry either because of epidemics, malnutrition or catastrophes such as drought or floods. There are many people who are living below the poverty line and even close to destitution. Many families are cramped into small, dark and intolerable living quarters, while others live in comparative luxury and worry about how often to change the color of the wall-to-wall carpeting. There are gross inequities existing in our world in which the truly human needs of many are not being met. Unfortunately, most of the developed nations of the world are often using the developing nations and preventing these people from having those things which are necessary for truly human existence.

4. How does the false understanding of life manifest itself in our country?

Within our own country there are many people who live below the poverty line and do not have the food they need or proper health care or educational facilities. Too often the attitude toward welfare is that people should be able to help themselves, and we have no obligation to help out those people who are lazy or just do not want to work. Implied in this is the concept that human dignity depends on what one does or accomplishes. Compare the amount and the way in which government funds are given to university research and industrial development with the amount of money and the way in which it is given to the basic human needs of people in our society.

Another area of concern embraces those who are not contributing members of our society. Immediately one thinks of the aging and the elderly who are becoming more numerous but who no longer positively contribute in the way of work and often seem isolated and in great need of affection and care. Many people in our society also suffer from different physical and mental disabilities because of which they are often institutionalized. Here too there arises a conspiracy of silence to put these people away in some rural setting and forget about them. The mentally retarded are also in great need of care and affection even though they might not be able to contribute very much to society in the way of wealth. We all know situations in which they have been the occasion of greater understanding of what Christian love really means.

Special mention must be made of those who lack power in a particular society, for these are often the victims of oppression in all its different facets. Think, for example, of all the problems of a minority group in any society, especially our own—Black, Indian, Spanish-Americans. Above all think of the lot of the prisoner and how the administration of penal justice does not always respect the dignity of human beings who do not lose that dignity just because they might be imprisoned.

5. What constitutes the Christian response to this?

The sensitive Christian conscience should see in many areas of our life these signs of sin—our failures to live in accord with the Christian understanding of respecting the life of all especially those most in need. To overcome this present situation we must use all the means at our disposal, but the ultimate solution will never be found merely in technology. In the last analysis the sin-filled situation in which we live can only be changed through a continuing and radical conversion or change of heart which is the fundamental moral message of the Scriptures. The radical change calls for us to give less emphasis to ourselves and more to the needs of our neighbor.

In the ethos of our consumer society we so easily become involved in fulfilling the false needs that are created that we truly forget the human needs of many others. From a collective viewpoint we Americans as the richest nation in the world must be willing to do with less so that others might have the bare minimum in keeping with their basic human dignity. We cannot continue consuming forty per cent of the world's resources when we form only a comparatively small percentage of the world's population. Christians must make a special effort to say "no" to false needs and concern themselves with the true needs of others. But again the only way in which this can be brought about is through a radical conversion or change of heart. The manifold questions affecting human life are very complex and involve many political, social and economic realities and relationships. There will never be any simple solutions to these complex questions, but a start must be made. The first step must involve the recognition of all of us of our individual sinfulness and the need to change our hearts so that we truly respect human life and strive to promote and defend human life especially among the weak and poor.

6. Can these demands be specified in greater detail?

Yes. Both now and throughout the centuries of the Christian tradition, many detailed questions implied in the general words of the fifth commandment have been addressed and analyzed. We shall summarize many of these, loosely grouping them under five topics: killing itself, death and dying, care of health and medical ethics, genetics, and peace and war. Under the first topic we shall now consider the moral questions of suicide, murder, killing an unjust aggressor, capital punishment, and abortion.

"YOU SHALL NOT KILL"

7. Is suicide a permissible option for the Christian?

The Christian tradition has condemned suicide as wrong because man received life as a gift from God, and his stewardship does not give him the full dominion to take his own life. Suicide is often an expression of desperation and indicates a loss of hope. Canon Law forbids Christian burial to suicides, but this must be interpreted in the light of the actual dispositions of the person. The general pastoral rule is that there is usually great doubt that the person was fully responsible for the suicide so that a Christian burial should not be denied especially in the light of the needs of the family.

Christians, however, must always take into consideration the biblical text from John 15:13 that greater love than this nobody has than that one lay down one's life for a friend. The Christian tradition does not make an absolute value of human life, even one's own physical life. The tradition has acknowledged that conflict situations can arise when my individual act might have a number of effects, one of which is my own death. The Catholic approach to this question has been based on the distinction between the direct and indirect effect as enunciated in the principle of double effect.

8. How is this distinction used in the question of suicide?

Direct suicide occurs when the killing is intended either as a means or an end in itself. Indirect suicide is morally permitted when the following four conditions are fulfilled: 1) the act itself is good or indifferent; 2) the intention is good; 3) the good effect occurs equally as immediately as the evil effect so that the evil effect is not the means by which the good effect is obtained; 4) there is a proportionate reason to justify the indirect taking of life. In extraordinary situations the tradition also acknowledged the fact that God, who is the author of all life, could give a private inspiration to an individual to take one's own life.

Manuals of moral theology point out cases of indirect suicide. In the first book of Maccabees 6:43–47, Eleazar killed the opposing king by courageously fighting his way under the king's elephant and thrusting his sword through the soft underbelly of the elephant with the knowledge that the elephant would collapse on him and kill him. Kamikaze pilots in the Second World War were also judged to be only indirectly killing themselves. However, most authors would not allow the spy or the saboteur to take a pill to kill himself lest secrets affecting the lives of many other people be revealed. In this case the killing of self is the means by which the good effect is accomplished. In the other two cases the effects are equally immediate, and the good effect is not produced by the means of the bad effect but might even have come into existence if the bad effect did not occur.

9. Is this distinction still used the same way?

Today a good number of Catholic theologians are questioning the adequacy of the distinction between direct and indirect, since it is primarily based on the physical structure of the act itself and does not give enough importance to the complexity and multiple relationships involved in human actions. They deny the absolute validity of the distinction between direct and indirect as it has been proposed in the tradition. On the basis of proportionate reason the spy can take a pill to end his life and thus conceal knowledge which would be detrimental to the lives of many other individuals. In such conflict situations between my life and the lives of others, there could be a proportionate reason to justify the taking of my life. But again one recognizes the value here must be commensurate with the value of human life.

10. Does the fifth commandment forbid all killing?

Based on the fact that a human being does not have dominion over the life of another, the Catholic tradition has clarified the generic fifth commandment to read that the direct killing of innocent life is always wrong. Catholic theology with its emphasis on human reason maintains that all human beings can come to this same conclusion on the basis of their rational understanding of reality. The tradition has justified the indirect killing of innocent persons if there is a proportionate reason. For example, in everyday life, people drive automobiles even though indirectly some people are killed in automobile accidents.

One type of conflict situation that the tradition acknowledged was the killing of an unjust aggressor. If necessary one may kill an actual unjust aggressor if this is required to save life or spiritual or material goods of great value. Note that here Catholic theologians have been willing to admit that other values such as spiritual goods (e.g., use of reason, reputation, etc.) or material goods of great value could be as important as physical life itself.

Some theologians maintain that it is indirect because one can never intend the death of another human being, but others say that it is direct and intended because the death of the aggressor is the means by which I defend myself. In my judgment, if one is going to retain the accepted understanding of direct as that which is intended either as an end or as a means, then the killing in this case is direct.

12. Is it necessary that the unjust agressor be aware of his evil?

No. It is important to note that the unjust aggression here does not refer to a formal unjust aggressor—that is one who is subjectively guilty of unjust aggression. The primary moral consideration is not whether the person is subjectively guilty but only whether the person is bringing about an objective conflict situation. In the light of these refinements we would understand murder as the unjustified killing of another. In conflict situations in which one's life or other goods of commensurate value are being threatened, then one could be justified in taking the life of another as a last resort.

13. What about capital punishment?

Traditionally, Catholic theology in the light of the state's obligation to protect the common good has accepted the right of the state to resort to capital punishment in cases of proportionately grave crimes. Today many theologians would disagree with the older teaching. Prudentially and historically it does not seem that capital punishment can be justified. One would have to justify capital punishment on the basis of the reasons for which punishment exists.

One of the purposes of punishment is corrective, but capital punishment obviously does nothing to rehabilitate the offender. Second, capital punishment is often defended as a deterrent—only the death penalty will deter people from the most horrendous crimes. But I would argue that the death penalty has not served as a salutary deterrent in the past. A third reason invokes a concept of justice which demands there be vindication for the injustice done. The person who takes another life must forfeit his own. But this is not the only way of vindicating justice. Why should another life be taken if this is not necessary? The original victim is not brought back to life by the death of the assailant. Often such a concept of vindictive justice seems closer to revenge than a just form of punishment. Since human life is so important a value, I do not think that the state should take human life when it cannot be shown to be absolutely necessary. But the arguments as proposed in favor of capital punishment do not in my judgment prove the need for capital punishment.

14. What about abortion?

Roman Catholic teaching has consistently applied its understanding of respect for life to unborn life in the womb. In the whole historical development as well as in the contemporary discussions there are two important questions on which one's teaching on abortion hinges. The first is: when does human life begin? The second is: how does one solve conflict situations involving human life?

The authoritative, hierarchical teaching of the Catholic Church solves the problem of the beginning of human life by saying that in practice one has to act as if human life is present from the first moment of conception, but in theory many Catholics have maintained that human life is not present at the very beginning. Thomas Aquinas, following the traditional teaching proposed by older biological authorities such as Aristotle and Galen, maintained that animation takes place (the soul is infused into the body) or human life begins for males at forty days and for females at eighty days after conception. (I do not know what empirical data they had for their teaching, but I am sure they did share some anti-feminine prejudices which entered into such a judgment.) Today some Thomistic philosophers still maintain the theory of delayed animation.

As might be expected, there are two possible explanations for Aquinas' teaching. Some maintain that Aquinas based his teaching on the poor biological knowledge which was then accepted as true. The only active element in human reproduction according to their knowledge was the male element. The very word "semen" comes from the agricultural analogy whereby the seed is placed in the ground, dies and then new life shoots up. Until a few centuries ago we knew nothing of the active female element—the ovum—and the union of ovum and sperm. Thomas could not hold that human life begins at conception because at conception there is only the semen which is now present in the uterus of the female. But contemporary knowledge and especially modern genetics prove that from the first moment of conception there is a unique genetic package that is never to be duplicated—except in the case of twins.

The other interpretation gives a more philosophical basis to Thomas' teaching. Thomistic metaphysics accepts the theory of hylomorphism according to which matter and form are the constitutive causes of being. There is a reciprocal causality between matter and form so that the form can be received only into matter that is capable of receiving it. This printed page cannot receive the form of a human soul or even the form of a piano because the matter is not disposed to receive it. So, they argue, in the very beginning the conceptus is not capable of receiving a human form—the soul. Only after some time is the matter disposed to receive such a form. (My difficulty here is that I do not see that there has been a significant development in the matter in the first forty or eighty days after conception so that it is now disposed for human form whereas before it was not.) It is important to realize that at least in theory there has been this long discussion about the difficult question of the beginning of human life.

Today there are many non-Catholics and even some Catholics who cannot accept the Catholic teaching that in practice one must act as if human life is present from the moment of conception. However, it is also important to point out that many other people join the official Catholic teaching in condemning direct abortion. There are three generic approaches to the way one determines the beginning of human life—the relational approach, the individualistic-biological approach and the process approach.

15. What is the relational approach to determining the beginning of life?

The relational approach maintains that biological or genetic data alone can never determine the beginning of human life. The human being is more than just the biological or genetic. The new life must be recognized as such and accepted by the parents into a loving relationship. I cannot accept the relational criterion in this case. First, nobody seriously proposes that such a relational criterion be employed after birth so that in practice these people do accept a biological criterion such as birth as marking a point after which there is human life. Second, a fully human relationship must be reciprocal, but it is obvious that there is a point after birth before which the fetus cannot respond in a human manner. Third, in determining the time of death, all contemporary approaches use an individual-biological criterion—heartbeat or brain waves. Fourth, the rational criteria would be rather nebulous and very difficult to apply in practice. When precisely is the relationship present and what are the criteria by which one can determine the presence of this relationship? Although one must recognize the greater importance attached to relationality in contemporary moral thinking, when one is talking about the very minimum required for human life I do not think that a relational criterion is fitting.

16. What is the individual-biological approach?

The second generic approach employs an individual-biological criterion to determine the beginning of human life. Some choose birth, but it seems that birth tells more about where the child is than what it is. There is just not that much difference between the unborn child one day before birth and the born child one day after birth. Others choose viability, but again this tells more about where the baby can live, and in the light of medical advances viability is a very relative criterion which will occur increasingly earlier in the life of the fetus. Quickening also seems inadequate because it merely records the mother's perception of movement. Some ethicians argue for the presence of brain waves or the early development of the cortex of the brain or the rudimentary formation of the basic systems of circulation, respiration and brain activity. On the basis of such criteria human life begins at about eight or ten weeks after conception. But in my judgment these developments do not really constitute such a qualitative difference between human life and no human life. At this early stage human brain activity is not an actuality but now becomes a possibility;

but even before, in terms of evolutionary development, there was also this possibility. In my judgment there is here a question of evolutionary development but not the qualitative difference between human life and no life.

The strong reason for saying that life is present from conception, with strengthening support from modern genetics, has already been mentioned. But there are some Catholic theologians who do not accept this. They hold that human life begins about the fourteenth day after conception. All descriptions of human beings seem to insist on individuality as a fundamental characteristic, but individuality is not present and achieved before that time. The phenomenon of identical twinning can occur up to fourteen days after conception. Likewise science has discovered the less frequent occurrence of two fertilized ova joining together to form one being before the fourteenth day. Thus there are strong indications that individuality is not present before that time. A confirmatory reason comes from the fact that many fertilized ova are spontaneously aborted without the mother's even being aware of it in those first fourteen days. In practice these theologians maintain that human life is not present until the fourteenth day after conception. At the present time their view has only limited practical applicability—after rape or concerning use of "contraceptive" devices which really prevent fertilization.

17. Is the process approach really plausible?

Some prefer to adopt the third model of process or development. At first sight there seems much to commend such an approach, but in the last analysis this approach must be reduced to one of the other types and must face the question of when in this process of development human life does begin.

18. What about that second important question?

The second fundamental question in abortion concerns the solution of conflict situations involving the fetus (and presupposing now it is human life, for if it is not human life then the dilemma is no longer of such great magnitude). In the past Roman Catholic teaching condemned all direct abortion but allowed indirect abortion if a proportionate reason was present. The two most common examples of indirect abortion are the cases of the cancerous uterus and the ectopic pregnancy. As mentioned above, many contemporary theologians reject the concept of direct and indirect as a solution to conflict situations. As in the question of unjust aggression, if there is an objective conflict so that the fetus is causing harm to the mother, they argue that the abortion can be justified to save the life of the mother or for some other value commensurate with physical life. Recall that in other conflict situations other values such as spiritual goods or material goods of great value were equated with physical life itself. Thus, for example, if it was in accord with the best medical indications and understanding that the pregnancy would mean that a mother of three would be physically disabled for a very prolonged number of years (not just a temporary depression), then they would reluctantly justify the abortion.

19. Is this solution the common teaching of theologians today?

Yes and No. Many Catholic moral theologians writing today disagree with the solution of conflict situations by the application of the concept of direct and indirect as it has been understood in the manuals of theology. To a considerably lesser extent there is also some dissent from the authoritative teaching on the practical acceptance of conception as the beginning of human life.

The teaching on abortion is not a matter of faith, and dissent remains a possibility for the Catholic. But the dissenter must also be aware of the dangers involved. In general in our society, I am convinced there is a tendency to deny the humanity of the fetus because it produces nothing and one cannot see or hear the fetus so that the temptation to abortion is often very strong. The Church should continue to teach in this area and in other areas but always trying to read the signs of the times in the light of the tradition. In teaching on such specific moral problems, as illustrated by the debate about the beginning of human life and solution of conflict situations, the hierarchical Church does not claim that its teaching is so certain that it excludes all possibility of error and the option of dissent.

DEATH AND DYING

20. What about the second general topic falling under the fifth commandment: death and dying?

Death is a subject which is no longer taboo in our society. A Christian's understanding of death in my judgment recognizes the many complex aspects of the reality. Death is something which is natural for every created thing. The Christian tradition has also seen death as intimately joined with sin and effected by sin, for we are reminded in the Scriptures that through sin death came into the world. This aspect of death causes even the Christian to experience it as a break with the past, and death is accompanied by sentiments of fear and trepidation even for the Christian. But death is also seen in the light of the redeeming love of God, for he has transformed death in the resurrection of Jesus. Death transformed by love is the way to life. Death for the Christian does not deny all that went before in life but rather it breaks with the past in order to transform what went before into the newness of life. The Christian understanding of death must take cognizance of all these aspects of the reality of death, and individual Christians must come to grips in their own existence with the thought and the fact of their dying.

Christian thought about life and death has tried to hold in balance two basic truths—there must be a great respect for life and the need to preserve life; but death is not the greatest evil in the world, and one does not have to avoid death at all costs. A technically precise theological statement of this attitude is that we have an obligation to use ordinary means to preserve life, but we have no obligation to use extraordinary means.

21. How should ordinary and extraordinary means be distinguished?

The ordinary means of preserving life are best described as those medicines, treatments and operations which offer a reasonable hope of benefit for the patient and which can be obtained and used without excessive pain, expense or other inconvenience. Since the Christian has no obligation to use extraordinary means to preserve life, there is for the Christian the right to die.

The description of ordinary means originally emphasized the question of excessive pain, expense or inconvenience; but in the last few decades with the increasing realization that medicine can keep people alive for a few more hours or days theologians have added the criteria about some reasonable hope of benefit for the person. If a person will only live for a few more hours or days, then one cannot consider the treatment obligatory. The Christian recognizes there is a time when the respirator can be shut off and the intravenous feeding pulled out. There is no obligation to prolong death but only to take ordinary means of preserving life. Naturally there will be differing prudential judgments about what is an ordinary means, but the right to die has been an accepted part of the Catholic tradition.

The Catholic tradition, by accepting the distinction between ordinary and extraordinary means, has also recognized the importance of the quality of life and denied the absolute value of physical life itself. For example, a person has no moral obligation to move to a different climate and location if this is necessary to add some years to life but will involve proportionately grave inconvenience for the person and family involved. Allowing to die exists not only with the elderly but even with newborn children, who, for example, need an operation to sustain life but are very severely malformed.

22. What about euthanasia or the active and positive interference to bring about death?

Traditionally Catholic teaching and the hierarchical teaching authority have opposed euthanasia. Two reasons are frequently given. First, the individual does not have full dominion but only stewardship over one's own life and therefore cannot directly interfere with life. Second, there is a great difference between the act of omitting an extraordinary means and the positive act of bringing about death. To allow one to die is not the same as positively interfering to cause death especially as it concerns the intention and act of the person performing the deed.

Some contemporary theologians do not think that these two arguments are absolutely convincing in all cases. Human beings do have some dominion over life and death; for example, by refusing extraordinary means one can intend to die and efficaciously carry out that intention. They grant there is an important difference between the act of omission and the positive act of killing, but in their judgment at the point in which the dying process begins there is no longer that great a difference between the act of commission and the act of omission. They acknowledge problems in determining when the dying process begins (some could argue it begins at birth), so they practically identify the dying process with the time that means can be discontinued as useless but having in mind such means as respiration, intravenous feeding, etc. In practice there will always be a difficulty in determining just when the dying process begins so that one must recognize the potential problem of abuse that can arise and the difficulty in determining laws in this matter. The matter is so complex that the present teaching as proposed by the authoritative, noninfallible magisterium, to its credit, does not claim to exclude the possibility of error.

23. Do any other contemporary questions fall within this topic?

Yes. Other questions, concern the definition of death and the test for death. These questions arise today precisely because the older sign or test for death was often the lack of a heartbeat, but now one recognizes that the heart can artifically continue to beat while the person is really dead. Likewise, the problem has arisen, in the light of heart transplants, of making sure that one person is already dead before the heart is transplanted. There is a tendency today to accept brain death as the best criterion or test for determining whether or not death has occurred. However, even with this criterion or test for death, one could still accept the definition of death as the beakdown of the three major systems—heart, lungs and brain, or revise that to the death of the brain alone. From the perspective of moral theology there is no difficulty with accepting these revisions which have lately been put into practice.

CARE OF HEALTH AND MEDICAL ETHICS

24. What about the third general topic: care of health and medical ethics?

The Christian view recognizes the value of human life and the consequent obligation to care for the health of the total person—body and soul. The Christian approach, while acknowledging the importance and value of health, never absolutizes what is itself relative. Risks to health are permitted if there are proportionate reasons to justify them. In this connection questions have arisen about the morality of cigarette smoking and boxing or prize-fighting. Can one take the risk to health in these things? In all questions of this type there is need for a prudential judgment, but one must also honestly evaluate the scientific data and not merely accept things because everyone else does them. There is evidence that smoking does constitute a risk to health. There could be other reasons which would justify this risk, such as the mental good of the person or the lack of anxiety, but the danger of self-deception is again ever present.

25. Can Christians really support the use of alcohol and drugs?

The use of alcohol and drugs also involves care for one's health and sanity. Here too the traditional approach has avoided the extremes of total condemnation or of blanket acceptance, since the guiding principle is the relationship of drugs and alcohol to the good of the individual person. Alcohol as a part of creation is a good that can be used for either good or ill. A moderate use of alcohol can be a salutary and helpful thing for the good of the whole person. Even the social drinking of alcohol can be a good thing. Likewise drugs can be used to eliminate pain and bring relief from stress and strain, but the danger of abuse is ever present in both drugs and alcohol.

Both alcohol and drugs can readily be used as a neurotic form of escape. Both can create a dependency by which the person loses truly human dignity and freedom becoming a slave or an addict. Abuse of such things can be destructive both for the individual, all those related to the individual and society itself. Also the availability of drugs and alcohol is one of the problems of an affluent society. Especially in the context of our consumer society, one can easily create a false need for alcohol and drugs. In the case of drugs this does not only refer to hard drugs but also to the tendency of so many Americans to be dependent on many different forms and types of drugs. Obviously the problems of addiction, dependency and long-term self-destruction are much greater with the use of hard and habit forming drugs. The use of alcohol and drugs is governed by the Christian virtue of temperance which justifies them in terms of the good of the total person. However, it must also be recognized that an individual for many different reasons might truly feel a personal call to greater abstention in the use of drugs and alcohol.

26. What are the moral obligations of the medical community?

As already mentioned earlier in this chapter, the primary moral question in my judgment concerns the need to insure that all people in society and in the world have available to them proper medical care. The focus now will be on proper care for the health of the individual. Here the Christian tradition operated within what might be called the eschatological tension between doing everything possible to overcome sickness and insure health and yet realizing that suffering of some form will always be part of the Christian life, since our life is intimately associated with the Paschal Mystery of Jesus. Sickness and dying often unite the Christian with the death and resurrection of the Lord. Vocations in service of the sick have been continually encouraged in the Christian tradition. Hospitals first came into existence under Christian auspices and continue to be sponsored by Christians. Medical and nursing professions constitute two forms of service to fellow human beings and the Christian reality sees in them a Christian vocation in the service of mankind.

27. What was the contribution of traditional medical ethics to the understanding of this moral obligation?

In general, medical care and treatment for the individual did not usually occasion many ethical problems. The doctor was guided by the good of the patient, and that is the same norm as the ethical criterion. Traditionally medical ethics was treated under the rubric of mutilation of the body which can be justified for the good of the whole. Catholic theology developed the principle of totality which maintains that a part could always be sacrificed for the good of the whole to which it belonged. Ethical problems could arise only in terms of prudential judgments of what was truly for the good of the individual. The relationship of doctor and patient introduced ethical questions based on that relationship itself with special emphasis on the moral obligation of the doctor to tell the truth to the patient (especially the dying patient) and to obtain the consent of the patient or guardian for operations insofar as this is possible. Especially in cases of newer or experimental procedures used for the good of the individual, the patient has a right to know all the possibilities and risks before making a decision. Special problems arose in Catholic medical ethics when the generative organs were involved. The older teaching maintained that the generative organs could never be sacrificed for the good of the individual or for the good of the marriage itself. Many contemporary moralists say sterilization, like contraception, can be justified either for the good of the individual or for the good of the marriage, but these problems are treated elsewhere in greater detail.

28. Did the principle of totality adequately deal with all the issues of medical ethics?

New questions came to the fore in medical ethics when the individual was mutilated or treated not for his own good but for the good of another or the good of the species. Pope Pius XII maintained that the principle of totality could not justify transplants because the organ was taken from one person not for the individual's good but for the good of another. However, on the basis of charity or an extended version of totality, Catholic teaching today justifies organ transplants. An individual may give an organ (usually one of a pair of organs) to another provided that the individual's health and bodily integrity are not seriously or disporportionately jeopardized. The highly publicized heart transplants create different types of problems. The donor must be dead before the heart is taken. The recipient must know precisely and exactly what the chances of success are. Also there is the broader societal question of perhaps devoting an inordinate amount of money and talent to such extraordinary operations while neglecting ordinary medical care for the total population.

Medical experimentation done for the good of the species or the good of another also raises some problems because again the individual is subject to danger not for personal good but for the good of others. There must be a proper proportion between the good to be achieved and the risk for the individual whose bodily integrity cannot be seriously jeopardized. Above all the individual must be in a position to freely consent to the experimentation (i.e., have the necessary knowledge and freedom). Some would argue that children and those who cannot consent on their own should never be used in experimentation. I would maintain that children can be used in experimentation if there is no discernible risk to them, and their parents consent. Problems can more readily arise with prisoners and people who are institutionalized, since their ability to consent freely is severely diminished. Society must be vigilant so that the weak and the poor are not taken advantage of in the name of scientific discovery and advancement.

29. Does that exhaust the questions of medical ethics?

No. Another contemporary problem in medical ethics concerns the allocation of scarce medical resources. If there are five people who need a certain piece of lifesaving equipment and there are only three pieces of equipment available, who should receive the lifesaving treatment? The first judgment is medical—only those who can truly profit from it. But there still might not be enough equipment for all the people who need it. In this type of situation I uphold the equal dignity of all and acknowledge the great difficulty in most cases of deciding which life is more important. The system of first come first served is probably the most just procedure in ordinary circumstances.

GENETICS AND THE FUTURE OF HUMANITY

30. What about the fourth general topic falling under the fifth commandment: genetics and the future of humanity?

In the last few years new questions have arisen with the advent of new knowledge and technology in the area of genetics and the human future. Human beings today have more power and knowledge to make a better future for the whole human race, but we can also never forget our limitations and the sinful abuse to which power can be put.

There are three generic types of questions raised by such advances. First, genetic engineering or gene surgery tries to change the genetic makeup of the individual which causes certain diseases or conditions. Such procedures should be guided by the medical ethics governing all procedures for the good of the individual and based on the proportionate good to be obtained. The second type of question can be described as euphenics in which the genotype is not treated but rather the phenotype, as in the case of eyeglasses or insulin for diabetes. Here again, since the treatments are employed primarily for the good of the individual concerned, the regular moral principles for medical ethics apply.

The third generic question is called eugenics, or good breeding, based on a recombination of genes to bring about a better human species in the future. Eugenics is either negative (to eliminate bad genes from the human gene pool) or positive (to create a better type of human being). It also provides opportunities for couples to have children who are not now able to have children through the ordinary process of procreation. There are three possible forms that eugenics can take—artificial insemination with sperm that have been stored in sperm banks, *in vitro* fertilization and subsequent implantation of the fertilized ovum in the womb, and cloning which is the process whereby a genetic twin is produced from just one "parent"—this latter process has been referred to in popular parlance as the Xeroxing of people.

31. What is the moral judgment regarding eugenics?

Much of the discussion is futuristic at the present because only artificial insemination with sperm is now possible and feasible although attempts are being made (possibly even successes) to bring about fertilization in a test tube and then implantation of the fertilized ovum in the womb of a woman. Scientists continue to debate the possibility and feasibility of cloning human beings. At the present time I believe we should say "no" to positive eugenics even if it were possible because there are too many unanswered questions at the moment. Even from a genetic viewpoint positive eugenics might rule out the benefits of hybrid vigor as exemplified in the problem of inbreeding through marriages of close relatives. In addition, because something is possible genetically does not mean it should be done humanly. Think of all the psychological problems for the individuals involved if there were 10,000 identical twins of Einstein. What is possible from the genetic viewpoint cannot always be identified with the ultimate human good, but rather all other considerations must also be taken into account. Even more importantly, who would direct the genetic future of the human race and choose the types to be reproduced? If our genetic planners are no better than our foreign policy planners, then there is need for great caution. Here too there is always the danger of thinking that science and technology will be able to solve some very basic human problems which the Christian ultimately believes lie at a level deeper than science or technology can ever touch.

32. What about such measures being used to provide individual couples with the possibility of having children if they are not able to have children or to have healthy children through the normal process?

In accord with the teaching proposed by Pope Pius XII, some would argue that the natural law demands that conception takes place through the act of sexual intercourse by which male semen is deposited in the vas of the female. Some would maintain that the child must always be the fruit of the love and the bodies of the parents so that the sperm must come from the husband and the ovum from the wife. Other theologians agree that this is the ideal way, and there are many important values connected with it, but they do not make an absolute out of this.

However, there are other significant ethical questions which must be resolved in the case of *in vitro* fertilization with implantation and cloning. What about mishaps? One cannot merely discard human beings if the experiment does not work out. Also what about possible harm to the individual which will only show up later in life? Before even such experiments are morally justified, the risk of mishaps or future harm to the individual must be no greater than such risks in the ordinary process of procreation. Again, society has to be aware of the danger of trampling on the rights of individuals in the name of medical science and the advancement of the human race as a whole.

PEACE AND WAR

33. What about the fifth general topic: peace and war?

The Christian vision of the world recognized the great need and im
portance of peace for the good of all human beings. But again the
question arises if there are any other values or reasons which might
justify the use of force and war. Christian teaching in the course of
history has proposed three different approaches to this very vexing
question.

34. What is the first approach?

The first approach can be described as witness pacifism, and is best
illustrated by the pacifism of some of the Protestant sects such as the
Mennonites. Pacifism is a requirement of the Christian gospel, and
our lives must always bear witness to that gospel. Such an approach
does not rest on the assumption that pacifism will always be an
effective means of achieving justice here and now or that it will be
accepted by all human beings. In fact, such sects usually separate
themselves from the world because life in the world will sooner or
later involve compromises with the biblical ethic in the form of violence or some type of accommodation. In my opinion, Christian
witness pacifism is not the only possible approach for the Christian.
Such an approach absolutizes peace at the expense of other values
such as justice. Sometimes force can be used in the service of justice
in this world. Individual Christians, however, can feel a personal
vocation to bear witness to this important aspect of the Christian
message and embrace pacifism just as others are called to embrace
poverty. I do not think that the total Church can adopt such an
absolutist approach even though the Christian Church must always
strive for peace and justice.

35. What is the second approach?

The second approach can aptly be described as the use of non-
violence as an effective means of social change and has been associated
with Gandhi, Martin Luther King and the Berrigans. The basic roots
of this teaching are three: the gospel calls for non-violence; non-
violence can be a very effective way to overcome injustice as illustrated
in the success of both Martin Luther King and Gandhi; violence
always escalates and tends to become counter-productive. Again,
there are many important values in such an approach and one can

appreciate the fact that some Christians feel called to adopt this policy, but in the last analysis I cannot accept it. First of all, effective non-violence cannot be called *the* Christian or gospel approach as opposed to all other approaches. In fact it must be recognized that non-violence in this case is proposed as an effective form of resistance. The Sermon on the Mount seems to call for non-resistance, not just for non-violence. For conceptual clarity the primary distinction exists not between violence and non-violence but between non-resistance and resistance. Both violence and non-violence are types of resistance, so that the difference between them, while great, is not as generic or great as one might at first think.

Such an approach, since it claims to be effective, tends to give way to the use of force if force is the only effective way of preventing injustice. This was true historically in the cases of Dietrich Bonhoeffer and Reinhold Niebuhr. Both came to the conclusion that only force and violence would be effective in preventing the injustices wrought by Hitler. Such a theory rightly points out all the problems and dangers connected with violence and killing, but reluctantly the Christian because of the need of justice can on occasion justify the use of violence.

36. What is the third approach?

The third approach which acknowledges that at times force may be used in the cause of justice has been accepted by the Roman Catholic Church and most other Christian churches and developed in the theory of just war. The conditions for a just war call for justice in going to war *(ius ad bellum)* and justice in the waging of war *(ius in bello)*. Justice in going to war involves the following conditions: a proper intention; declaration of war by legitimate authority; a just cause; war is a last resort when all other means have been exhausted. In the light of the growing escalation of war, the teaching of the recent Popes especially Pope Pius XII has restricted the just cause to defense against unjust aggression. Recognizing the dangers and problems connected with violence and killing, this theory insists that war is the *ultima ratio,* and other means for a peaceful settlement must first be exhausted. Here too one must acknowledge the importance of prudence in applying this and other criteria.

37. What does this just war theory imply?

Justice in war calls attention to two principles. The principle of proportionality maintains that war is justified only if the good to be attained outweighs the evil which will accompany it. The Catholic tradition has also insisted on the principle of discrimination, although a few theologians today question the absolute force of this principle. According to the principle of discrimination force can only be employed against the bearer of force. Non-combatants are immune from direct attack, but some non-combatants unfortunately may be killed indirectly if their killing is proportionate to the good to be attained. For example, one can drop a bomb on a military installation even though some noncombatants who are working on the premises in different capacities will also be killed. Their killing is only indirect because the bomb is directly targeted on the military installation and not on a non-military target. However, the saturation bombing of European cities by the Allies during World War II and the dropping of atomic bombs on population centers in Japan constitute severe violations of the principle of discrimination. To their great credit some American Catholic theologians such as Francis Connell, John Ford and Paul Hanly Furfey spoke out during World War II to condemn such bombings.

In the light of the principle of discrimination together with the principle of proportionality, I conclude that the use of large nuclear weapons is always morally wrong. The problem we are facing today is that of possessing and threatening to use weapons which we have no moral right to use. At the very least, Christians should strive to do away with our dependence on the deterrent value of possessing such weapons and ultimately aim to destroy the weapons themselves.

38. Does the just war theory solve all the problems?

There are dangers in accepting the just war theory, starting with the risk of self-deception, since as human beings we are always tempted to justify the wars in which our country is engaged. There is also a great danger of escalation toward nuclear weapons and the fear that violence will get out of hand. Often the possibility of war tempts the strong and powerful nations to make force more important than justice. But on the other hand, the just war as Augustine pointed out is not against the Christian notion of love. In this imperfect and sinful world in which we live one is often confronted with more than one neighbor in need. If a neighbor is being attacked by another, love can urge that one use force to save the neighbor who is being attacked. I accept the theory of just war but emphasize the fact that it is a last resort and involves many possible pitfalls.

39. What about revolution?

Whoever accepts the just war theory must also accept the justified revolution and tyrannicide. The justification and the conditions for the justified revolution parallel those of the just war. The justified revolution avoids two of the problems associated with just war—the chances of escalation to nuclear weapons are not present because revolutionaries usually do not possess such weapons and the danger that the force which will be used by the strong and powerful to oppress the weak and powerless is not present because the revolutionaries are themselves the ones who are usually weak and oppressed by others. The justified revolution like the just war can readily go against the principle of discrimination which tries to limit the extent of violence. Thus putting a bomb in the Tower of London or hijacking an international airliner filled with innocent passengers are immoral means. The question arises: who are the bearers of force? Does every single person participating in and enjoying the fruits of an unjust society become a bearer of force against the oppressed? In my judgment this might be true in some cases to a certain extent, but not to the extent that I could justify killing people who are not actual bearers of force. Revolutionaries or Freedom Fighters might be justified in using violence against the property of such people who are clearly leaders in the process of oppression.

The Christian with some reluctance recognizes the need that at times violence, killing and force might be needed in the cause of justice. Unfortunately, both in the question of war and in the question of revolution or liberation there is a constant temptation to romanticize and glorify violence. Violence must always be a last resort because it entails killing and suffering and should never be glorified. The whole Christian message calls upon all of us to strive with every possible means to achieve peace and justice in our society.

Human Sexuality
The Sixth and Ninth Commandments

1. What is the Christian meaning of human sexuality?

With all men of good will, we Christians search for a better knowledge of the human person and his or her sexual endowment. We do not always have ready answers about specific norms of behavior but through divine revelation, we do have a fundamental orientation to meaning and values. Scripture tells us that the human sexual endowment is willed by God and is therefore good. "And God said, 'Let us make man in our image and likeness, male and female' " (Gen. 1:26).

All of revelation tells us that God is love and that man becomes more an image of God as he becomes more able to reciprocate love and to discern what is truthful love and what is counterfeit. God created human bisexuality not only for reproduction but also, and above all, to help mankind to grow in mutual love.

Revelation as a whole teaches us formally that the full activation of sexuality has its legitimate and dignified place in marriage. There the two meanings—the bodily expression of love and the transmission of life—find their synthesis in a total sharing of life, values and ideals. This synthesis, in a perspective of redeeming and redeemed love, is the heart of a Christian understanding of human sexuality.

2. What is the virtue of chastity?

Chastity is not something besides or beyond love. It is that respectful self-control that preserves one's capacity to see and to fulfill one's sexuality, in a perspective of love. It is also a result of growth in truthful love for the other person. It has nothing to do with distaste for sexual pleasure. Sexuality, with the joy and pleasure it brings, is good when it is integrated in the mutual and responsible expression of love.

The virtue of chastity is possible only if one overcomes selfishness and grows in deep respect for one's own body and person and that of all others. One who is chaste will never consume or abuse another in selfish pleasure-seeking. Chastity also excludes the possessive approach to another person of the opposite sex or of the same sex. In a final analysis, chastity lives for love and through love, as well as through and for self-respect and respect for other persons.

3. Why is chastity a Christian virtue?

Chastity is a virtue common to both Christians and non-Christians. Many who do not know Christ or who do not believe in him have a deep understanding of chastity. They live and love according to its profound meaning.

What, then, is specifically Christian? Through revelation we know explicitly about the lofty dignity of our sexual endowment and its relation to our highest vocation, to grow in love and to become ever more an image or, as it were, a sacrament of God who is love. But we also know explicitly from revelation that sexuality, like the whole human person, is in need of redemption. Our attitude toward our own and others' sexuality is constantly threatened by sin: that selfishness which is not only in one's own heart but also somehow invested in the human environment. Yet the final tone of the Christian approach is not pessimism but rather trust in redemption. We believe that people can gradually overcome their selfishness and, in the freedom of the children of God, come to love in the true meaning of sexuality.

4. Why is virginity a Christian value?

In most primitive cultures, virginity was strongly requested of the woman. Among the many reasons, a main one was the concept of male superiority. Men did not want their future spouses to be sexually possessed or used by others. The family therefore carefully guarded a girl's bodily virginity, and girls were given in marriage very early. There were several noble motives as well, but the fact that pre-marital chastity often was not requested of the male shows that the meaning of virginity was not fully grasped. In a Christian evaluation, male dominence must be excluded, since it is the outcome of sinfulness (Gen. 3:16).

In a Christian perspective we distinguish between virginity as pre-marital chastity and virginity as freely chosen for a lifetime. Pre-marital virginity takes its Christian value from a high reverence for marriage. Since marriage means "becoming one body," where the mutual self-bestowal is part of the covenant, both men and women preserve themselves for the future partner in marriage. Virginity can also mean an equal openness and readiness for celibacy or for marriage, both understood as a calling (vocation) coming from God.

Virginity for a lifetime is a specifically Christian choice. In no way does it negate or disown one's sexual endowment; rather, it is a witness that the person can come to his or her personal fulfillment without genital activation of sexuality. Christ gave himself totally to the service of his gospel, and those who have found their greatest joy in the gospel of Christ, and are ready to consecrate or dedicate their whole life to the kingdom of God, can renounce marriage and family. It is essential, however, that these persons remain fully capable of loving others affectionately. The value of virginity depends above all on the capacity to love sincerely, and to love especially those with whom nobody falls in love.

5. What is the special value of celibacy?

It is essentially the same as that of virginity. It is a free renunciation of marriage. The word is sometimes used, however, simply in the sense of being celibate or unmarried.

If a person is unable to marry because "he was so from the mother's womb" or "was made so by man" (by unfavorable environment and/or education) it can mean great suffering. To be celibate in this sense is not a value but a non-value. However, it can be transformed into a value if it is accepted in faith and united with the passion and death of Christ in the hope of resurrection. Similarly, an abandoned spouse who cannot remarry may be able to grasp the situation as a call to give himself or herself totally to the kingdom of God.

Celibacy is a specifically Christian value if it is freely chosen or at least accepted in the freedom of the sons and daughters of God. We have to distinguish its intrinsic value from the particular legislation of the western Latin church, which makes celibacy a condition for admission to the ministerial priesthood. This law is by no means essential. Throughout the centuries, the church has taken diverse approaches to this question, and will be equally free in the future to change legislation. However, such a change must by no means darken the intrinsic value of freely chosen celibacy as a witness to the gospel and to our hope of resurrection.

6. What is the Christian meaning of marriage?

Each marriage is meant to be a way of growth and salvation for the people involved. It is a covenant of faithful love that should enable them to grow in their capacity to reciprocate genuine love and to enrich future generations with this most gracious talent. In every good marriage there is a presence of God who helps the spouses to become more effectively what they are meant to be: an image and likeness of God for each other.

A Christian marriage is distinguished by awareness that Christ is present with his redeeming love. "As God of old made himself present to his people through a covenant of love and fidelity, so now the Savior of man and the Spouse of the church comes into the lives of married Christians through the sacrament of matrimony. He abides with them therefore so that, just as he loved the church and handed himself over on her behalf, the spouses may love each other with perpetual fidelity through mutual self-bestowal" (*Pastoral Constitution on the Church of Today,* Art. 48). This awareness of Christ's presence in a Christian marriage encourages shared prayer, which is a shared searching for God's will: how to please him and to render him thanks by the whole life together.

The main purposes in a Christian marriage are to help each other to know and to love God more vitally, to learn to love all people in this great school of love, and to transmit life and educate their children to maturity, discernment, commitment to the common good, and to awareness of God's presence.

7. What is conjugal chastity?

Conjugal chastity is, above all, an expression of faithful love. The more the spouses love each other and are able to discern genuine love from its counterfeits, the more they will be chaste. Conjugal chastity cannot be defined by only prohibitive laws or by abstinence from certain acts. Primarily it is the fostering of those attitudes which help husband and wife to progress in mutual respect, love and fidelity. It includes a conditioning of the whole life, the daily situations which promote respect and therefore chastity. Then, negatively, we can say that conjugal chastity forbids possessive and exploitive attitudes toward one's own body and that of the spouse.

Real conjugal chastity harmonizes somehow the unitive values and the procreative values of marriage. This does not mean, however, that each conjugal act should be sought or considered as actual transmission of life. Rather, the whole of the married life is directed, by wisdom and prudence, toward its two main purposes: to grow in love and to transmit life—but not only biological life—and to fulfill the high vocation of parenthood.

8. What are the principal sins against chastity?

Holy Scripture condemns, above all, adultery, and not only the external act but the root of it: the lack of fidelity in thought, desire and purpose, the whole attitude that tends to use others instead of giving one's self faithfully to the spouse. Within marriage, too, there can be a striking lack of chastity if each partner is seeking his or her own pleasure and self-fulfillment instead of expressing tender, attentive and respectful love for the other.

Sins against chastity in the sexual encounters of unmarried people can be of various levels and degrees. The most degrading form is prostitution, often more sinful for those who abuse the prostitute for either sexual pleasure or financial gain. Next is promiscuity, the changing of sexual partners with no commitment to each other, though perhaps with some mutual affection but without that love which engenders responsibility and fidelity. Traditionally, these acts are called "fornication." Concubinage can be a long-lasting relationship but without intention of permanence or at least without commitment to fidelity.

Modern psychology deals with a number of deviant sexual behaviors such as homosexuality, lesbianism, transvestism, and so on. In some cases it can be almost impossible to discern what is psychological defect, what is suffering, and what is sin.

9. What is the Catholic attitude toward adultery?

Since marriage is meant to be a witness to the covenant fidelity between God and the church adultery thoroughly belies the sacramental commitment. It is a grave break in the promises made before God and man; it often is the first step towards divorce; it almost inevitably causes numerous lies and deceitful attitudes toward the spouse; and it can bring in its wake the temptation of abortion.

However, condemnation of this very grave sin does not suffice. The Catholic attitude is to call the sinner to repentance, which should eliminate the roots of these sins: selfishness, superficiality, irresponsibility, and especially lack of true love. From the very beginning, the choice of a future spouse should raise the question of whether union with this person will facilitate fidelity or possibly make it difficult.

While we consider adultery as one of the gravest sins, we should not forget that there are other forms of misbehavior in marriage, such as cruelty, constant manifestation of disrespect, calculated loveless-ness, which can harm the other person and destroy a marriage even more effectively than an individual act of adultery.

In the case of adultery, the spouse should try to dispose himself or herself to be ready to forgive and to heal the wounds, and also to examine his or her conscience about any possible contribution toward the other's failures. Thus both can join in a deeper conversion. We are all challenged by the increasing trend toward infidelity in marriage because of the permissiveness of our society and the many quasi-institutionalized temptations. For each of us and for the whole com-munity and society, the question is: what can we do to remove or at least to diminish the temptations in the environment.

10. What is the Catholic attitude toward divorce and remarriage?

Among the Jews of Jesus' time, divorces was rather frequent. The husband could divorce his wife on almost any ground. Jesus severely condemned this male-centered behavior with its unjust, irresponsible attitude toward women. The husband is as much obliged to fidelity as the wife.

The Christian community is sharply challenged by a very high divorce rate even among believers, due to our unstable culture, the trend to consumerism, and a general selfishness. The church is always obliged to do all she can to prevent divorce. She has to give high priority to better preparation for marriage, through education for fidelity and for readiness to forgive and be reconciled. She should also provide well-trained marriage counsellors. If our lives are guided by the principle, "forgive us our trespasses as we forgive those who trespass against us," many marriages can be saved.

In past centures the church has justified separation of spouses on various grounds. The separation, however, excluded remarriage. One reason for this was the hope of future reconciliation. In a patriarchal family system, the separated or abandoned spouse was reintegrated in the original family. In today's urban society with its nuclear family, the abandoned spouse is often left alone, exposed to many frustrations and temptations. This has led many Christians to think that, for some divorced people, it would be better to remarry than to "burn." The issue is under theological, pastoral and canonical investigation, and sharply divides the different currents in the church. All agree that divorce must be avoided wherever humanly possible. There seems also a consensus that the abandoned spouse should try to live a celibate life if reconciliation is impossible. Many would, however, apply here the word of the Lord, "Not everyone can accept this teaching, only those to whom it is given to do so . . . Let him accept this teaching who can" (Mt. 9:11–12).

The Orthodox churches tolerate or even allow a remarriage when the first one is hopelessly dead and a remarriage is, all things considered, a lesser evil or the better solution for the person and the community. This solution, documented since the third century, is based on their understanding of the divine *economy* of salvation. In the Roman Catholic Church, the only solution that authorizes a remarriage is the canonical annulment of the previous one. This practice is firm since the 12th century. However, through the centuries, there is considerable diversity in the transmission of motives and reasons for annulment.

The new cultural and social situation, the insights yielded by the behavorial sciences, and the understanding of marriage as it is officially presented by Second Vatican Council are gradually leading to a new approach to this difficult problem. The question, "Which are the anthropological conditions for an indissoluble marriage?" is a great and complicated one. A number of theologians and canonists suggest that the church should not forbid a remarriage where there are strong, though not proven, reasons for considering the previous marriage invalid. However, all these discussions should strengthen rather than weaken the church's efforts to do all possible to promote the stability of the Christian marriage.

11. What is the Catholic attitude toward artificial insemination?

Pius XII spoke very forcefully against artificial insemination in the case of a donor other than the husband. With respect to insemination with the husband's sperm, the wording of his declaration left some openings. There is surely an essential difference between the two situations.

For married couples who are unable to have children without artificial insemination, the best solution is adoption. The adopted child is as much, and even more, the child of the adopting parents than a child conceived by an anonymous donor's sperm. The idea of sperm banks —of men selling their sperm for unknown women—is repugnant and in contrast to our idea of responsible transmission of life in response to God and in loving response of the spouses to each other. Artificial insemination with a donor's sperm could also result in marriages between close relatives without awareness of the relationship.

Traditional Catholic teaching has objected to massage by which the husband obtains the sperm for insemination. It has been considered as masturbation and therefore an intrinsic evil. However, this question is now under open discussion. For many it does not evidence the masturbation syndrome, since there is no selfish intent in it.

12. What is the Catholic attitude toward fertilization in vitro?

The experiments have a considerable potential for progress in embryology and might detect many reasons for infecundity. Some of the experiments were motivated only by search for scientific knowledge about the development of the zygotes. Others are now directed toward the implantation of the blastocyst in the mother's womb around the eighth cell division. Some scientists are already dreaming of a "steel womb" (artificial placenta) so that women would be liberated from child-bearing.

The whole presentation and prospect of these experimentations pose enormous moral questions. What are the risks, biologically and psychologically, for this prefabricated man? Those who are firmly convinced that the zygotes are not endowed with the spiritual life-principle before implantation—that they are not yet persons—would see lesser difficulties than those who consider the product of artificial fertilization as already a human being in the full sense. It is true that many fertilized eggs are lost before implantation: the estimates are up from 30 per cent to 50 per cent. Would the percentage of failures not be considerably higher in the case of fertilization in vitro? At any rate, there is a fundamental difference. It is an arbitrary risk with grave consequences. In the case of a deformed embryo, who would decide to continue or to stop the process? The idea of the steel womb seems to be a striking invention of the technical age which so easily forgets the uniqueness of the human person who is in need of a loving environment from the very onset of life.

13. What is the Catholic attitude toward birth control?

There are two fundamental but different questions: first, whether spouses should control the transmission of life; and second, if so, what means are morally acceptable.

The first question is answered clearly and firmly by the Second Vatican Council: the transmission of life, the size of the family, and the interval between pregnancies are matters of responsible, conscious deliberation by the spouses. We do not consider as ideal in our times the attitude, "let children come as God sends them." God has given people intelligence and wants them to be sharers and co-workers in his creative love according to that intelligence. Nobody can decide the family size except the couple themselves. They should take into account their whole situation, their capacity not only to give shelter and food to the children but to educate them harmoniously and, above all, to transmit to them the greatest gift, faith in God, and the capacity to love their fellowmen. They should also consider the social situation. In over-populated countries and areas it might be a virtue not to have too many offspring. However, those who are surely able to give their children a good secular and religious education and formation are contributing very positively to the welfare of their society. To make a mature decision on such an important question, Christian spouses will pray and search together before God. For them it is a response of gratitude for the gift God has bestowed on them.

The second question about the means is causing a certain pluralism within the Catholic church. There is a firm consensus, however, that abortion must be thoroughly excluded. This makes it advisable for us to avoid even the term "birth control" and to prefer expressions like "regulation of conception" or "contraception." Thus we exclude, in the very use of concepts, the tendency of some planned parenthood advocates to consider abortion as just one of the different means of birth control.

Once human life is conceived, man has no right to control birth. Since Pius XII (1951) the papal magesterium approves the calculated use of "rhythm" as a legitimate means of regulation of conception, provided the spouses have good motives for not transmitting life here and now. But since this method causes psychological and other difficulties in some cases, which can endanger the very marriage, and since it cannot be used by people of some cultural backgrounds, a number of episcopates, most moral theologians, and marriage counsellors would consider other means of contraception licit, or at least tolerable, when there is a *conflict* between responsible transmission of life and the exigencies of conjugal harmony and love. Catholics have to learn to live with this pluralism in mutual respect. Meanwhile, each couple should act according to its own well-informed conscience.

14. What is the Catholic attitude toward sterilization?

We have to distinguish carefully between therapeutic and non-therapeutic sterilization. Therapeutic sterilization is to be judged by the same principles as any other therapeutic intervention. However, there is some disagreement among the various schools of Catholic theology about what can be understood as therapeutic. Some would define health, sickness and therapy only in view of the biochemical, physiological aspect of the human body: a concept that corresponds to a rather materialistic concept of medicine. We have also to consider the mental health. Whenever sterilization is the best possible and most indicated therapy for restoring the total health of a person, there can be no moral objections. Non-therapeutic sterilization cannot be justified and is generally judged negatively within the Catholic church.

It is a serious infringement of the fundamental rights of the human person if a government or another social agency imposes sterilization as a means of birth regulation.

15. What is the Catholic attitude toward premarital sex?

God entrusted to mankind the creative flame of human life and thereby gave joy, dignity and an awesome responsibility to human sexuality. From the beginning the Catholic church has taught—and still teaches—that the sexual union must be reserved for marriage. It is the expression of "one body" which has its true dignity and full meaning only if there is already the community of life and commitment to fidelity.

The term "pre-marital sex" is generally understood as sexual intercourse by anyone who is not yet married. The word "fornication" describes the disorder of intercourse by unmarried people. Yet the pre-marital sex of a betrothed couple who love deeply though imperfectly should not be labelled with the same words as the loveless acts of prostitution or promiscuity. It is a moral disorder but not "fornication" in the same sense. It is not enough, however, just to condemn it. Young people have to be motivated and helped to understand that the church's doctrine does protect their dignity and their true freedom. The one who suffers most often under the consequences of extra-marital intercourse is the woman.

In our superficial society, where sex is considered by many as merely an "article of consumption," only those who are educated to a profound sense of the dignity of the human body, of the sexual endowment, of transmission of human life, and of the vocation of marriage will be sufficiently motivated to follow the doctrine of the church.

16. What is the Catholic attitude toward homosexuality?

Holy Scripture gives us a clear picture of how Israel defended itself against homosexuality, which was a widespread phenomenon in the surrounding pagan cultures. Saint Paul's decisive point in Romans 1:18–27 is that the deviant sexual behavior—homosexuality, lesbianism, etc.—is a result of the total alienation of mankind or of a culture from God. "Although they knew God, they did not adore him or give him thanks."

Generally speaking homosexuality is not inherited: most homosexuals do not beget children. It is chiefly a symptom of our culture, caused by the many tensions, family quarrels and/or by erroneous sex education that presents the other sex as threat. Abuse of young people by persons of the same sex who are in positions of authority can also lead to a homosexual trend. In other cases the trend is initiated by curiosity and then fostered by homosexuals who, once a person has come into contact with them, often try to block the person's efforts to regain his or her freedom.

Well-trained psychotherapists can be very helpful if a person is not too old and truly wants to overcome the homosexual trend. Those who can be healed should seek help for their own benefit and the benefit of others. It is a great handicap not to be able to come to a balanced marriage and family life because of homosexual fixation. For those who cannot be freed from the trend, it is of paramount importance to accept and understand the traditional conviction that a person can come to his or her maturity and human fulfillment without sex activity. Overt homosexuality does not make people happy.

The basic principle is that homosexual persons must make the same honest effort to control their trend as heterosexual persons have to make for their self-control. However, if a homosexual makes an honest effort and does not succeed, especially if he is plagued by other psychic or social handicaps, he should not be driven into guilt complexes. Homosexuals should not concentrate all their attention on this problem but rather use other existent freedom in those areas in which they can make their contribution to the common good. They should be offered friendship and respect.

17. What is the Catholic attitude toward masturbation?

Masturbation is a very complex phenomenon. Therapy and moral judgment are impossible without discernment. Among preadolescents and adolescents, masturbation can be a transitory phase, worsened by an early sexual masturbation and a delayed personal development. In our culture, youth is now sexually mature three or four years earlier than previously, while our whole style of culture often postpones a balanced social and emotional maturation.

In some cases, frequent masturbation is caused by physiological irritation. In other cases it is the consequence of a disturbed economy of hormones. Inappropriate or totally lacking sex education can contribute to it. Most frequently, young people have difficulty in overcoming the masturbation phase because they have not received enough of the right kind of love; they do not feel accepted. In all these situations it is senseless to cause a guilt complex. The main educational effort must be orientation toward altruism. The young people need understanding, acceptance, respect, and have to learn how to acquire the same attitude toward others. When they do, they will overcome one of the chief sources of the masturbation syndrome.

A one-sided pedagogy of fear often blocks the therapy, causes anguish, and becomes a cause of frustration that explodes in masturbation. There are even many adults who have not overcome masturbation in spite of all their efforts. A person should not feel worthless if he has difficulty in this field if, at the same time, he has developed the capacity to love others generously and commits himself to worthwhile causes for the common good.

18. What is the Catholic attitude toward obscenity?

One of the main foundations of chastity is reverence for the mystery of the human person, including his or her body and sexual endowment. Obscenity in look, in exhibition, pictures and reading is manifestation of a lack of this respect and reverence. It can be, besides, a severe temptation for others, at least in the sense that they, too, gradually lose respect for the mystery of human sexuality. Obscenity is expressed in a particularly debasing form in pornography, where ruthless business men exploit people's weakness and vulnerability.

19. What is the Catholic attitude toward immodesty?

Immodesty is not so much a matter of mode or fashion as a way of presenting one's self or looking at and treating others: an attitude that takes advantage of the vulnerability of others. It is a manifestation of immaturity in sexual matters. The Christian is called to glorify God in his body. This should be the main criterion regarding motives as well as external behavior, modes and fashions.

20. How does the virtue of chastity extend to internal thoughts and desires?

The gospel teaches us that impurity, like purity, comes from one's heart, from one's innermost desires. Christ teaches us to make the tree good and it will bear good fruit. We cannot change the external behavior profoundly unless we change thoughts, desires and purposes in the right direction.

21. Is there parvity of matter in sexual sins?

All commandments of God are thoroughly serious, and mankind has to strive in all fields to do God's will whole-heartedly. But Christian life is an ongoing conversion. In many things we fail not because of bad purpose but because of human weakness, and this is particularly true in matters of the sixth commandment. The possibility that many sins are not mortal, but are less or more grave venial sins, stems from man's imperfect liberty.

Sexual sins have to be judged like all other sins. The most important law is the law of love of neighbor. If there can be parvity of matter in other sins against love, respect, justice, why not in matters of sexual sins? The sixth commandment has to be treated like all the other commandments of God.

If, after a fault, a person wants to know whether he or she has committed a mortal sin or a less or more serious venial sin, the main criterion is the following: Is my moral life on a road of progress or am I on a downward path? If the sin were mortal, there would be a decline of morality and freedom also in other matters. Another criterion offered by tradition gives persons of good will considerable encouragement. It says, if someone, immediately or very soon after the sin, makes an act of sorrow and of serious purpose, there is great hope that the sin was not a mortal sin although it might be a grave venial sin.

Justice and Truth

The Seventh (Tenth) and Eighth Commandments

SEVENTH COMMANDMENT: "YOU SHALL NOT STEAL"

1. What are we taught by the seventh commandment?

We are taught to respect the rights of all our fellow human beings with regard to material goods. It has been the constant teaching of Christendom that all things on earth were made for the good of all human beings, and that ordinarily a person can obtain certain of these goods for his own exclusive use. Such property rights are not absolute, but are true rights, subject to the needs of individual fellow humans or of a human community.

This right to private property can be acquired in many ways such as, by gift, by contract, by inheritance, by prescription, by occupation, and so forth. Civil laws constitute legitimate determinations of these means of acquiring title to material goods, and at least to this extent they bind in conscience.

2. What is forbidden by the seventh commandment?

The seventh commandment directly forbids theft, that is, taking what belongs to another against the owner's reasonable wishes. This may be called by other names, such as theft, robbery, embezzlement, larceny, looting, pilfering, confidence game, welching on a contract, fraudulent labeling, use of false weights or measurements. Indirectly the commandment also forbids other sinful actions by which one knowingly and willingly causes a person a loss in material goods to which he has a strict right. Such actions are against this commandment as well as against the law of love and whatever other commandment is violated; for example, the fifth commandment, by physically injuring a person so that he cannot perform his regular job and get his pay or, the eighth commandment, by sinful racial discrimination which causes a person a material loss.

The gravity of the matter in violations of the seventh commandment has been widely discussed in the past. One who truly loves God above all things will not want to violate any divine commandment even slightly. To try to draw a fine line between grave and less than grave matter is impossible. It depends on circumstances. In general, the matter is grave if it causes gravely evil effects on the victim or to the thief, or to the common good. Of course, for a person to be guilty of any mortal sin in any matter, the act must be done with full realization of its grave sinfulness and with a fully free choice of the will.

3. Under what conditions is one obliged to make restitution in material goods to a victim?

Restitution can be obligatory either for unjust possession or for causing a loss. If one possesses what belongs to another against the owner's reasonable wishes, even if one originally received it in good faith, one must restore the property to the rightful owner.

If one has caused a loss to another in material goods to which that other has a strict right one can owe restitution in several ways: by strict commutative justice, in legal justice, in charity, or not at all.

One owes restitution in strict commutative justice for a loss caused, if one causes the loss (a) with theological fault—that is, deliberately doing what one realizes was unjust; (b) efficaciously—the mere desire that a neighbor suffer a loss from some other cause is objectively sinful but does not entail an obligation of material restitution; (c) in goods or property in which the other had a strict right—and not just an outside chance of acquiring.

Even when such a loss is caused without theological fault, the one who has caused such a loss will be obliged in legal justice to make restitution if: (a) a legitimate court so orders; and, (b) there is at least juridical fault; that is, when one has been objectively negligent and should have avoided the damaging act.

When a loss occurs by complete accident without theological or juridical fault, but the result entails great need on one side, the other will be obliged in charity to help if this can be done without serious loss to him or herself.

4. Does not the fact that a victim's loss is covered by insurance relieve a damager of any obligation to make restitution?

If one has sinfully caused a loss, that is, with theological fault, he is bound to restitution even if the damage was covered by insurance. In this case, the actual loss is to the insurance company, which has the right to collect restitution from the damager, or from the victim if the restitution comes to him. So also if there is juridical fault and the court so orders. One would be exempt from any obligation in damage that was completely accidental, or which was done with only juridical and not theological fault and restitution is not ordered by a court.

5. Is it all right to collect insurance over and above actual damage?

It is a form of theft to obtain insurance payments fraudulently. However, if an insurance company agrees that its coverage will include complete repainting of a house, for example, when only a part was scorched, the victim may freely accept this as due him from a proper understanding of the policy, which is a form of contract.

6. Am I entitled to whatever I can get in a suit for damages?

If I have suffered a true loss because of the objective negligence of another, I am entitled to sue him in court to recover what I have truly lost. If there was evidence of malicious intent in the damaging, I may also sue for punitive damages. A just court sentence in such matters can give the plaintiff a true title to the damages. If the sentence was unjustly arrived at by my fraud, I acquire no right.

7. May I sue for more than what I honestly believe is my loss on the basis that most juries reduce the amount asked?

If circumstances are such that I am fairly sure that the amount will be reduced, I may sue proportionately higher. However, if I deliberately sue for more than I honestly think I should get and am awarded that higher amount, I should return or waive the surplus, taking into account the possibility of just punitive damages.

8. Do contracts regarding material goods or services bind in conscience?

A contract is an agreement between two or more persons (individuals and/or moral persons such as companies, societies and such) to exchange a right to material goods (including money) for other goods or services. As long as both parties agree on the meaning of the terms and are dealing honestly regarding materials or services over which they have control, a contract does truly bind the parties.

9. Have I a right to keep what I win in gambling?

Gambling is a contract in which it is agreed that money or something of value will be given by one party to the other, the direction being dependent on the outcome of an uncertain event. In itself it can be a legitimate and binding contract provided that both parties agree on the risk, that the risk is equal or proportioned to the amount wagered, and that each can legitimately afford to pay if he loses. Insurance contracts are actually a form of gambling. Because of the great dangers associated with gambling, especially with commercial gambling, civil laws in many jurisdictions prohibit or strictly regulate ordinary gambling, and often make a gambling contract void or unenforceable in court. It can be argued that civil laws do not bind with regard to private acts between consenting adults.

To bet on a sure thing is usually sinful and null and void as a contract, and collecting on such a bet usually is a form of theft, since the nature of a gambling contract is that the event be uncertain. If one party is warned that the other is certain and still insists on betting, it can be considered a donation.

10. Is cheating in games against the seventh commandment?

Cheating in games on whose outcome something of material value depends is a form of theft or cooperation in theft. Prizes are offered for winners and bets made on games with the understanding that the game is fair. Even shading the score of a game or contest can cause bettors to lose by changing the conditions of the contract without their knowledge and consent.

If nothing of material value depends on the outcome of the game, intentional cheating is still a form of dishonesty, at least against charity, and perhaps against the eighth commandment in depriving a person or team of an honor which should rightfully have been theirs.

11. Is cheating on taxes against the seventh commandment?

Sacred Scripture tells us that we should pay just taxes and there is a natural obligation that everyone should pay his fair share of necessary government expenses. This would seem to be an obligation indirectly under the fourth commandment, among the duties of citizens towards legitimate governmental authority. Many writers, both theo-logical and legislative have debated greatly on the justice of modern tax structures; yet all agree on the general obligation of citizens to pay a fair share of the costs of government. Dishonesty will always be wrong, and evading taxes does not extinguish the obligation to do one's fair share.

Obviously to steal from the government, directly or by cheating on government contracts, or, on the part of civil servants, by extortion or graft, is a violation of justice and does oblige to restitution.

12. How does the seventh commandment apply to business practices?

The general principle that taking what belongs to another against the owner's reasonable wishes is theft and against the seventh com-mandment applies very definitely to business dealings, whether the victim be an individual buyer, a company or the general public. For example, to list on a business expense account expenses with no connection to the business is stealing from one's company. To substi-tute cheaper materials than specified and charge for the better materi-als is stealing. To charge the price of a good used car for a car that is substantially defective is stealing.

13. What constitutes a fair price in selling?

It is impossible to draw fine lines in determining a just price. A seller who is doing a service for others is entitled to a reasonable living from his work, and therefore to a reasonable profit on his sales. Any fraud or deception in selling will be equivalent to stealing. A seller has no right to increase a price because of the need of the buyer, since the buyer's need is in no way the property of the seller. Usually common prices in a free competitive market will be just. Anti-trust laws try to prevent the temptation to set artifically high prices. Rare curios and objects of art are not necessities even in the broad sense of the word, and so any price agreed on will be just provided that there is no fraud or deceit.

14. Does an agent acting for another or others have special obligations under the seventh commandment?

An agent is obliged to act for the best interests of those for whom he acts, whether he is acting for an individual person, for a company, for a governmental unit, or for an ecclesiastical division, such as a parish or diocese. The agent should not allow himself to be influenced by considerations for his own interest to the detriment of his principal(s). For example, to place an order with one company because he has received an expensive gift from it, when the best interests of his principals would demand placing the order with another company, is unjust and amounts to stealing from his principals. If there is no appreciable difference in value to his principals among several possible companies, choosing one over the others because of a personal gift would not of itself be unjust, but it is so open to abuse that in many matters civil law prohibits civil officials from accepting such gifts.

To offer such a gift to an agent in a position of trust in order to influence him to do business with you amounts to bribery and is unjust, if you are trying to get him to make a decision which he should not make.

For an agent to demand payment from anyone other than his principal, for doing what he should do anyhow, or for doing an unjust act, is extortion, and is a form of stealing. The acceptance of payments in bribery or extortion in a public office is graft, and is unjust.

Extortion also includes any form of unjust demand of payment under threat of unjust action against the payer. Ransom demands in kidnapping and hijacking are forms of extortion and are sins of theft as well as violations of justice and the fifth commandment in threatening death or harm to innocent human beings.

15. Do copyright and patent laws bind in conscience?

It seems only just that an author, artist or inventor should profit from his/her work. On the other hand, publishing a work is, in a sense, giving it to the public. Copyright and patent laws have been enacted to encourage creativity and publishing. With the advent of Xerox and other duplicating machines that have made copying printed material so much easier and more economical than formerly, the question of the rightness or wrongness of copying and distributing copyright matter has become a topic of lively discussion. Simple pirating of books, booklets, music and such, and selling them for profit, is clearly unjust. To duplicate an article or chapter of a book and distribute copies to a class or other group without material profit, to serve as the basis of study or discussion would not seem unjust in itself, if the members would not otherwise buy the originals. Whether civil laws bind to the extent of making such use immoral is much discussed and disputed. The least that can be said for the binding force

of the law is that it does give a title to the author to share in any
monetary or material profit gained from his work for the period of
years specified in the law. Copyright laws do not bind beyond fifty-six
years, so there is no difficulty about copying printed material older
than that.

16. Are there exceptions to the prohibition against stealing?

Granted the definition used in question n. 2, it would be hard to see
how there could be exceptions. However, there are situations, in
which taking what belongs to another is not a violation of justice.
Some of these are the exercise of the right of eminent domain, occult
compensation, bankruptcy, and cases of extreme necessity.

17. What is the right of eminent domain?

It is the right of a unit of civil government to take the property of
a private or moral person which is judged necessary for the common
good. This can take the form of condemnation proceedings to obtain
land for a necessary highway, school or such or the nationalization
of an industry, where this is deemed necessary for the good of all.
Ordinarily the government should give adequate compensation to the
owner of his property.

18. Does the legal process of declaring bankruptcy extinguish the obligation to pay just debts to the full?

It is generally held that a civilly adjudicated declaration of bankruptcy extinguishes debts beyond what the court assigns to be paid.
This is considered an exercise of eminent domain in charity to a
person who honestly cannot meet his financial obligations, in order to
give him a fresh start and promote trade and commerce. Wherefore,
even if the bankrupt later makes much money, he is not obliged in
justice to pay in full debts declared extinguished by bankruptcy. He
may be obliged in charity if he easily can pay and his former creditor
is in dire need. Contracts are presumed to be implicitly conditioned
on the possibility of bankruptcy.

19. What about occult compensation?

Occult compensation means taking from another what is due in
justice to the taker. Ordinarily we may not take from another what
he possesses against his reasonable wishes even if what we take is due
to us in justice. Such taking would usually fail against charity and may

fail against justice as well. If the debtor can and should give me here and now what he owes me and unreasonably refuses to do so, my first recourse should be to legal proceedings. If somehow recourse is practically impossible or unreasonable, my taking what is due me would not violate justice, but might still be a failure in charity.

20. If all material things are meant for the good of all, and I am in extreme need, may I legitimately take what I need from one who has plenty?

Since there are means by which I can ordinarily get help when I am in need (for example, Red Cross, Catholic Charities, Salvation Army), it would be wrong of me on my own authority to take what belongs to another. If conditions are such that I must take some material goods to save my life, and taking them will not put the owner in similar need, and there is no available way to get what I need by asking or by applying to public sources, then I do not violate justice in taking what I need. However, even in such a case, I must restore what I have taken if it is afterwards possible.

THE TENTH COMMANDMENT:
"YOU SHALL NOT COVET YOUR NEIGHBOR'S GOODS"

1. What does "covet another's goods" mean?

The word "covet" can mean simply "desire," or in the sense of this commandment, "desire what belongs to another." Covetousness, or, in its more modern synonyms, avarice or greed, is usually numbered as one of the capital sins, as being more often a source of sin rather than a formal sin in itself. The mere feeling of desire for the goods of another is not a sin, but if it is recognized and deliberately fostered, it would be a violation of this commandment. It is to be noted that this concerns desire for the actual goods of one's neighbor, not merely the desire to have something of the same kind. Also any internal sins, such as the deliberate intention to commit an act of theft, even if prevented from being carried out, is a sin against this commandment. In general, what is forbidden by the seventh commandment in act, is forbidden by this commandment in deliberate desire or intent.

EIGHTH COMMANDMENT:
"YOU SHALL NOT BEAR FALSE WITNESS AGAINST YOUR
NEIGHBOR"

1. What are we taught by the eighth commandment?

By the eighth commandment as illuminated by other parts of Sacred Scripture, we are taught to be truthful and to respect the reputation or good name of all our fellow men. This commandment directly forbids calumny, that is, lying in a way to harm another's good name or common esteem in the community. Indirectly, it forbids all forms of lying and commands due respect and esteem toward all fellow humans unless they have forfeited such a right by becoming dangerous to others.

2. What lies are forbidden by the law of God?

The notion of lying seems to be a very simple one and yet it must be defined carefully if it is to signify something always forbidden by the law of God. We cannot simply say that is uttering misleading or untruthful words. Jesus himself apparently used misleading words at times; for example, "I am not going up to this feast"—"And he also went up to that feast" (John 7:8, 10). Language is conventional in essence and all recognize some conventional uses as truthful, even when literally contrary to the truth. No one would accuse a person of lying if he said that the sun rises in the east, even though the speaker was aware that the sun merely appears to rise and that actually the movement of the earth gives this illusion of sunrise. Some polite usages are called white lies or fibs with the understanding that they are not morally wrong. Others prefer to call anything required by politeness merely a conventional usage and not a lie at all. Such would be telling a hostess that you enjoyed her dinner even if you did not. Most would recognize the sin of lying if one went far beyond the demands of politeness without truthfully meaning what one said. No one will accuse an actor playing a role on stage, screen or television of lying, no matter how much of what he says departs from the truth.

These examples should make it clear that the circumstances of a situation greatly modify the moral quality of any disagreement between a speaker's words and his internal mental judgment. It is impossible to predetermine for every possible case, what will or will not be objectively sinful speech. One accepted way of defining a lie is to say that it is saying what one knows to be false when all objective external circumstances suggest that the speaker intends to communicate what is in his mind. This would always be morally wrong. But it can be difficult or impossible to apply this strictly in every case.

3. What is the respect and honor which we owe to all fellow humans?

We owe ordinary respect and honor to every human being as made in the image and likeness of God. Although in the Old Testament this was sometimes applied only to members of the chosen people, Jesus taught that it applies to all humans even those whom we may consider enemies (Matthew 5:43–44). Christian tradition and papal teaching have insisted that the obligation to show honor and respect to all fellow humans is an obligation not only of charity or love but also of justice—that every human being has a basic right to common honor and respect. This is a God-given right and is forfeited only by serious sin against one's fellows. This basic respect and honor include what we might call politeness towards all, seeing all as God's children, regardless of race, color, creed or national origin.

4. What are offenses against this honor and esteem?

The principal sins in this matter are:

a. contumely or insult: Treating another person with contempt for no reason or for an irrelevant reason, like difference in race, color, social standing or such.

b. calumny: Lying about a person so as to deprive him of due esteem of his fellows.

c. rash judgment: Judging that a person is a sinner, criminal or inferior person without sufficient reason. Many acts of racial discrimination are based on rash judgments.

d. detraction: Destroying or diminishing the esteem due another by revealing secret defects of his without sufficient reason.

5. Why is detraction a sin if it is telling the truth?

A person does not lose his right to ordinary esteem and honor just because he is of illegitimate birth or because he has committed some sin or sins which are in no way a threat to others. But to broadcast such facts about him will ordinarily cause the loss of such esteem and honor. Therefore, one is obliged to avoid such foreseen damage unless there is a proportionate reason for telling: for example, being questioned as a witness in a court trial, or protecting a prospective spouse who would have a right to know.

6. Does the law of God oblige us always to tell "the truth, the whole truth, and nothing but the truth"?

The law of God forbids us to tell lies in the strict sense given above in question n. 5, but it does not oblige us to tell everything we know. Some things we are obliged not to tell, still other matters can fall into the category of things which we may conceal, but we are not obliged to conceal. The former come under the heading of secrets; the latter are matters of privacy.

Secrets are generally considered to be of three different and possibly overlapping types, according to the basis or foundation for the obligation of keeping them: (1) natural secret: based on the very nature of the matter; it is a fact whose revelation would harm a person by causing a loss of something to which he has a right, whether material goods, position, or good name; (2) promised secret: based on fidelity to one's word: when, after learning something, I promise another person I will keep the matter secret; (3) and committed secret: based on justice: when an understood or explicit contract or agreement not to tell is present before learning the matter in question. More than one of these bases can be present in one secret matter. For example, if I learn of a friend's illegitimate birth only because he has told me as a counselor and then asks me to explicitly promise him afterwards that I will not tell. The matter itself would be a natural secret since its public revelation could hurt his reputation; a contracted or committed secret since he approached me as a counselor; and a promised secret, because after learning the matter I promised not to tell.

7. How serious is the obligation to keep a secret?

The seriousness of the obligation differs greatly according to the matter and the basis of the obligation. There can be a prevailing obligation to reveal some secrets. A promise to keep a matter secret is not meant to bind to a point of risk to the promiser of any grave consequence, unless this is explicitly a condition of the promise. Committed secrets are more seriously binding in that they are based on a relationship of trust. In these, the gravity of the obligation increases in proportion to the importance of that relationship. One friend asking advice of another without explicit agreement beforehand is the lowest in the scale of committed secrets. A recognized position of trust creates a greater obligation. This constitutes a so-called professional secret and exists in varying degrees and positions such as physician, counselor, psychiatrist, spiritual director, minister or priest. The confessional secret is strictest of all, even apart from the very strict regulation of Church law on the point.

8. What sort of matters fall under the obligation of professional secrecy?

In general, the recipient of confidential information in a trust relationship should not reveal anything so learned without the free and informed consent of the revealing party. The consent should be explicit especially for matter that can be harmful or embarrassing to the revealer. This applies also to information learned by use of special techniques of the professional; for example, a physician discovering pregnancy in a woman patient, or a venereal disease, which by law must be reported to the proper authorities, but should not be revealed to others without the patient's freely-given consent.

Secrecy applies in a special way to those who use hypnosis, narcotherapy (use of so-called "truth serum"), psychological tests of varying kinds, that may reveal secrets of a person's interior life without his realizing that he is revealing such things. Informed consent to use these means in the first place requires that the person know the sort of thing that may be revealed to the professional. And consent to use the means does not imply any consent to divulge the results to others unless this is freely and explicitly agreed to also.

If the examinee is clearly mentally incompetent, consent should come from the responsible guardian, that is, parent, next-of-kin, religious or ecclesiastical superior or legal guardian.

9. Can anyone ever be justified in revealing a committed professional secret?

The understood commitment of most professions would leave some possibilities open. A physician is not understood to agree to conceal what civil law obliges him to reveal; for example, a gunshot wound or a venereal or other serious contagious disease. A spiritual director or priest would rarely if ever be justified in revealing any confidential non-confessional matter, and a priest may never reveal confessional matter unless the penitent has given clear and free consent to do so.

Popes and theologians have agreed that the spiritual director of seminarians may not reveal what he has learned in confidence, even to prevent the ordination of an unworthy candidate, so important is confidentiality in these matters.

10. What is allowed in protecting legitimate secrets?

It is generally permissible simply to deny knowledge of secret matters. However, in some cases this may not be enough to put off importunate questioners. Moralists of times past suggested what they called a "broad mental reservation" which would allow the secret-holder to use equivocal statements, which would have a meaning that would agree with the facts, but another intended and more obvious meaning besides. For example, when hiding a person who was being unjustly pursued, the host might answer the pursuer, "I saw him go down that street and turn west," meaning that he had once seen the man go that way, but not recently.

Modern theologians have been in general agreement that whatever words are necessary to protect a legitimate secret are allowable, whether they have such a true sense or not. It would take a genius to think up equivocal answers to fit the broad mental reservation. One explanation why a false statement in such a case would not be a lie is that external objective circumstances do *not* indicate that the speaker intends to communicate what is in his mind.

The use of false statements is morally justified only in protecting legitimate secrets, including matters of privacy. Since such statements do lead the recipients into false judgments and so may be said to be physically harmful, they should be kept to a minimum. If "I don't know" or "no comment" will suffice, further fabrications would be against charity at least, if not also against truthfulness.

11. Has everyone a right to privacy?

Natural or God-given rights as distinguished from acquired or civilly-granted rights are based in some way on the nature of man as created by God and as destined by God to work out his salvation according to his nature. God endows man with a right to whatever is necessary for him to live a decent human life. Christian teaching has always held that a certain amount of privacy is a necessity for a decent human life. Earlier theologians did not treat the matter in any great detail, speaking in this regard mainly of one's right to the privacy of his privately written words in letters or notes. Beginning with Pope Pius XII and the invention of means to invade a person's privacy, more has been taught about the right to privacy, especially with regard to such means as wiretapping, "bugging," recorders, "truth serum," polygraphs ("lie detectors"), personality inventories, and psychological testing.

12. What does the right to privacy imply?

It implies the right of every human being to keep a sector of his life to himself and another part to be shared only with his family and a few chosen friends or confidants. This implies, further, the obligation incumbent on all not to invade this privacy; not to listen in secret to private conversations whether these are face to face or over the telephone; not to read private letters or notes without the consent of the author or the one to whom they are addressed; not to spy, by special lenses or secret openings, on the private actions of others; not to pry into the private affairs of others by importunate and nagging questions, even of a public figure; not to plant listening devices or recorders to hear or to record private conversations; not to try to trick a person into revealing private matters by questionnaires, hypnosis, truth drugs or lie detectors.

13. Is a person ever justified in prying into another's private affairs in any of these ways, or revealing what he has learned in such ways?

If one accidentally learns something of the private life of another, he will be bound by the general rules governing secrets. Explicit or reasonably presumed permission of the person will justify passing it on to others. Natural secrecy will dictate not revealing what can be harmful or embarrassing to the other. A person may show by clear outward actions and words that he does not care what is revealed about his private life, but this must not be easily presumed.

Apart from such permission, prying into the private words or actions of another, especially by the means mentioned in question n. 12, is justified only if there is a well-founded reason to suspect that injustice is being plotted by the other person. Civil law in this country takes a similar stand, surreptitious entry, "bugging" and wiretaps may be used even by government agents only after showing probable cause to believe that illegal actions are being committed or plotted on the premises.

Recording of a telephone conversation even by a party to the conversation should not be done without the other party's knowledge and consent. Civil law requires a regular intermittent beeping sound if such a recording is being done. Similar principles are applicable to recording any private conversation.

It might be noted that parents should respect the right of their children to some privacy.

Among matters which might be considered as sharing in the right to privacy is the right not to have to incriminate oneself.

14. What is the basis for the right not to have to incriminate oneself?

The strongest of human instincts, that of self-preservation, exerts its powerful influence also in this field. Recognition of this often overpowering instinct has led both Church and State to enact laws exempting anyone from having to give evidence in a court trial which might incriminate himself. Moralists have long taught that one may simply deny guilt when questioned by private individuals. Authorities differ as to whether this applies also to questioning of a child by its parents, or to questioning of a cleric or religious by his/her legitimate superior outside of a judicial setting. It is at least probable that no one is obliged to admit his own guilt unless he has willingly set up circumstances in which this would be expected. Such circumstances would be especially realized in approaching the sacrament of penance. And even outside of confession, self-incrimination can be the more perfect choice.

15. To what extent do pledges or promises oblige in conscience?

A pledge or promise made by a private individual binds as he intends it to bind: gravely, lightly, or not at all. If it is a promise made to another person, both should agree on what is promised and how serious the promise is meant to be. Unless the promise is specified as gravely binding, it is presumed to bind only lightly or not at all. If meant not to bind at all, it would be better called a resolution. To make any kind of promise or resolution with no intention of fulfilling it is a lie. To promise something immoral cannot bind in conscience.

A public pledge or promise will bind according to the way it is presented. For example, the pledge of the Legion of Decency is considered by the bishops' committee that proposes it to be a mere resolution to observe morality in entertainment and not to add any new obligation. A pledge to give money in a parish drive is ordinarily lightly binding, and ceases to bind if one's circumstances change, either financially or in location.

A promise can amount to a contract and be binding as such, if it is so intended and is made known to and accepted by another person, especially if it is in consideration of something of value received. Church law specifies that a promise by a priest to say Mass on receipt of a stipend binds gravely in conscience, even if the amount of the stipened is small. A promise to say Mass without acceptance of a stipend, binds lightly in fidelity and ceases to bind in the face of any unforeseen inconvenience, unless the priest intends to bind himself more seriously.

A promise by an employee to keep trade secrets is practically a contract, since it is a condition of his receiving his salary. The secrets are also committed secrets, and should be kept, even if the employee changes to another company.

The Just Society

1. What is social justice?

The term social justice in a Catholic context refers to that aspect of Church teaching and Christian life which seeks to apply the Gospel command of love to the structures, systems and institutions of society which are the framework in which all human relationships (personal, political, economic, cultural) take place. The object of the virtue is systemic, structural relationships; the agent of social justice is usually people organized in some form of group activity working through the political process.

2. Can we find a basis for the idea in the Scriptures?

Yes. The fundamental meaning of the term can be found in the prophets (e.g., Isaiah, Amos) who constantly tested the fidelity of the chosen people in terms of its social relationships. The Gospels do not mention the term as such but the basic perspective of social justice as a demand of the New Covenant and a central dimension of the ministry of Christ pervades the Synoptics (cf. Lk. 4:18ff; Mt. 25:31ff).

To grasp the themes of social justice fully one needs to read the Gospels in light of the prophetic literature.

3. Where do we find the meaning of social justice in Catholic teaching?

It is primarily to be found in the body of papal, conciliar and synodal literature of the last eighty years which comprises "the social doctrine" or "social teaching" of the Church. Pre-eminent among these documents are the following: *Rerum Novarum* (1891); *Quadragesimo Anno* (1931); *Christmas Messages* of Pius XII (1940–57); *Mater et Magistra* (1961); *Pacem in Terris* (1963); *Gaudium et Spes* (1965); *Dignitatis Personae Humanae* (1965); *Populorum Progressio* (1967); *Octogesima Adveniens* (1971); *Justitia in Mundo* (1971).

The key document in this line of development was *Quadragesimo*

Anno in which Pius XI began to speak specifically about a structural analysis of society as a framework for interpreting justice. The line of growth and continuity between this initial structural insight and the method of analysis employed in the Synod document of 1971 *(Justice in the World)* is very striking.

4. How does social justice relate to the other dimensions of the virtue of justice?

Justice traditionally has been distinguished into three parts: *commutative,* relating to contractual obligations between individuals involving a *jus strictum* and the obligation of restitution; *distributive,* the relationship between a government and its people regulating the burdens and benefits of societal life; *legal,* regulating the relationship of the individual toward society.

Social justice is often perceived as having evolved from legal or general justice; it has, however, a distinct meaning of its own, more precise than legal or general justice. It seeks to assess the worth of social systems in view of how they impact the lives of people in them, and it calls for a sense of responsibility by the individual for the structures in which he or she lives. The purpose of the social teaching of the Church has been to make explicit by what *criteria* and in terms of which *issues* Christians should form their consciences regarding social justice.

5. What is the relationship of justice and charity in Catholic teaching?

The synodal document *Justice in the World* says, "love implies an absolute demand for justice, namely a recognition of the dignity and rights of one's neighbor." The meaning of this absolute demand is that justice is the foundation of charity, i.e., it is absolutely required that I respect the rights and meet the needs of my neighbor if I am to say that I love him or her. If justice is lacking between people, groups, societies, then charity is impossible; since charity theologically means the giving of self to others (agape) it is impossible to reach this stage without first sharing with others what is due them by *right* (justice).

Conversely, justice reaches its fulfillment in charity; once the demands of justice are met, there is still room in a Christian view of human relationships to go beyond what is due others by right and share with them in the self-giving manner in which Christ gave himself to us and for us through his life, death and resurrection. Briefly, charity excuses us from none of the demands of justice; rather it calls us beyond justice to sacrificial service of others in imitation of the Suffering Servant.

6. What is the authority of social teaching for the Catholic conscience?

In answering this question two parameters are useful guides. First, the content of the social teaching is not optional; it articulates responsibilities which arise from the fundamental Gospel command to love our neighbor. The Christian who neglects his temporal duties, neglects his duties toward his neighbor and even God jeopardizes his eternal salvation (*Gaudium et Spes,* n. 43). Social justice is loving our neighbor in and through the complex relationships of societal structures from the local to the global level of life. Secondly, because of the contingent nature of many socio-political issues treated in the social teaching, the degree of authority of Church teaching varies with the nature of the subject: principles have a high degree of authority (e.g. each person has a right to a just wage) application of principles requires much discussion and debate (e.g. what constitutes a just wage).

7. Why is the social teaching not more explicit?

The purpose of the social teaching is primarily to set forth the values, norms and principles by which socio-economic and political issues are to be evaluated. When this has been done there is still the need for personal collective decisions to reduce the norms and principles to specific issues. As Paul VI said: "In concrete situations and taking account of solidarity in each person's life, one must recognize a legitimate variety of possible options. The same Christian faith can lead to different commitments." (*Octogesima Adveniens,* n. 50).

8. How important is the social teaching in the life of the Church?

The most specific and authoritative answer to this question is found in *Justice in the World* which describes the work of justice as a *constitutive element* in the ministry of the Church. The implications of this statement cannot be overestimated; it means that work for justice has equal value with the two other constitutive dimensions of Catholic faith: the celebration of the sacraments and the preaching of the Gospel. In summary, work for justice is essential to the ministry of the Church and is the task of all baptized Christians, not simply the work of a few specialists.

9. Does the social teaching manifest a process of development?

There has clearly been a broadening and deepening process at work since 1891. In general terms, one can trace a movement from a primary emphasis on the national society as a unit of analysis *(Rerum Novarum* and *Quadragesimo Anno)* to the global community or international society as the focus of analysis *(Pacem In Terris* and *Justice in the World).* Similarly, one can trace a movement from concern for economics *(Mater et Magistra)* to a move beyond economics to political issues *(Octogesimo Adveniens).* On specific issues like private property and pacifism it is also possible to trace a process of development at work.

10. Is the phrase "the social Gospel" an adequate description of the social teaching and ministry of the Church?

No. The phrase is confusing on two counts. First, it is identified with a specific period of Protestant theological thought which had merit but also many inherent difficulties. Secondly, it conveys the impression that questions of justice, peace, etc. are to be understood as a segment of the Gospel or an extension of the real (i.e. preaching and sacramental) ministry of the Church. Instead of "the Social Gospel," it is much more accurate theologically to speak of the Gospel which is thoroughly social in its meaning and extension.

11. What is "political theology?"

The phrase is commonly associated with a body of writing emerging first from Europe, then some of the developing countries after Vatican II. Its stated purpose was twofold: to carry out an internal critique of Christian theology in light of the social perspective of the Gospel ("deprivatize" theology); and to provide the Church with a theological stance which would allow it to fulfill more aggressively the role of a social critic in society.

12. What is "the theology of liberation?"

The phrase is primarily associated with a theological orientation emerging from Latin America which is based on two principles. Methodologically, it seeks to have theological reflection arise experientially from its cultural context; Latin American theologians take as a starting point the dependent character of the socio-economic situation of their societies. Substantively, in response to a dependent status, these writers seek to articulate and make operative the liberation themes found in the Exodus-Resurrection motifs of the Scriptures.

Liberation is explored both theologically and sociologically in this literature.

13. What is the place and role of natural law in Catholic social teaching?

The affirmation of a second source of wisdom beyond revelation has been a traditional part of Catholic social thought. Natural law, understood as a reflective analysis of the normative meaning of the human person and human society has provided much of the specific content of Catholic social teaching. The most fully developed articulation of this picture of the person and society is found in *Pacem In Terris.* More recent social teaching has tended toward a more biblical, less philosophical style of presentation as exemplified in *Populorum Progressio* and *Justice in the World.*

14. What are the basic concepts which are the foundation of the Church's social teaching?

Theologically, God is depicted in the Old Testament as "liberator of the oppressed and defender of the poor, demanding from man faith in him and justice toward man's neighbor"; Christ is seen in the Gospels as uniting "in an indivisible way the relationship of man to God and the relationship of man to other men." The Church, continuing the liberating ministry of Christ in her ministry, seeks to defend and promote "the dignity and fundamental rights of the human person" (cf. *Justice in the World,* II).

Philosophically, the Church seeks to explore what the dignity of the person means, which rights this dignity demands, and who is responsible for fulfilling these rights.

15. What is the basis of the dignity of the person?

Theologically, the dignity of the person, that which sets the person apart from the rest of creation, is the belief that the person is made in the image of God. This affirmation in Catholic thought gives the person a pre-eminent status. In Pius XII's words, the social order should have the person as "its subject, its foundation and its end." To protect the dignity of the person, he or she must be endowed with a spectrum of rights.

16. What are rights?

Rights are moral claims which the person can make on other persons and society in general; every right has a corresponding duty (e.g. the right to bodily integrity implies the duty to care for one's body). Moreover, the right of one person creates a duty for others to respect, foster and fulfill this right. Hence each person has both rights (claims) and duties (responsibilities); a basic duty of civil authority is to provide for the equitable coordination and adjudication of the rights and duties of its members.

17. What are some of the rights of the person in society?

A sampling of the spectrum of human rights would include economic rights (to work, to a just wage, to property); political rights (to participation, to judicial protection); cultural rights (to education, freedom of speech); social rights (to assembly, free association); also the right to worship; the right to emigrate and immigrate. In Catholic teaching the concept of rights is also applicable to rights of nations in relation to one another.

18. What is the right to development?

In *Justice in the World,* it is defined as "a dynamic interpenetration of all those fundamental human rights upon which the aspirations of individuals and nations are based." In defining the right the interplay of liberation and development is made explicit: development is a means of achieving liberation. Moreover, in all of the social teaching since *Mater et Magistra,* a constant theme has been the right of developing nations and people to control and direct their own process of development, even though foreign capital and technical assistance are also part of the process.

The concept of local control and the correlative idea that liberation of the person and society includes but transcends economic growth are both essential to an understanding of the right of development. Hence, the right of development includes both economic growth and political, social and economic participation by the citizenry in the process of development.

19. If the person and personal rights are so important, why do we stress the social teaching of the Church?

At the heart of a Catholic conception of the nature and dignity of the person is the conviction that the person can develop fully only in a societal context. Indeed, the person is social by nature; hence the quality of life in society, the justice of its mode of organization, the orientation of its structures and systems (political, legal, economic, social) will either enhance or retard the full human development of the person. Hence the need for the Church and all Christians to bring the structures and systems of society under scrutiny, precisely because we are concerned about the good of the person.

20. What are some of the structures and systems which the Chruch examines in her social teaching?

Some examples of systems and structures include the *wage system* in an economy *(Rerum Novarum);* the structural pattern of *economic growth and development* within a country *(Mater et Magistra);* the structure of the *international economic system (Justice in the World* and *Populorum Progressio);* the balance between individual freedom and public authority *(Pacem In Terris);* the system of trade relationships *(Populorum Progressio);* and the *structure* of public authority, nationally and internationally, in relation to the needs of the common good *(Pacem In Terris);* finally, patterns of *socio-economic organization (Octogesima Adveniens).*

21. What is social sin?

Social sin is a situation in which the very organization of some level of society *systematically* functions to the detriment of groups or individuals in the society. The sinfulness lies in the way social relationships are contrived or permitted to exist; the responsibility to change the situation rests upon all who participate in the society: some are called to assert their rights which are being systematically denied; others are called to recognize their responsibilities to change existing patterns of social relationships.

22. What is society?

Society is constituted by the total complex of social, political, cultural and economic relationships which are necessary for full human development.

23. What is the state?

Although it varies greatly in form, the state is the center of coercive power in society; it is entrusted with the authority to procure those aspects of societal life which involve the role of law and may even require the use of force. The role of the state as a part of society is most clearly delineated in Catholic teaching in *Pacem In Terris* and *Dignitatis Personae Humanae.*

24. What is the content and meaning of the principle of subsidiarity?

The principle of subsidiarity, first enunciated by Pius XI in *Quadragesimo Anno,* seeks to adjudicate and regulate a balance between individual initiative and governmental assistance and intervention in socio-economic activity. It seeks to answer the question how much state intervention is necessary and/or legitimate in societal affairs. The principle is a "conservative" principle of socio-economic organization since it holds that the presumption is in favor of personal or voluntary action; the state should intervene only when lesser bodies cannot fulfill a given task required by the common good.

25. What is meant by the process of socialization?

The term socialization was first used by John XXIII in *Mater et Magistra.* He defined the process as "the growing interdependence of men in society giving rise to various patterns of group life and activity and in many instances to social institutions established on a juridical basis." The process both arises from and evokes increasing state intervention in the socio-economic order. The encylical gave a cautious but clear approval to this increasing role for the state because of the new complexities of the modern socio-economic system.

26. What is the relationship of the principle of subsidiarity to the process of socialization?

The basic question which both subsidiarity and socialization address is the degree of state intervention which is necessary to achieve the common good while not unduly restricting the right of personal and group initiatives. The thrust of the subsidiarity approach places the burden of proof for intervention on the higher body, principally the state; hence the orientation of this principle tends to restrict state action. The acknowledgement of socialization as a beneficial process in society legitimates as a matter of principle the expanded intervention of the state to accomplish tasks which are judged to be beyond the scope of individual initiatives in the modern world. The two principles ought to be understood in a relationship of tension, the judgment on what degree and type of intervention is justified should be made in light of the "conservative" orientation of subsidiarity but also in light of the "liberal" understanding of the complexity of the modern economy conveyed by socialization.

27. What is the common good?

The common good is usually defined as the complex of spiritual, social and material conditions needed in society for the person to achieve integral human dignity. In the social teaching of John XXIII important developments in both the *substance* of the concept and its *scope* of extension are evident.

Substantively, John XXIII specified the idea of the common good by linking it directly to human rights: "It is agreed that in our time, the common good is chiefly guaranteed when personal rights and duties are maintained" *(Pacem In Terris)*. John XXIII also expanded the *scope* of the concept by speaking of the *international* common good, a phrase which does not appear in Catholic thought prior to *Mater et Magistra*.

28. Who is responsible for achieving the common good?

Generally speaking it is the work of the whole society; individuals, voluntary associations, professional organizations and public authorities are all responsible in different ways for contributing to the common good. Specifically, the state has a unique function in the achievement of the common good. On one hand the state is entrusted with preserving those conditions of *public order* which are essential elements of the common good; these include perservation of public peace, care for public morality and the establishment of conditions leading to justice. On the other hand, if other groups cannot by themselves realize those conditions which supplement public order with a fuller conception of the common good, the state as a final resort must intervene. In determining when this should occur, the concepts of subsidiarity and socialization provide criteria for policy.

29. What is Catholic teaching on private property?

The basic affirmation has two dimensions: first, the right to own private property is regarded as a natural right flowing from the nature of the person and conducive to protecting the dignity and freedom of the person; secondly, all property, even private property, is regarded as having a social function. Hence the ownership and use of private property must be evaluated in terms of both the needs of the individual and the needs of the wider society. In the social encyclicals of Leo XIII and Pius XI, while both dimensions were recognized, the stress of the teaching was upon the right of ownership; this was due in part to distinguish Catholic teaching from some of the premises of nineteenth-century socialism in Europe.

The more recent Catholic social teaching has laid increasing stress on the social obligations of ownership, while still not denying the natural right. Hence, Pius XII taught that the principle that the goods of the earth are intended for all and should be used to provide for the subsistance of all is prior to all other economic rights, even the natural right of private property.

It is in the teaching of Pope Paul VI, however, that the social responsibilities of property are most clearly set forth. Using the teaching of the Church Fathers, he subordinates the right of private property and free commerce to the universal principle that the goods of the earth must serve all and he clearly indicates that property rights are not absolute rights." No one is justified in keeping for his exclusive use what he does not need, when others lack necessities." *(Populorum Progressio,* n. 23).

30. What is Catholic teaching on the status of unions?

From the encyclical *Rerum Novarum* (1891) to the teaching of *Gaudium et Spes* (1965) the recognition of the right to organize workers' unions as a basic human right flowing from the nature of the person has been constant. On this question as on other issues of justice the Church performs a service by articulating the moral principle of the right to organize; what is equally critical, however, is that she manifest her commitment to this right in her own institutions.

31. Does the Church endorse a specific form of socio-economic organization in society?

No. The primary purpose of Catholic teaching is to set forth norms and principles which are to be used in judging all human systems of socio-economic organization. The process of carrying on work of discernment testing the various ideologies and systems of organization, pointing out their theoretical and practical failings and urging the same kind of discernment by Christians throughout the Church is a major element of *Pacem In Terris, Populorum Progressio* and *Octogesima Adveniens.*

In this process of discernment elements and principles of all existing systems come under scrutiny. For example, in discussing the theory of Liberal Capitalism, Pope Paul VI says: "the baseless theory has emerged which considers material gain the key motive for economic progress, competition as the supreme law of economics and private ownership of the means of production as an absolute right that has no limits and carries no corresponding social obligations . . . One cannot condemn such abuses too strongly because—let us again recall solemnly—the economy should be at the service of man." *(Populorum Progressio,* n. 26).

32. What is the status of the nation state in Catholic teaching?

Catholic social teaching has accepted the nation state as a factual reality in the contemporary world, but its primary emphasis has been to assert the *relative* moral value of the nation state. Concretely this means affirming that the nation state stands under the judgment of the moral law (cf. *Pacem In Terris,* n. 80) and calling for a form of international organization which goes beyond the present nation state system.

In *Pacem In Terris,* Pope John linked the structure which public authority should possess to the objective needs of the common good. He illustrated that in today's world a structural defect exists because the needs of the international common good go beyond the ability of the nation state to meet them. In light of this gap between objective requirements and existing structures, both *Pacem In Terris* and *Gaudium et Spes* call for the establishment of some form of world-wide public authority which could aid and assist the national authorities in meeting their responsibilities.

The pastoral implication of this teaching of the nation state calls for the cultivation of a more discerning form of patriotism. Such a view could affirm the real but limited value of one's own country while opening the consciences of people to the solidarity and responsibilities which bind them to those of other nations.

33. What is Catholic teaching on the morality of modern war?

Contemporary Catholic teaching moves between two positions: the Just War doctrine and Christian Pacifism. On the one hand while condemning the destructiveness and waste of war, Church teaching continues to affirm the tragic possibility and necessity of a legitimate right of defense. In this perspective the categories of Just War teaching would be used to determine which resorts to force could be considered morally legitimate.

In recent Catholic teaching, however, another perspective has been introduced. *Gaudium et Spes* speaks of the need "to undertake an evaluation of war with an entirely new attitude" (n. 80). This is coupled with statements which praise those "who renounce the use

of violence in the vindication of their rights" and which call upon
public authorities to make provision in civil law for those who because
of reasons of conscience refuse to bear arms.

In light of these perspectives, it seems accurate to say that there
are two options open to Catholics today: a proper use of the Just
War doctrine (admitting the use of force as an ultima ratio but
seeking to limit its destructive consequences) is one posture; it is
clear, however, (as it was not always clear in the past) that conscientious objection to any use of force is also a legitimate position
for a Catholic to assume.

Within the context of these two broadly stated positions, other
significant specific positions include: (a) a condemnation of total war;
(b) a similar condemnation of acts of war aimed indiscriminately at
the civilian population; (c) a vague acknowledgement of the fact of
deterrence which preserves "peace of a sort"; (d) an indictment of the
arms race as a treacherous trap wasting vitally needed funds; (e) an
affirmation that those in military service who fulfill their role properly
"are making a genuine contribution to the establishment of peace"
(Gaudium et Spes, n. 79).

34. Distinguish conscientious objection (C. O.) and selective consci-entious objection (S. C. O.).

Conscientious objection is a form of pacifism; stated in Christian
terms, it is a rejection of all use of military force as incompatible with
the Gospel. Selective conscientious objection is a conclusion drawn
from the application of Just War criteria to a specific war. The decision is made that while some uses of force are legitimate, this one is
not, hence the person refuses to bear arms in the conflict.

35. What does Catholic teaching say about the United Nations?

Since the inception of the United Nations it has received Catholic
support in the form of Church statements and through official Catholic participation. The most explicit support for the idea of the United
Nations and its concrete programs is found in *Pacem In Terris* and
in the Address of Paul VI to the General Assembly (1965).

In *Pacem In Terris,* Pope John went beyond his call for a form of
universal public authority to a specific endorsement of the United
Nations as a step in that direction: "It is our earnest wish that the
United Nations Organization—in its structure and in its means—may

become ever more equal to the magnitude and nobility of its tasks. May the day soon come when every human being will find therein an effective safeguard for the rights which derive directly from his dignity as a person, and which are therefore universal, inviolate and inaliena- ble rights" (n. 145).

PART FIVE
Moral Education

Moral Education

Concept and Components

1. What is the relationship of moral theology to religious education?

The purpose of moral theology is to investigate human activity in the light of the Gospel and to communicate the results of its investigations to the Church at large. It utilizes the tools of modern scientific research to arrive at conclusions of varying probability and certitude regarding man's basic posture toward God, creation and his fellow men. It also investigates the morality of various actions and situations as these relate to man's fundamental stance toward God and men. Moral theology is, therefore, a highly cognitive enterprise which communicates its findings for the service of the people of God.

Religious education has a broader and more immediately pastoral objective. Its purpose is to help believers grow in faith. As *Christus Dominus* put it, "Catechetical training is intended to make men's faith become living, conscious and active through the light of instruction" (n. 14). The cognitive is but one element among others which the religious educator uses to help Christians mature in living faith. The affective and attitudinal aspects of human growth are at least as important as the rational to the process of religious development. Solid catechetical programs must, of course, be based on sound moral theology if serious mistakes are to be avoided. Certainly catechists should have a firm grasp of those aspects of moral theology which affect their area of work. However, the task of the religious educator is not merely to transmit moral truths to the learners. His criterion in selecting which doctrinal or moral insights should be stressed must be based on whether these truths help his students mature in faith at this particular time in their human development.

2. What are the principal changes in moral catechesis in recent years?

Moral education has been influenced by developments in moral

[291]

theology and other fields especially developmental psychology and educational theory. Chief among the new emphases in moral formation are the following:

1) **Stress on the freedom of the Christian.** An indoctrinational methodology which sought to impose values from without has given way to a more "discovery" style of education which seeks to help the learner discover and freely choose values from among alternatives. At a time when young and old alike are confronted with a plurality of conflicting value systems, "those engaged in the ministry of the word must never forget that faith is a free response to the grace of the revealing God." (*General Catechetical Directory* n. 3).

2) **Utilization of the psychological profile of the learner.** Research in developmental psychology has demonstrated that human beings progress through rather clearly defined stages of emotional and intellectual readiness for various kinds of learning as they grow from infancy to adulthood. This knowledge must be used by catechists if they are to deal with students effectively. For example, since young children are incapable of abstraction, it is at best a waste of time to have them study or memorize abstract moral principles.

3) **Attention to the social implications of the Gospel.** Earlier catechetical texts tended to stress only individual morality, that is, the duty of each man to lead a personally blameless life. Seldom treated were the moral dimensions of such questions as war and peace, race relations, distribution of wealth or the relationship of the richer nations to the poorer nations. Such complex topics seldom admit of simple or univocal solutions. At least some of the controversy surrounding contemporary religious education is attributable to the efforts of teachers to apply the Gospel and the social teaching of recent popes to institutional and societal problems.

4) **Situating moral catechesis in a more biblical perspective.** The biblical renewal with its stress on covenant influenced moralists to explain man's relationship to God in the model of interpersonal relationships rather than in the traditional model of law. Thus sin can be seen not primarily as breaking a law but as a personal and radical turning away from a loving relationship with God. This insight in turn helped religious educators to present moral behavior as a loving response to a gracious Father rather than a series of duties which must be performed for fear of punishment.

5) **Ongoing rather than terminal education.** Educators in general are coming to the conclusion that it is no longer possible during the

years of formal education to impart a fixed body of knowledge which will adequately serve a student for the rest of his life. Technological, scientific and socio-cultural changes are accelerating at an exponential rate. As a result, a student in school today may well spend most of his adult life using yet uninvented skills in a technology or a profession which has not yet even been dreamt of. In such circumstances educators see themselves more as facilitators of learning rather than transmitters of information. Their main task is to help students learn to go on learning so they can cope with the future.

Applied to moral education this means that the religion teacher can not possibly give a student prefabricated answers to all the moral problems he will encounter in his life. Most of the ethical questions of tomorrow have not yet even been raised much less answered. What the teacher can do is to help the student search honestly and dialogically for answers to today's questions with the hope that he will continue the search in the world of tomorrow. Hence ongoing adult education programs are one of the great needs of the time.

3. Why don't teachers simply tell young people what is right and wrong instead of discussing it with them?

The goal of the religion teacher is the personal growth and development of his students—not control over their consciences. Therefore, he should help them as fairly and honestly as he can to form their own consciences. In so doing the teacher will communicate those general laws and moral principles which embody the insights of the tradition of the Church. However, the closer principles come to actual concrete situations, the more difficult it becomes to apply them. Individual actions are frequently complex and ambiguous as the traditional principle of the double effect attests. Often there is not one but many seemingly competing principles which apply to a particular action or situation.

Some contemporary moralists argue that there are no human actions, taken just in their physical structure, which can be neatly labeled as always good or always evil. More traditional moralists would hold that apart from such intrinsically evil actions as adultery or direct homicide, most actions are indifferent and take on their moral character from the motive of the person acting and from the circumstances surrounding the action.

Even if it were possible to issue a catalogue which authoritatively graded actions as mortal sin, venial sin and no sin, such a catalogue would be of limited usefulness. Students need to analyze not only the individual action and the circumstances surrounding it, they need even more to be able to anaylze their own motivation. For example, no discussion of the Sunday Mass obligation is going to be of any value unless students honestly confront the reasons why they do or do not participate in the Eucharist. And beyond the question of motive is the far more radical question of fundamental option. Why one should attend Sunday Mass takes on it full significance only in the context of what the fundamental direction of his life is. It is only in a wholistic moral context that analysis of individual actions will promote the moral growth of the person.

4. Is it not dangerous to teach people about fundamental option and that a single act can not be a mortal sin?

It is certainly dangerous to teach material to students who are not mature enough to assimilate its meaning and who may only caricature it. Hence teachers have to be careful to coordinate their material with the psychological development of their students.

It is even more dangerous to oversimplify the theory of fundamental option so that it is reduced to meaning that no single human act can ever be indicative of a change of one's basic relationship with God. Most explanations of fundamental option teach that a single act which seals or ratifies a series of unloving actions can indeed be a serious sin which ruptures the Christian's relationship to God. The married man who leaves for the weekend to carry on an adulterous relationship with his secretary ill understands fundamental option if he argues that such a single weekend affair can not possibly be a mortal sin. It may well be an activity which seals and ratifies a whole series of exploitive actions on his part.

Far from encouraging people to sin, fundamental option compels them to confront the basic direction of their lives. Thus moral activity can be seen not as a series of isolated good or evil actions, but as a positive living out of the fundamental commitment of one's life. Mortal sin can be seen in its full dimension as not merely a breaking of a law but a radical rupturing of one's relationship with God.

5. Should students be taught the moral teaching of the Church or the opinions of theologians?

Students should certainly be instructed in the moral doctrine of the Church. The opinions of theologians should not be presented as the official teaching of the magisterium unless and until the Church has accepted these opinions and incorporated them into her official teaching.

To distinguish the opinions of the theologians from the teaching of the magisterium does not imply that the former are devoid of all practical value for the Christian community. In accord with their age and development, students should be acquainted with the relevant teachings of the moralists for the following reasons:

1) The moral pronouncements and directives of the magisterium need knowledgeable explanation and interpretation. It is to the moral theologians that the religious teacher must turn for such help. Where there is consenus among theologians on a particular point, this should be explained to students. When there is a plurality of opinions and explanations among responsible moralists, this too should be communicated to students. It is patently unfair to present one particular theological opinion as *the* Catholic position when there are several or many Catholic positions all situated within the parameters of orthodoxy.

2) In officially approving the moral system of St. Alphonsus Ligouri, the Church accepted probabalism as an operative principle for conscience formation. This means that when the meaning or binding force of a law or ethical principle is disputed by moralists, the stricter interpretation can not be insisted upon as binding in practice. Because the Church has come out so strongly on the side of human freedom, Catholics have the right to know not only the laws and moral principles of the Church, but how these laws and principles are interpreted in practice.

3) Because of the nature of their work, moralists are usually in touch with developing trends in ethical thought. Teachers who keep abreast of the writings of the moral theologians are not only able to present the position (or positions) of the Church on various moral questions, but can alert students to possible future developments as well. Thus students can be more realistically equipped than were their predecessors to anticipate and cope with change.

6. Should Catholics be taught to follow their own consciences or the authoritative teaching of the magisterium?

Every man must honestly form his own conscience so that he always does that which he personally judges to be morally correct. Since man is a social being, he can not form his conscience in a purely antonomous fashion. He must consider not only his own insights into the situation but the common experience and judgment of his fellow men. As a Catholic he has the guidance of the accumulated moral wisdom of the Judeao-Christian tradition which includes the authoritative teaching of the magisterium. Hence as a Catholic he must take into serious account the teaching of the magisterium.

But if the Catholic conscience is not purely autonomous, neither is it purely heteronomous. The authoritative pronouncements of the magisterium do not absolve the individual from the duty of honestly judging what is right and wrong. He must personally appropriate and interiorize the values expressed in the particular moral teaching of the magisterium.

Since a Catholic believes in the abiding presence of the Spirit in the Church, it is to be normally expected that he will agree with the various moral pronouncements of the Church. However not all moral pronouncements of the magisterium are of equal weight and none is infallibly defined. Hence it is possible that the Catholic might disagree with a particular statement of the magisterium or judge that the statement does not apply in the complex and conflicting circumstances of his concrete situation.

Hence there is no conflict in principle between freedom of individual conscience and the authoritative teaching of the Church. The moral guidance offered by the Church is a priceless help to the Catholic in freely forming his conscience.

7. Should moral education be centered around the Ten Commandments?

Christians should certainly be acquainted with the Ten Commandments as part of their religious heritage. The general moral insights expressed in the decalogue retain their basic value and are reminders to sinful men when they refuse to respond in love.

Christianity is first and foremost a religion of love, not a religion of law. Consequently while the Commandments should not be neglected, neither should they be at the center of moral education. In the past manuals of moral theology as well as catechetical works taught morality within the context of the Ten Commandments. That is, they gathered the various virtuous or sinful activities and placed them under one of the Ten Commandments as actions commanded or forbidden by the particular commandment. This was a somewhat arbitrary arrangement, and it sometimes extended the meaning and binding force of the individual commandment far beyond what an accurate exegesis of the scriptural text could sustain. This method did, however, provide a handy pedagogical framework for teaching morality.

The danger in teaching morality almost entirely in the context of law is legalism which concentrates on the letter of the law to the exclusion of the spirit or purpose of the law. Such an approach all too often engenders a mentality of moral minimalism which is a far cry from gospel injunction to "love one another as I have loved you." As long as men are sinners they will need laws to point out when they are not listening to the Spirit. In the final analysis, however, the ultimate law of the Christian is the Spirit himself. The center of gravity in moral education must, therefore, be situated within the context of loving response to the invitations of the Spirit rather than in any lesser law.

8. Why do not religious educators give more attention to fear of God as an effective motive for obeying the moral law?

If religious educators are to help Christians mature in faith, they must take into serious account the psychological profile of the learner. They must understand how human beings learn and perceive reality at different stages of their development. Unhealthy religious attitudes can unwittingly be instilled if threatening concepts are introduced before students are capable of understanding them or integrating them into their personalities. Great harm can be done, for example, if young children are told about mortal sin too soon or if they are given graphic descriptions of the eternal fires of hell. Rather than help children grow morally, such manipulative techniques tend to fixate them at an infantile level. The resulting image of God can often be that of the arbitrary tyrant who lurks in the shadows waiting to catch one of his creatures violating the moral law. While such pedagogy may prove effective in promoting behaviorial conformity with the law, it is ultimately a failure because it distorts the Christian idea of God.

The dominant image of God which emerges from the New Testament is that of gracious, loving father. It is this image which should be communicated, and it is this image which forms a healthy base for moral growth.

9. Should catechists stress God's just punishments as well as his love?

Students should be helped to understand their responsibility for their own actions and for the consequences of those actions. Moral catechesis will differ markedly as a person develops from early childhood to mature adulthood. All must gradually and in accord with their psychological development be led to appreciate that at times they deliberately refuse to respond lovingly and that such refusals not only hurt others but retard their own moral growth and the deepening of their union with God. When they are mature enough they should be helped to understand that each man must from the depth of his personality choose for or against God, which choice is inseparably linked to his choice for or against others. The ultimate consequence of a fundamental option or choice which turns away from God and man is expressed in the traditional concept of hell. It affirms that basic human freedom is such that it is at least possible that man can turn away from God at the deepest level of his being and that God will honor this ultimate choice.

To describe the existential consequences of rupturing one's fundamental relationship to God as "God's just punishments" can be misleading. Sometimes anthropomorphic scriptural passages describing God's anger have been too literally interpreted as indicating vindictiveness on God's part. God is always loving even toward sinners. Therefore he does not punish in the sense that he becomes vindictive. In willing a certain order of creation, God has willed the consequences which are concomitant upon violation of that order. The man who refuses to eat will get sick. His sickness, however, is not a vindictive punishment from God but the inevitable consequence of the man's refusal to conform to the present order of creation. Similarly the sinner who steadfastly refuses God's loving invitation to respond in love suffers the consequences of selfishness, unhappiness and ultimate separation. He suffers, however, not because God is vengeful or vindictive, but because he freely places himself outside God's gracious order.

10. Does the Church require that children receive the sacrament of penance before making their first communion?

The law of the Church does not demand that anyone make a confession of devotion before receiving the Eucharist. The decree on Frequent Communion of 1905 states that "no one who is in the state of grace and who approaches the holy table with a right and devout intention can be prohibited therefrom."

Some confusion has arisen because of varying interpretations of a 1973 joint declaration from the Sacred Congregations for the Clergy and for the Discipline of the Sacraments. The declaration, entitled *Summus Pontifex,* noted the introduction of certain new practices which permit first reception of the Eucharist without prior reception of the sacrament of penance. The declaration stated that an end must be put to the experiments and concluded: "The Decree *Quam Singulari* is therefore to be obeyed everywhere and by all."

Some thought this document meant that all children were now obliged to confess before first communion. Such an interpretation would have meant that of all the sinners in the Church, only the seven-year-olds were obliged to make a confession of devotion before communion.

It is evident from the conclusion of *Summus Pontifex* that no new legislation has been enacted. What Rome is insisting on, rather, is that the old legislation contained in the Decree *Quam Singulari* of 1910 be obeyed. This decree affirmed the right rather than the obligation of children from about the age of seven to receive the sacrament of penance. It censured the practice of not allowing children to go to confession or of not giving them absolution if they did confess. It is one thing to say that priests should not refuse to hear children's confessions; it is quite another to conclude that children are, therefore, obliged to go to confession. Hence in ordering an end to certain experiments, the Holy See was apparently referring to any sacramental programs which are not in accord with *Quam Singulari,* that is, any programs which do not genuinely respect the child's right to the sacrament of penance.

In a reply to the Canadian Bishops the Congregations for the Clergy and the Sacraments clarified the matter:

> The declaration does not aim at compelling or regimenting every child to receive first penance before first communion. Neither does the declaration desire to foster conditions which would prevent children from receiving the sacrament of penance before their first communion . . . but to emphasize that during the one and same initiation period, children should be given a positive and pastoral catechetical preparation for the fruitful celebration of these two sacraments. (*Origins,* Dec. 13, 1973)

11. At what age should children make their first confession?

The Code of Canon Law in Canon 906 requires all Catholics to confess their sins once a year. Commentators of this Canon have always taught that one is obliged to confess annually only if he has committed serious sin. Canon 856 enjoins all who are conscious of serious sins to confess before receiving the Eucharist except in extraordinary circumstances. Authorities today commonly teach that children are not able to commit mortal sin until much later than seven years of age. Most psychologists and moralists would agree that even early adolescence is not usually accompanied by that fullness of the use of reason necessary for the formal guilt of grave sin.

The relevant sections of Church law do not, therefore, settle the question of the age for first confession. The time for first penance should be determined according to principles of sound pastoral theology. The most appropriate age is when the child is old enough to appreciate the nature of sin and the meaning of forgiveness and reconciliation with the Church. Since children develop at different rates, no hard and fast norm can be established. As a rule of thumb, however, most authorities recommend about nine or ten years of age—always allowing for individual differences among children.

The recently revised rite of penance stresses the importance of the social aspect of the sacrament. Thus the sacrament is to be seen as expressing not only reconciliation with God but also with the people of God, the Church. Before children can appreciate reconciliation to a group, they must have developed a consciousness of group dependence. Usually children have not developed this consciousness much before about fourth grade. The experience of communal penance celebrations is an excellent way of helping children from first grade on to grow in an understanding of the social dimensions of sin and reconciliation.

Contributors

Gregory Baum is a Professor of Theology at St. Michael's College in the University of Toronto, consultant to the Secretariat of Christian Unity in Rome, and author of *Man Becoming, The Credibility of the Church Today.*

Eamon R. Carroll, O. Carm., is a Professor of Systematic Theology at the Catholic University of America, Past President of the Catholic Theological Society of America, and contributor to *Marian Studies, Theological Studies,* etc.

Charles Curran is a Professor of Moral Theology at Catholic University of America. Past President of the Catholic Theological Society of America, he is the author of *A New Look at Christian Morality, Contemporary Problems in Moral Theology,* and most recently *New Perspectives in Moral Theology.*

John F. Dedek is a Professor of Moral Theology at St. Mary of the Lake Seminary, Associate Editor of *Chicago Studies,* author of *Contemporary Sexual Morality, Human Life,* and *Titius and Bertha Ride Again.*

Avery Dulles, S.J. is a Professor of Theology at Woodstock College, Associate Editor of Concilium and author of *Revelation Theology* and many other books and articles.

George J. Dyer is the Dean of Faculty at St. Mary of the Lake Seminary, Mundelein, Illinois, editor of *Chicago Studies,* and contributor to *Theological Studies, American Ecclesiastical Review, Theological Education,* etc.

Joseph V. Farraher, S.J., is Dean of Faculty at St. Patrick's Seminary, Menlo Park, California. Formerly Professor of Moral and Pastoral Theology, Alma College, California, he was the author of the "Moral Notes" in *Theological Studies.*

Bernard Haring, C.S.S.R., is a Professor of Moral Theology at the Accademia Alfonsiana, Rome. Author of the *Law of Christ* and many other books and articles. Frequently a visiting professor and lecturer in the United States.

J. Bryan Hehir is Director of the Division of Justice and Peace of the
United States Catholic Conference, and a visiting Lecturer in
Social Ethics, St. John's Seminary, Brighton, Mass.

Monika K. Hellwig is Associate Professor of Theology at Georgetown
University and author of *What Are the Theologians saying?*, *The
Christian Creeds.*

Richard P. McBrien is a Professor of Theology at Boston College,
President of the Catholic Theological Society of America, and
author of *Do We Need the Church?*, *Church: The Continuing
Quest.*

Richard A. McCormick, S.J., is the Rose F. Kennedy Professor of
Christian Ethics at the Kennedy Institute for Bioethics, George-
town University. Author of the "Moral Notes" in *Theological
Studies.* Past President of the Catholic Theological Society of
America he was the recipient of its Cardinal Spellman award for
the best theological writing of the year.

Charles R. Meyer is a Professor of Systematic Theology at St. Mary
of the Lake Seminary, Mundelein, Illinois, author of *A Contemporary Theology of Grace, The Touch of God, Man of God: A
Study of the Priesthood.*

Norbert Rigali, S.J., is Chairman of the Department of Religious
Studies at the University of San Diego. He is a frequent contributor to *Chicago Studies* and other theological journals.

Thomas F. Sullivan is Associate Superintendent of Schools for the
Archdiocese of Chicago. Member of the Editorial Board of
Chicago Studies, he is the author of *Focus on American Catechet-
ics.*

Cornelius Van Der Poel, C.S.Sp., Director of the Family Life Bureau
for the Archdiocese of Detroit, teaches Theology at St. John's
Provincial Seminary in Plymouth, Michigan. He is the author of
God's Love in Human Language, The Search for Human Values,
and *Religious Life: a Risk of Love.*

Jared Wicks, S.J. is a Professor of Historical Theology at the Jesuit
School of Theology in Chicago, author of *Man Yearning for
Grace* and the forthcoming *Reader in Reformation Controversy.*

John H. Wright, S.J. is a Professor of Systematic Theology at the
Jesuit School of Theology at Berkeley, immediate past president
of the Catholic Theological Society of America, author of *The
Order of the Universe in St. Thomas Aquinas,* and contributor to
Gregorianum, Theological Studies, etc.

Index